THE

ACTOR'S

CITY

SOURCEBOOK

THE ACTOR'S CITY SOURCEBOOK

A COMPARATIVE GUIDE TO AMERICA'S BEST PLACES
TO WORK AND LIVE AS A PERFORMING ARTIST

ANDREA WOLPER

BACK STAGE BOOKS
AN IMPRINT OF WATSON-GUPTILL PUBLICATIONS/NEW YORK

Edited by Tad Lathrop
Cover and book design by Areta Buk

This edition first published 1992 by Back Stage Books,
an imprint of Watson-Guptill Publications, a division of
BPI Communications, Inc., 1515 Broadway, New York, NY 10036.

Library of Congress Cataloging-in-Publication Data
Wolper, Andrea.
      The Actor's City Sourcebook : a comparative guide to America's
best places to work and live as a performing artist / Andrea Wolper.
         p. cm.
      Includes bibliographical references and index.
      ISBN 0-8230-7591-5
      1. Acting—Vocational guidance. 2. Cities and towns—United
States. 3. United States—Description and travel—1981- I. Title.
PN2055.W65 1992
792'.028'023—dc20   91-39622
                                        CIP

Manufactured in the United States of America

First Printing, 1992

1 2 3 4 5 6 7 8 9 / 97 96 95 94 93 92

FOR SHERRY EAKER.
AND FOR ACTORS EVERYWHERE.

TABLE OF CONTENTS

PREFACE

Once upon a time, nearly everyone who was serious about an acting career called New York or Los Angeles home. Moving to either coast in no way guaranteed success, but living anywhere else made it unlikely that acting would ever be more than a sometime thing. More recently, however, changes in the theatre, film, and broadcast industries have turned several other regions into major venues, at times actually stealing production—and actors—away from our two first cities of show business. From the ever-changing regional theatre movement to the increasingly decentralized film and broadcast industries, the nation's eyes are no longer fixed solely on the Big Orange and the Big Apple.

Certainly Hollywood and New York remain our busiest and most visible centers of production, where actors play for the biggest stakes. But while every year thousands of performers head east for snow and stage, or west for sun and screen, many others choose to begin—or breathe new life into—their careers in San Francisco, Philadelphia, or Chicago. Some actors, itching to move out of the regions and into the big time, know they'll never be satisfied if they don't give New York or L.A. their best shot. Others, intimidated by those cities' demanding lifestyles, prefer to stay away, reaching for the stars from places where life on earth isn't quite so hectic; still others, weary of the crowds and competition on either coast, decide to try their luck elsewhere. But making a move—whether from one's adopted city or one's home or college town—is a big decision, especially when the reason for the move is the pursuit of an acting career.

Rumors fly about the state of the business in cities from Seattle to Dallas to Boston. In waiting rooms and audition halls across the country, actors trade information and speculation about life and work in Florida, the Twin Cities, Washington, D.C.: "The entire film industry will have moved to Florida by the end of the decade." "If you didn't get started in Chicago theatre five years ago, you're too late." "In New York, you have to line up for auditions by 6 a.m." The actor in search of a new home base, whether temporary or long-term, needs to sort through speculation and hearsay, separate fact from fiction, and make a reality-based assessment of living and working conditions.

This book offers an actor's-eye view of the state of the business in Boston, Chicago, Dallas, Los Angeles, Miami, Minneapolis/St. Paul, New York, Philadelphia, San Francisco, Seattle, and Washington, D.C. Here, you'll learn which markets are busiest in each city, which "types" work most frequently, how the agent/casting director system works, what sort of training is available, and how to make contacts and get started. You'll also read about opportunities for ethnic minority actors, female actors, actors with disabilities. And since, even for the most devoted actor, work isn't everything, you'll learn about each city's character and social atmosphere, costs of living, crime rates, climate, and much more.

ACKNOWLEDGMENTS

With great generosity and good spirit, the people named here welcomed me to their homes, offices, and theatres to speak with me about their lives and work. They're actors, directors, talent agents, casting directors, union representatives, journalists; some are friends who let me sleep in their extra beds, eat their food, and run up their phone bills. The people in the first list offered assistance above and beyond any I'd asked for or dreamed of getting; they chauffeured me around town, gave me theatre tickets, and made sure I found the people and information I needed. To everyone on both lists, my deep gratitude and best wishes. To readers, my hope is that you'll read through this admittedly long list, for everyone named deserves thanks and recognition for sharing their knowledge and experience.

Barbara Capell, Carole DeNola, Pam Dougherty, Scott Glasser, Pat Hilton, Ed Hooks, Caroline Jack, Cecilie Keenan, Diana Gershon Knight, Abel Lopez, Rebecca Richards, Lillian Rozin, Felicia Von Drak, Mark Waldstein

---

Iris Acker, Kurt Ackerlind, Colleen Aho, John Allen, David Alt, Benny Sato Ambush, Mary Beckwith-Allen, Deborah Biron, Sandy Blaine, Jim Bodge, Warren Bowles, Judy Braha, Deidre Ann Brodeur, Valina Brown, Barbara Callander, Valerie Cates, Jill Charles, Phyllis Cicero, Mary Collins, Scott Colomby, Tad Currie, Edmond Dante, Estelle Davids, Harrise Davidson, Timothy Davis-Reed, Rafael de Acha, Franchelle Stewart Dorn, Nancy Doyle, Ann Drymalski, Kathleen Dunn, Ross Eatman, Victoria Eide, Eric Fergusen, Hallie Frazer, Ken Freehill, Marla Freeman, Burton Frink, Cathy Fuller, Nat Fuller, Stuart Weinberg Gershon, Marc Goldberg, Gretchen Grant, Tammy Green, Joan Greenspan, Evelyn Guerrero, Sue Harloe, Jonathan Harris, Nancy Hayes, Steven Hendrickson, Diana Hill, Tony Hazapis, Diane Hogan, Patty Holland, Debra Hopper, Ray Houle, Jeffrey Hutchinson, Johanna Jackson, Sharon Jensen, Terry Joe, Craig Jones, Dennis Jones, Mona Jones, Vicki Juditz, Patti Kalles, Tracy Katz, Dana Keeler, Madeleine Kelly, Rody Kent, Lotis Key, Robin Kilrain, Bea Kiyohara, Tom Kouchalakos, Kat Krone, Leslie Krensky, Greer Lange, Serena Lee, Michael Lemon, Sherron Long, Tara Lonzo, Tish Lopez, Gary Lowery, Kellie Lowery, Carol McCormick, NaDean McInnis, Susan McMath, Joe Minjares, Jim Monitor, John Moore, Scott Morgan, Gene Morrill, Ginger Moss, Cyndi Mulkern, Paula Muzik, Ken Narasaki, Carole Ness, Mary Beth Noll, Dean Nolen, Steve Olsen, Fred Ornstein, Luis Oropeza, Harriet Oser, Mary Otis, Yvonne Paradise, Elaine Park, K.T. Patt, Larry Paulsen, Michael Pedretti, Tawnya Pettiford-Wates, Carolyn Pickman, Cynthia Pleasant, Allan Poe, Leslie Rapp, Helen Reece, James Ridge, Kim Roberts, Lars Rosager, Brenda Rosario, Marcia Ross, Alison Roth,

Patty Royall, Karen Rushfield, Mario Ernesto Sanchez, Jean Schiffman, Robyn Sue Schmidt, Ann Sebastian, Martha Sherrat, Chuck Smith, Kelly Smith, Dona Sommers, Betty Spiegel, Lynn Steele, Billy Strong, Catherine Struzynski, Randall Stuart, Will Stutz, Bernadette Sullivan, Ellen Taft, Lisa Tejero, Jon Tindle, Jane Titus, Michael Torrey, Jackie Townsend, Dee Ulsaker, Summer Uzell-Selby, Michael Van Duzer, Carol Waaser, Edwin Wald, Jeff Wallach, Thomas Walsh, Brannon Walker, April Webster, Susan Weider, Ellen Weiner, Harry Winter, JoAnne Winter, Brent Whitney, Dagmar Wittmar, Lori Wyman, Ronnie Yeskel. And to all the actors who filled out surveys, my thanks.

Thanks also to Jerome Weeks of the *Dallas Morning News,* Phil Anderson of *City Pages* (Minneapolis/St. Paul), Jim Knipfel of *Welcomat* (Philadelphia), and Peter Keough of *The Boston Phoenix* for movie recommendations. And finally, thanks to my editor, Tad Lathrop.

The Actor's City Sourcebook is an overview of living conditions and professional opportunities for actors in eleven U.S. cities. It was written for experienced actors and newcomers, for women and men, union and nonunion actors, actors of any ethnic background, actors with or without disabilities. It was written for you if you're

- mid-career and wondering if there's life and work beyond New York and L.A.;
- just out of school and unsure about where to get started;
- thinking about moving to New York, L.A., or another city, and aren't sure which is right for you;
- planning audition trips to regional theatre cities;
- anywhere, wondering what it might be like to try your luck somewhere else.

Each of the eleven cities is covered in a separate chapter. Each chapter is divided into two parts. The first part, "The City," addresses the quality of life, offering information about the social climate, public and private transportation, the weather, housing conditions, employment, crime and safety, and so on. It cites addresses and phone numbers of libraries, post offices, information centers, and more. The second part, "The Business," addresses the strengths and weaknesses of the various union and nonunion markets; it offers suggestions on meeting and working with agents and casting directors, and includes information on auditions, training opportunities, casting diversity, and networking. Lists of casting resources, including trade publications, hotlines, auditions, and useful books and periodicals are provided, as are addresses of bookstores, talent unions, and professional organizations and support services.

As careful as I've been to include only up-to-date information, you can bet that something will have changed between the time I finished writing and you started reading. A theatre I've mentioned will have closed its doors, while a new, important one will have come into being. Union contracts may have been renegotiated, affecting who can and can't work on certain productions. (Union members who have *any* questions about whether or not they may accept employment should check with their local office or liaison.) A popular "actors' bar" will have gone out of favor; a bookstore or professional association will have moved to a new address. Since I know how frustrating it can be to consult a resource book only to find that listed phone numbers have changed, prices have risen, and stores have gone out of business, I've avoided listing data that is particularly time-sensitive. I tell you, for example, if you need a token to board the bus, but I don't tell you what that token costs. I rarely mention the names of top agents and casting directors because, though such information is useful, agencies split, casting directors move around, power and popularity wax and wane. Still, it seems inevitable that there will be some changes, and I hope any you encounter won't cause too much difficulty.

To get the most from *The Actor's City Sourcebook,* please start by reading the following explanations and elucidations:

RECOMMENDED READING

Each chapter includes two *Recommended Reading* lists. The first, in "The City," is eclectic, and may include literature, memoirs, unusual guidebooks, and history. The second, in "The Business," includes readings directly related to the acting profession in each city or region; those listed in the Los Angeles and New York chapters represent just a few of the many available books. These lists do not include newspapers and periodicals, which appear in each chapter under *Looking for Work.* For books that are national in scope, please see Appendix A.

MOVIES

Some movies are recommended because they take the viewer inside various aspects of life in a particular city, some for their historical perspectives, others simply because they show what the city or region looks like.

CENSUS

Population figures and percentages are based on the official 1990 census. The figure in parentheses following the total population shows the increase or decrease since 1980.

CLIMATE

The *Normal Temperatures* tables show the cities' average daily high and low temperatures for the coldest and hottest months of the year.

The *Temperature Extremes* tables can be confusing at first glance. The first table shows the mean number of days per year in which the temperature reaches 90° or higher, and the mean number of days in which the temperature reaches *no higher than* 32°. The second table shows the mean number of days per year in which the *lowest temperature* is 32° and below, and the mean number of days in which the lowest temperature is 0° and below.

HOUSING AND COSTS OF LIVING

The *Intearea Shelter Indexes* offer rough comparisons between housing costs in metropolitan areas. The numbers shown in the tables are not dollar amounts. Rather, for purposes of this study (see *Sources of Information* in the back of this book), Philadelphia was assigned a base value of 100. Looking at the Boston table, you'll see that in that area, housing costs are about 27 percent higher than in Philadelphia. In the

Minneapolis area, costs are about 8 percent lower. (Bear in mind that figures reflect conditions in entire metropolitan areas, except in the cases of Los Angeles and New York, which are broken down into urban and suburban areas.) Figures in the "Owners" columns reflect the fair market *rental equivalent* of owner-occupied housing; they do not indicate mortgage or purchase rates.

Although cost of living figures are included here, they're reliable only up to a point. The Bureau of Labor Statistics warns that "special care should be taken when analyzing . . . the CEX [Consumer Expenditure Survey] . . . the sample size is relatively small for some metropolitan areas . . . these tables should NOT be used . . . to compare across MSAs [Metropolitan Statistical Areas] because the demographics are not the same in all areas . . . (and demographic) characteristics will affect expenditures."

EMPLOYMENT
Employment and earnings statistics should be used for comparative purposes only. "Average Annual Pay" data are based on earnings of all employees covered under state and federal unemployment insurance programs.

CRIME
Crime figures are taken from offenses reported to the FBI by law enforcement agencies throughout the United States. Violent crime includes murder, rape, robbery, and aggravated assault. Property crime includes burglary, larceny theft, motor vehicle theft, and arson.

A city's crime statistics are meaningful only in relation to the size of its population. Again, the suggested use here is comparative. The second and third lines in the crime tables in each chapter show my own calculations using 1990 crime and population statistics. Please remember that in most cities, the majority of crime statistics are generated from certain specific areas, and every city has relatively safe and relatively dangerous neighborhoods.

MISCELLANEA
Listings of museums and religious organizations are limited to those that are performing arts-related.

TALENT UNIONS
Membership figures reflect the most current totals (of paid-up members) available at the time of publication (AEA: November 1990; SAG: October 31, 1990; AFTRA: May 1990). Actors' Equity liaisons' (see *Explanation of Terms* at the end of this section) addresses and phone numbers are not listed in this book; Equity members who need further information may contact an Equity office or call their local Equity hotline.

HOTLINES

Telephone hotlines announce upcoming auditions in a given city or region. Many are for use by talent union or professional association members only. For that reason, while all hotlines are listed by name, only a few actual telephone numbers are included.

BULLETIN BOARDS AND BINDERS

This entry lists bulletin boards on which audition notices are posted, and binders (maintained at some union offices) containing current audition announcements.

TALENT BOOKS AND TALENT BANKS

Talent books are compilations of pictures and résumés that are distributed to casting and industry personnel. Actors pay to be included. Talent banks are files of pictures and résumés (and in a few cases audio- and videotapes) that are made available to casting and industry personnel. In some cases, inclusion is open to all actors, while in others, only to members of the sponsoring organization.

TALENT SHOWCASES AND COMBINED AUDITIONS

Talent showcases are presentations of scenes (and sometimes songs and monologues) performed for casting personnel, artistic directors, and others. Combined auditions are (usually annual) events at which directors, artistic directors, and casting directors from several theatres gather to see many actors perform monologues and/or songs; several take place throughout the country primarily for casting summer stock, while others are organized on a local level by theatre alliances and actors' associations. Showcases and combined auditions specific to a city or region are listed in full within each chapter. Others are listed by name only; detailed information can be found in Appendix B.

FILM AND TELEVISION

Information under this heading refers to movies, television series, and movies-for-television.

CORPORATE AND COMMERCIALS

Many people are replacing the term "industrial" with "corporate." Both terms, used interchangeably in this book, refer to productions—from live shows to training films to on-site sales videos and so on—produced by corporations, companies, and public or private agencies.

TRAINING

The mention by name of classes, schools, and instructors implies neither recommendation nor endorsement. In most cases, addresses and phone numbers of listed colleges and universities are for their theatre departments.

NETWORKING AND SOCIALIZING

For networking opportunities in addition to those listed under this heading in any given chapter, look through the chapter's *Other Associations* and *Additional Opportunities* listings.

▰▰▰ EXPLANATION OF TERMS

Actors' Equity Contracts, Codes, and Agreements.1 The Equity *COST Contract* (Council of Stock Theatres) covers Non-Resident Dramatic (or Musical) Stock. It may be used by commercial or not-for-profit theatres, but must have a season of not less than two consecutive productions, or in the case of a unit tour not less than two consecutive weeks. The *Guest Artist Agreement* (GA) may be used by not-for-profit educational or community theatres to hire an individual Equity actor. The benefits and protections of an Equity contract are provided for the actor working in a nonprofessional situation. The *League of Resident Theatres (LORT) Contract* is used by not-for-profit regional theatres throughout the United States. Some employ resident companies each season, though most job in actors on a show-by-show basis. The five categories, which determine salary and manning requirements, are based on actual weekly box office gross receipts averaged over a three-year period. *The Small Professional Theatre (SPT) Contract* may be used in theatres of less than 350 seats, in areas outside of New York, Chicago, and Los Angeles. The contract may be used in both commercial and not-for-profit situations and for both seasonal operations and unit productions. The ten salaried categories are based on potential box office gross income. A *Letter of Agreement* (LOA) is used by Equity in a developmental situation to allow a theatre the time and flexibility needed to grow into a standard Equity contract. Each LOA is individually negotiated, and the terms vary from theatre to theatre (and from year to year for each theatre). The *Members Project Code* is available only in Liaison Areas and is for member-produced projects where all members involved in the production are considered, as a group, to be the producer. The *New York Showcase Code* is available within the city of New York for theatres of ninety-nine seats or less. There is a Tiered Code for Funded Nonprofit Theatres and a Basic Showcase Code for commercial, single productions. The *Production Contract* is primarily used for Broadway shows, National and International Tours, and Bus and Truck Tours. It is also used for productions done at large Performing Arts Centers. The contract is used by both commercial and not-for-profit Producers. The *Theatre for Young Audiences (TYA) Contract* covers productions of plays or material expressly written, created, or adapted to be performed for children through high school level.

Franchised Agent. Approved by one or more of the performers' unions, franchised agents "may solicit employment and negotiate contracts on behalf of performers they represent. Members may work only through such franchised talent agents. You are responsible for verifying that the agent is franchised before entering into any agency agreement."[2] In most cities, you can obtain lists of approved agents from union offices.

Liaison City. There are four Equity "office cities": Chicago, Los Angeles, New York, and San Francisco. An Equity "liaison city" is a city or area with a minimum of 100 paid-up members and at least one Equity theatre, in which members have requested liaison status. Members elect a committee to serve as a communications link between local membership and the national and regional Equity offices. The chairperson of a committee is known as the area liaison.

Presenting Houses. These are theatres that book, rather than produce, shows.

Sides. Sides are the pages of a script you'll be reading at an audition.

TDD. Telecommunications Device for the Deaf.

TTY. Teletypewriter.

Under Five. An under five is an AFTRA contract for speaking roles having five lines or less.

A final note: This book was written to be of use to *any* actor who seeks the sort of information it contains. As such, I've attempted to address numerous issues as they apply to actors with disabilities, to ethnic minority actors, to men, to women. I use the term "actors" to refer to both women and men (ever heard of a doctress?), and alternate the use of male and female pronouns from chapter to chapter.

---

[1] Definitions of Equity contracts, codes, and agreements are from an unpublished paper entitled "Equity Contracts" (New York: Actors' Equity Association, January 19, 1989).

[2] Bradley, Jacqueline, Charles Frederickson, Barry Gordon, Michael Harrah, and Mac Harris, eds., *The AFTRA-SAG Young Performers Handbook,* rev. ed. (1990).

BOSTON

Massachusetts has long been perceived as a bastion of both liberal politics and social conservatism. Think of Kennedys, then of shows "banned in Boston." Today, some blame an increasingly conservative social atmosphere on the state's ailing economy, and in 1990, voters did the nearly unheard-of and elected a Republican governor. State capital Boston, once the home of Paul Revere and the sight of that famous "tea party," is a city "forged by succeeding waves of newcomers—first Puritans, then patriots, then generations of immigrants."[1] Today, no matter which way the political and economic winds blow, Boston remains a city of both intellectuals, academics, and forward thinkers *and* easily-shocked traditionalists, those patrician "Boston Brahmins," the Beacon Hill bluebloods. Here's where L.L. Bean walks side by side with Gucci, where people move easily from sports to politics, from the galleries and boutiques of Newbury Street to the coffee houses and bookstores of Cambridge's Harvard Square.

Many find Boston a very livable city, whose culture and nightlife can satisfy true urbanites without overwhelming those who aren't. With Cape Cod two hours away and the North Shore beaches even closer, it's also well-situated for weekend frolicking. And by the way, Boston is the site of the nation's first free public school (the Boston Latin Academy, established by Puritans), as well as what one assumes must be the nation's only Sacred Cod (a model of a codfish that has been hanging above the Statehouse since the 18th century; representing the fishing industry, the Cod is a sort of Massachusetts mascot).

Boston actors benefit from being part of a community small enough to be manageable

FAST FACTS

1990 CENSUS
574,283 (+2%)

COUNTY
Suffolk

TIME
Zone: Eastern
Telephone: 637-1234

AREA CODE
617

BOSTON COMMON INFORMATION CENTER
146 Tremont Street
Boston, MA 02135

GREATER BOSTON CONVENTION AND VISITORS BUREAU
P.O. Box 490
Prudential Plaza
Boston, MA 02199
536-4100

1

and mutually supportive. At the same time, that community is small enough (and near enough New York) that actors may feel they don't get the recognition they not only deserve, but need in order to further their careers. Still, the sense of camaraderie is a strong one, and there are plenty of opportunities for networking and getting involved, if you know where to look.

RECOMMENDED READING

Charles Bahne, ed., *Car-Free in Boston: The Guide to Public Transit in Greater Boston and New England* (Cambridge, Mass.: Association for Public Transportation, Inc., 1990).

Mary Maynard and Mary Lou Maynard-Dow, *Hassle-Free Boston: A Manual for Women* (Lexington: Stephen Greene Press, 1984).

MOVIES

Between the Lines (1977), *The Bostonians* (1984), *The Good Mother* (1988), *The Verdict* (1982)

■■■■ CLIMATE

New Englanders are fond of saying "If you don't like the weather, wait ten minutes." Situated on the Atlantic Ocean's Massachusetts Bay and nearly surrounded by the Charles and Chelsea Rivers, the city is somewhat protected from the harshest of New England weather conditions. Still, coastal storms can produce plenty of rain and snow. Summers, though not excruciatingly hot, can be awfully humid; ocean breezes provide some relief. Pleasant fall days can turn quite chilly by evening. The Greater Boston Chamber of Commerce gets right to the point: "Long winters, short springs, fairly warm summers, bracing fall weather, abundant rainfall." *For weather information call:* 936-1234.

NORMAL TEMPERATURES	Average Daily High	Average Daily Low
January	36°	23°
July	82°	65°

TEMPERATURE EXTREMES

Maximum Temp.	Annual No. of Days	Minimum Temp.	Annual No. of Days
90° and above	13	32° and below	98
32° and below	27	0° and below	1

NORMAL WEATHER CONDITIONS

Clear	Partly Cloudy	Cloudy
99	104	163

ANNUAL PRECIPITATION	Days	Inches
All Precipitation	126	42
Snowfall	NA	41

◼◼◼◼ TRANSPORTATION

Boston is a city accessible by almost any means. Public transportation, combining commuter rail, buses, subways, and trolleys, is quite dependable and not especially formidable. Fairly compact, this is a good city for walking and bicycling, except for one thing: it's very easy to get lost. Certain areas aside, much of the city is laid out on anything *but* a grid pattern, making a map necessary until you really know your way around.

PUBLIC TRANSPORTATION

Massachusetts Bay Transportation Authority (MBTA). The T, as locals call it, consists of four color-named lines. The eldest is the subway/trolley combination Green Line which, with its older trains, rather rickety ride, and brightly-lit underground stations, has a certain undeniable charm. The Red, Blue, and Orange lines are more modern third-rail rapid transit. Either way, the system works pretty well and quickly except, perhaps, during rush hours. Buses run more slowly, of course, and with schedules changing every season, it's wise to refer to published schedules or call for departure times.

The MBTA fleet includes buses, trolleys, subways, commuter rail, and commuter ferries. *For information call:* 722-3200; 722-5000 (nights and weekends); 1-800-392-6100 (within MA); 722-5146 (TDD); 722-5218 (Pass Program/Pass by Mail).

Maps and schedules are available at
- MBTA Operations Center, 45 High Street;
- Park Street Station information booth (Green Line level);
- State Transportation Building, Tremont and Stuart Street, 2nd floor Library.

The above-ground trolleys take exact change or tokens; underground, tokens can be purchased at booths. On the Green Line, outbound street-level boarding is free. Local and express bus fares vary according to zone.

Children under five ride free; fares for ages five to eleven and students are discounted. Seniors and people with disabilities receive further discounts on the T and local buses. Monthly pass options are available, as are three- and seven-day tourist passes.

The following is a list of terminals and additional transportation systems:
Back Bay Station, 145 Dartmouth Street, Boston, MA 02116.
North Station, 150 Causeway, Boston, MA 02114, 227-5070 or
    800-392-6099.
South Station, Atlantic Avenue and Summer Street, Boston, MA 02110,
    482-4400 or 800-392-6099.
Amtrak, Back Bay Station and South Station, 482-3660.
Commuter Rail (MBTA Suburban Lines), Back Bay Station, North Station,
    South Station, 722-3200.
Greyhound, 10 St. James Avenue, Boston, MA, 423-5810.

TAXIS

There are plenty of taxis; how easy it is to flag one down depends on whom you're talking to, and on the time of day you're doing the flagging. Cabs are metered, and a taxi from one city cannot stop to make pick-ups in another, so there's no use trying to hail a Boston cab in Cambridge or a Brookline cab in Boston, although you can certainly travel from one city to another. (Brookline and Cambridge, though often considered parts of Boston, actually are separate cities.) Cabs also are available by phone order.

DRIVING

Though the city itself is very accessible by public transportation, most actors find they need a car. A number of theatres are outside the city proper, as are some commercial and corporate film production facilities. Boston has a reputation for maniacal driving, and the crazy cow-path of a street plan can make driving a bad dream and parking a nightmare. An October 1990 article in *USA Today* fingers Boston as the worst city for parking, where over "150,000 drivers compete each day for 35,000 downtown parking spaces. A single spot can sell (annually) for six figures."[2] When you'll be parking on the street, always allow extra travel time for the hunt.

HOUSING AND COSTS OF LIVING

Though the situation isn't as bad as in, say, New York and San Francisco, housing in Boston can be moderately expensive and hard to find. Many performers live in Boston, Cambridge, and Brookline, as well as in the more affordable (and almost as convenient) neighborhoods of Somerville, Central Square, Allston, and Briton. *Brighton* Also popular are several nearby suburbs only a few minutes from downtown by public transportation. Housing-hunters use roommate services and rental agencies, as well as the classified ads in *The Boston Globe* and *The Boston Phoenix.*

INTERAREA SHELTER INDEXES	Renters	Owners
Boston	127	153
(Philadelphia)	(100)	(100)

COSTS OF LIVING	
Total average annual expenditures	$30,361
Food at home	1,972
Telephone	548
Gas and motor oil	891
Public transportation	482
Personal care products and services	337

EMPLOYMENT

1989 Average Annual Pay
(Five counties): $26,915

1990 Average Unemployment Rates
Massachusetts: 6%
Boston metropolitan statistical area: 5.1%

1990 Average Weekly Unemployment Benefits
Massachusetts: $217.39

CRIME

Boston doesn't have a reputation as a high-crime city, and in general, residents aren't excessively concerned about crime and safety, though there are areas that are less secure than others. Among cities in this book for which statistics are available, Boston's murder rate is in the low-middle, its rape rate, the high-middle. The city has the fifth lowest rate of burglary and is tied with Dallas for the fourth highest rate of aggravated assault. The downtown theatre district borders on what locals call the

Combat Zone, meaning visitors after dark need exercise a little extra caution (though ironically, theatres in the district are commercial presenting houses that rarely employ local actors).

1990 CRIME RATES	Violent	Property
Total Crimes	13,664	54,393
Crimes per 100,000 People	2,380	9,476
Average 1 Crime per Every	42 people	11 people

MISCELLANEA

NEWSPAPERS
The Boston Globe (morning)
Boston Herald (morning)
The Boston Phoenix (weekly)

LIBRARY
Boston Public Library, Main Branch, 666 Boylston Street, Boston, MA, 536-5400.

POST OFFICE
General Mail Facility, Adjacent to the Rail Road Depot, South Station, Boston, MA 02110, 654-5083.

THE BUSINESS

Well, there's good news and there's bad news. The bad is that, in an atmosphere of traditionalism and poor economic health, Boston isn't the most nurturing place for artistic growth and experimentation. The good news is that hard times have inspired a certain amount of creativity, and that the performing arts community displays a strong belief in the benefits of mutual support and shared information. In an atmosphere of openness and camaraderie, there's ample opportunity for networking, from getting involved with play development groups to attending workshops and seminars. The majority of actors work in all venues. (Corporate and commercial work currently may not sustain quite as many actors as it has in the past, and very few actors can afford to work exclusively in the theatre.)

Boston is close enough to New York that its actors are sometimes overlooked by local and visiting producers and artistic directors who prefer to hire New York talent. Still, the situation (and resulting frustration) isn't quite as bad as it is in Philadelphia and, in fact, there has been some increased local hiring of late. In any case, the proximity to New York does allow quite a few Boston-based actors to shuttle between the two cities. Furthermore, the Boston-based actor's market covers a sixty-mile radius around the city and often extends to Connecticut, Rhode Island, Maine, Vermont, and New Hampshire.

Most newcomers probably will want to join StageSource (see *Other Associations* below) and/or buy a copy of *The Source* (discounted for members), which explains in depth and with humor just about everything the Boston-area performer needs to know, from how to ride the T to the names of theatres that have wheelchair access. Newcomers can also try to get involved with some of the many companies that develop new plays.

RECOMMENDED READING

Cyndi Mulkern, "Boston Is a Beacon for Actors," Back Stage (August 31, 1990).

Ellen Weiner, ed., The Source: The Greater Boston Theatre Resource Guide, 2d ed. (Boston: StageSource, 1992). Originally conceived by Marjorie O'Neill-Butler and Ingrid Sonnichsen, this comprehensive compilation of resources, hints, and inside information is truly amazing; a must for newcomers to Boston.

▉▉▉▉▉ PROFESSIONAL ASSOCIATIONS

TALENT UNIONS

Actors' Equity Association (AEA), Liaison City.
   Members: 550
American Federation of Television and Radio Artists (AFTRA), 11 Beacon Street, Suite 512, Boston, MA 02108, 742-2688.
   Members: 1,524
Screen Actors' Guild (SAG), same address/phone as AFTRA.
   Members: 896
American Guild of Musical Artists (AGMA), 11 Beacon Street, Boston, MA 02108, 742-0208.

OTHER ASSOCIATIONS

StageSource, One Boylston Place, Boston, MA 02116, 423-2475. Founded in 1985, StageSource is an arts advocacy, resource, and service organization for actors and other theatre professionals. Services include a casting hotline, picture and résumé file, a nontraditional casting file, and workshops. StageSource publishes *The Source*.

■■■■■■LOOKING FOR WORK

PUBLICATIONS

The Boston Phoenix. Boston actors look first to this weekly newspaper
for audition notices. It's published on ~~Fridays~~. *Thursdays*
Casting News, P.O. Box 201, Boston, MA 02134, 787-2991. Published
twice a month, *Casting News* is available by subscription or at a
number of newsstands in Boston and Cambridge and at some suburban
outlets. It includes resources, articles, events information, play
competitions, funding information, acting and musician auditions,
and more.
New England Entertainment Digest, Taylor Publishing, P.O. Box 313,
Portland, CT 06480, 203-342-4730. *NEED,* published monthly, is
available by subscription or at newsstands, and contains entertainment
news, an events calendar, press releases, and reviews. Audition notices
tend to be for community theatre, but press releases may contain
information useful to professionals.

HOTLINES

Actors' Equity Association, AFTRA/SAG (see *Talent Unions,* p. 7).
StageSource (members only)

BULLETIN BOARDS AND BINDERS

Baker's Plays (see *Bookstores,* p. 14)

TALENT BOOKS AND TALENT BANKS

AFTRA/SAG Talent Guide. For members only, this guide is published
every three years; a mid-term supplement updates information and
adds the names of newcomers.
StageSource. Membership dues cover inclusion of a P&R (photo/résumé)
in three categories of the talent bank; a small annual fee covers
additional categories. In conjunction with Playwrights' Platform,
StageSource maintains an Equal Opportunity P&R file for ethnic
minority actors and actors with disabilities; open to members and
nonmembers of StageSource.

TALENT SHOWCASES AND COMBINED AUDITIONS

National Dinner Theatre Association; New England Theatre Conference
(NETC); Straw Hat Auditions. (For addresses, see Appendix B.)
StageSource. Annual auditions are attended by local artistic directors,
producers, and others. The Equity-eligible auditions are open to all
eligible performers; non-Equity auditions are for StageSource members
only. Slots are filled on a first-come, first-served basis, with auditions
announced about six weeks in advance.

TALENT AGENTS AND CASTING DIRECTORS

At the time of this writing, only two of the approximately twenty Boston-area talent agencies are franchised by AFTRA/SAG; none hold Equity franchises. Most agencies have both modeling and talent and/or print divisions; franchises may be most necessary for those occasions when models do film and broadcast work. The fact is, it's possible for an actor to work in Boston without being listed with a single agent, though agents may provide access to print work and to film and broadcast projects whose budgets don't permit hiring casting directors. It's not a bad idea, then, for actors to send P&Rs, make some phone calls, and explore the benefits of listing with one or more of the franchised or legitimate nonfranchised agencies. AFTRA/SAG maintains a list of both; *The Source* also provides information about agents.

All actors who want to work in film and broadcast, however, need to be known to casting directors. A number of corporations and production houses do their own casting, but those that don't keep the independent casting directors pretty busy. Independent CDs rarely cast theatre, although area stages may turn to them when they have trouble filling a role. While StageSource lists ten casting companies, there are usually two or three that get the bulk of the work; at the time of this writing, Collinge/Pickman and Outcasting are busiest (but it's a good idea to ask other actors which companies are currently hot). Though some casting companies have a reputation for being less than accessible, others are quite open to newcomers, especially because clients tire of seeing the same actors over and over again. Send P&Rs, and follow up with phone calls requesting appointments. Recently, Outcasting has begun to hold biannual auditions; AFTRA and SAG members, keep an ear to the hotline.

THEATRE

Boston's theatre scene can be divided roughly into four categories. First are those regional theatres that operate under LORT contracts. American Repertory Theatre is known (and definitely not appreciated) for casting in New York; only the smaller roles are cast locally, and usually go to A.R.T. Institute students. The Huntingdon mixes some locals into their primarily-New York casts, and the Merrimack now uses all-Boston-area casts.

Category two includes local Equity theatres operating on COST and SPT contracts and LOAs. They may not pay much, but they cast locally, and some are quite successful. (Unfortunately, the Nickerson Theatres, two suburban houses that provided a lot of work for local actors, closed their doors in 1991.) Single-entity, often long-running, commercial productions like *Shear Madness* and *Nunsense* have put many locals to work.

Category three is non-Equity professional theatre. There are a number of such companies, ranging from those that produce sporadically to the well-established and respected companies producing on a regular basis. Actors usually receive some pay, if only a stipend, for their work.

The fourth category is community theatre, where many non-Equity professionals find the opportunity to build résumés, gain experience, and play some great roles.

Most theatres hold annual general auditions, and most send a representative to the StageSource auditions. Actors new to town can also contact theatres directly; send P&Rs and call to inquire about auditioning. Per-play auditions are nearly always by appointment; open calls are rare. Callbacks can be long, drawn-out affairs, with different pairings and combinations keeping actors reading for a good half day.

Comedy is especially hot in Boston, and there are a number of stand-up clubs. Performance art, movement theatre, and new vaudeville make a lesser showing, but the city does have its share of avant-garde and out-of-the-mainstream companies and performers.

████FILM AND TELEVISION

Although the budgetary axe has fallen on the Massachusetts Film Office, that agency can be credited with keeping area production alive, and Boston has been *relatively* successful in keeping a steady flow of production in the area. At the time of this writing, Boston could use a long-running TV series to replace "Spenser for Hire" and "Against the Law," but there's often something going on, from feature films to productions for *American Playhouse*. Local PBS and commercial television stations produce some dramatic shows that are cast locally, and from time to time there's talk of major studios or production companies settling in or near the city.

Visiting producers exhibit increasing respect for local talent: while locals have always been hired as extras and for very small parts, they filled nearly every non-star/guest-star role in the short-lived "Against the Law" and the 1990 feature, *Mermaids*. Local (especially nonunion) actors also benefit from increasing independent and student film (often SAG waiver) projects and cable television production.

████CORPORATE AND COMMERCIALS

There was a time in the mid-1980s when an actor could get work in corporate films almost without trying. That was during the "Massachusetts Miracle," when the economy was strong and spirits were high. When the recession hit, production and advertising budgets were slashed; even the big high-tech companies with in-house production facilities cut way back, and some production and postproduction houses closed. Actors certainly felt the pinch, as some projects were scaled down and others were cancelled altogether. Somehow, though, production has continued, and the greatest percentage of the earnings that pass through the local AFTRA/SAG office are from industrials. The road to full recovery is probably a long one but, by 1991, some people were seeing signs of a small comeback.

Union industrials are produced under both AFTRA and SAG contracts, with production under the former more frequent. Boston is a pretty strong union town so, despite the financial crunch, there hasn't been a big shift away from union production. But while that market dominates, there's a significant amount of nonunion industrial activity. Budgets for many of the nonunion productions are low enough that independent casting directors aren't part of the picture; it may be helpful, therefore, for the non-union actor to be listed with a legitimate nonfranchised agent and to make direct contact with independent production houses and with those companies that have in-house casting personnel and, in some cases, production facilities. Details and contact information can be found in *The Source*. Popular "types" for corporate production include the CEO, the thirty-to-fortyish manager, and the younger business person.

Few actors can make a living in commercials alone; those who do best have the versatility to do corporate and print work as well. It's not unheard-of for Boston actors to get national spots, but the city's proximity to New York means that many of the nationals that shoot here come for the location, and casting is done in New York; even some local and regional spots are cast in New York. Still, enough local and regional production is cast locally that there's work for Boston's commercial actors and, despite cutbacks, SAG earnings indicate a fairly substantial market. The voice-over and corporate and commercial print markets are quite strong.

CASTING DIVERSITY

There are a few constituent-specific theatre companies in Boston, like Black Folks Theater and The Company of Women. A few others, like Playwrights' Platform, utilize nontraditional casting. The Company of Women is committed to multiculturalism, and Wheelock Family Theatre is cited again and again for its absolute commitment to color-blind and nontraditional casting.

The corporate and commercial (including voice-over) markets remain predominately male, and employment drops off dramatically for women older than forty or forty-five. Ethnic minority actors find more work in industrials than in commercials. Apparently, more African American actors are being seen on camera, and StageSource gets more and more requests for referrals to older ethnic minority actors. Though there are few Asian, Hispanic, and American Indian actors in the area, calls for members of the first two groups are increasing steadily. Corporate producers regularly ask to see Asian and black actors, and there's a growing need for Spanish-English bilingual actors. AFTRA/SAG has at least a few members with disabilities, but opportunities for those actors are all but nonexistent.

StageSource and AFTRA/SAG have done a lot of outreach to both the ethnic communities and to theatres and producers. They've faced some resistance and lack of awareness on the part of the production community, and mistrust and discouragement on the part of some ethnic minority actors. Progress is being made, albeit slowly. AFTRA/SAG may create a Performers with Disabilities subcommittee under the unions' Equal Employment Opportunity Committee. StageSource encourages ethnic minority actors and those with disabilities to send P&Rs for inclusion in their nontraditional casting file.

ADDITIONAL OPPORTUNITIES

Cultural Education Collaborative, 201 South Street, Boston, MA 02111, 338-3073; 728-9187 (TTY). The CEC promotes "the cultural education of Massachusetts' diverse student populations through work with . . . artists," including performers, mimes, puppeteers, and dancers. Artists present their work to and/or work directly with students.

First Night Arts Celebration, Box 573, Back Bay Annex, Boston, MA 02117, 542-1399. Annually, from Dec. 29-31, this festival of visual, martial, video, and performing arts is presented in various locations. Participants include (among many others) storytellers, vaudevillians, performance artists, movement theatre artists, and musical groups. Applications are sent to artists; call to be put on the mailing list.

Museum of Science, Attn: Mike Alexander, Science Park, Boston, MA 02114, 589-0335. The museum hires actors to do short plays. Mr. Alexander generally works with an established pool, but accepts P&Rs from Equity and non-Equity actors.

The Open Door Theatre Company, P.O. Box 315, Jamaica Plain, MA 02130, 524-4007. This company performs outdoor summer theatre in a city-owned park. Casting is open each year; non-Equity only.

Playwrights' Platform, 164 Brayton Road, Boston, MA 02135, 254-4482. "A developmental theatre for new plays," its members include playwrights, actors, and directors. Sunday readings are a good place to meet people, as are monthly Playwright's Brunches. Equity and non-Equity actors may participate in readings; non-Equity only may appear in PP's two annual festivals (though this may change). P&Rs are kept on file; call for reading or brunch locations.

Revels, Inc., One Kendall Square, Building 600, Cambridge, Ma 02139, 621-0505. Twice a year, in December and in the spring, "through performance and participatory theatre, Revels blends song, dance, and drama into seasonal celebrations." Auditions are held for a volunteer chorus made up of professionals and nonprofessionals; call to be put on the mailing list.

Roxbury Outreach Shakespeare Experience (ROSE), 10 Orchard Street, Jamaica Plain, MA 02130, 524-3272. ROSE is an educational program that brings theatre to schools, prisons, churches, and other audiences, and does full productions of Shakespeare with mixed student/professional casts. Accepts P&Rs.

Theatre in Process, 220 Marlborough Street, Boston, MA 02116, 267-1053. TIP works on developing scripts, including some for the Wheelock Family Theatre. They do it all, from readings to full productions; P&Rs are accepted from Equity and non-Equity actors.

Until Tomorrow Productions, P.O. Box 1232, Boston, MA 02117-1232, 426-4737. UTP "develops and promotes integrated accessible theatre for the community," by supporting "select, innovative performers in the development and presentation of their work." UTP provides services to make performing spaces accessible to performers and audience members with disabilities.

▬▬▬TRAINING

Greater Boston is home to several colleges and universities of renown, and some, like Brandeis, Boston University, Emerson, and Northeastern, have highly-praised theatre departments. In addition, area theatres offer extensive training programs, classes, and workshops, including the New Theatre's two-year conservatory program. A hundred miles or so from Boston is the well-known Shakespeare and Co., which offers intensive workshops and summer training programs. One of that company's cofounders, Kristin Linklater, a nationally prominent figure in voice work, now teaches privately and at Emerson College in Boston. Several casting companies offer courses in on-camera technique, and though there are plenty of individual teachers and coaches teaching a variety of disciplines and styles, some people say there isn't enough selection for the *experienced* actor who wants to improve skills.

CERTIFICATE/DEGREE PROGRAMS
American Repertory Theatre, Institute for Advanced Theatre Training at Harvard, 64 Brattle Street, Cambridge, MA 02138, 495-2668.

The Boston Conservatory, Musical Theatre, 8 The Fenway, Boston, MA
02215, 536-6340 Ext. 16.
Boston University, School of Theatre Arts, 855 Commonwealth Avenue,
Boston, MA 02215. 353-3390.
Brandeis University, Department of Theatre Arts, P.O. Box 9110, Waltham,
MA 02254-9110, 736-3340.
Emerson College, Division of Performing Arts, 100 Beacon Street, Boston,
MA 02116, 578-8780.
Northeastern University, Department of Theatre and Dance, 360 Huntington
Avenue, Boston, MA 02115, 437-2244.

AFFORDABLE ARTS

Bostix, Fanueil Hall Marketplace, 723-5181. This program of ARTS/Boston
sells half-price day-of-performance tickets.
Arts/Mail, ARTS/Boston, Inc., 100 Boylston Street, Suite 735, Boston, MA
02116, 423-0372, 426-8966 (TDD). Subscribers can order advance
half-price tickets by mail; subscriptions are free as long as tickets are
purchased every six months.
StageSource. "Circle of Friends" cards are given annually to members of
StageSource and subscribers to participating theatres; they allow the
purchase of two tickets for the price of one at numerous area theatres
once each season.
First Night (see *Additional Opportunities,* p. 12), 720-3434 (ticket
information within Boston), 800-382-8080 (outside Boston). Admission
to most performances and events is free with a "First Night" button,
sold for a nominal fee at many locations, including BayBank branches,
visitor information booths, and the Bostix Booth.

RESOURCES

LIBRARIES
The Boston Public Library, 666 Boylston Street, Boston, MA 02116,
536-5400. This library has a good selection of plays

BOOKSTORES
Baker's Plays, 100 Chauncey Street, Boston, MA 02111, 482-1280. This is
a major play and performing-arts book publisher and mail-order house
that also carries plays and books by all major theatrical publishers.
They sell makeup kits as well.
Harvard Square. This area is abundant with bookstores, many of which
have good selections of plays and theatre-related books.

■■■■■NETWORKING AND SOCIALIZING

The acting community is small enough and friendly enough to make networking relatively painless. Quite a few theatre companies sponsor readings of new plays (see *Additional Opportunities,* p. 12 for details.) Getting involved at StageSource is another great way to meet people. Though many people express the wish for an informal actor's hang-out, none exists at the time of this writing.

New England Producers Association, 1380 Soldiers Field Road, Boston, MA 02135, 698-NEPA (6372). Some actors belong to NEPA for the chance to meet members of the producing community; a newsletter, *The Slate* (including "The Actor's Corner" column), keeps members up to date. Actor-Director Workshops allow acting and producing communities to meet and interact in low-pressure environments. Workshops open to NEPA members and nonmembers are announced on AFTRA/SAG and StageSource hotlines.

International Television Association (ITVA), 26 Constitution Drive, Southborough, MA 01772, 890-ITVA (4882). "Dedicated to the needs of the professional video communicator in nonbroadcast settings." As with NEPA (above), actors find that workshops and meetings offer good networking opportunities.

[1] *Metro Guide* (Greater Boston Chamber of Commerce).
[2] John Larabee, "In Boston, elsewhere, a constant quest for parking," *USA Today* (October 1990).

C H I C

Oh, that toddling town, one town that won't let you down! So the songs say and indeed, Chicago inspires the kind of love and loyalty that incites grown men to set their admiration to music. Here, the industrial North meets the Midwest, resulting in a sophisticated yet manageable metropolis. From O'Hare Airport (our nation's busiest) to the Loop, from Comiskey Park to the old stockyards, from blues music (this city even has a jazz hotline!) to deep-dish pizza, Chicago has a style and flavor unmistakably its own. It's a lively city, sexy in a friendly sort of way, comfortable without being dull.

The City of Big Shoulders may have a reputation for being hard-boiled, evoking images of tough union bosses and fedora-ed gangsters, but people who live here tell a different story. It's a great place to be, they say: affordable, livable, cultured. Sure it's the Midwest, but you can buy very cool clothes here, drink cappuccino in funky cafés and, best of all, maybe even earn a living as an actor. At the very least, you can live without starving as you might in New York (because you can't afford to eat) or L.A. (because you can't afford to gain weight).

Actors have an additional reason for loving Chicago: It's one of the few cities in which no small number of them actually earn a living working *on the stage*. Sure, plenty do commercials and industrials, and others have survival jobs, and there are actors who rarely work, struggling like actors everywhere. But a surprising number of people make it on what they earn on the boards alone. Just as important is the recognition and even

FAST FACTS

1990 CENSUS
2,783,726 (−7.4%)

COUNTY
Cook

TIME
Zone: Central
Telephone: 976-1616

AREA CODE
312

CHICAGO CONVENTION AND TOURISM BUREAU
McCormick Place on the Lake
Chicago, IL 60616
567-8500

CHICAGO OFFICE OF TOURISM
Historic Water Tower in the Park
806 N. Michigan Avenue
Chicago, IL 60611
280-5740

VISITOR INFORMATION CENTER
163 E. Pearson
Chicago, IL 60611
280-5747

respect actors receive in this, our nation's second city of theatre and
advertising. In Chicago, talent is nurtured, experimentation encouraged,
failure easily forgiven.

RECOMMENDED READING

Nelson Algren, *Chicago, City on the Make* (Chicago: The University of
  Chicago Press, 1987).

Glenn Bugala, *First Year: An Actor's View of Chicago and Its Theatre*
  (Glenn Bugala, 1990). This contemporary memoir is based on the
  journal of "a hick from Michigan in the big city."

Studs Terkel, *Chicago* (New York: Pantheon Books, 1986). This is Terkel's
  impressionistic view of the city, part history, part memoir, illustrated
  with black and white photographs.

Pearl Pacheco Williams with Aurelia Powell Henton, *The Black Experience
  in Little Theatre and the Richard B. Harrison Players* (published by the
  author). A memoir of Chicago theatre in days gone by.

MOVIES

. . . *About Last Night* (1986), *The Blues Brothers* (1980), *A Raisin in the
Sun* (1961), *V.I. Warshawski* (1991)

■■■■■■■CLIMATE

"Chicago is wonderful in September. You never want summer to end
because here there is no autumn—winter comes down your neck like
Madame Guillotine."[1] You think they were kidding when they dubbed
it "the windy city"? Winter temperatures rarely fall below the low 20s
to high teens, but strong gusts can turn otherwise run-of-the-mill days
into Arctic nightmares. Chicago gets a fair amount of snow, but the
real issue is that invisible force that, at its gustiest, can keep you rooted
to a single spot, struggling to take a step forward. Forsaking fashionable
wool coats for more practical down helps to make the season manageable.
Along the shore of Lake Michigan, the wind may be stronger, but it
actually raises the temperature a little. Summers range from hot and
lovely to hot and horrible; near the lake, though, that breeze moves the
air around, lowering the temperature and easing the sometimes-stifling
humidity. Those who can't afford to live along the lakeshore can visit

its beaches during the summer. Fall and spring can be lovely—and far too short. *For weather information call:* 976-1212.

NORMAL TEMPERATURES	Average Daily High	Average Daily Low
January	29°	14°
July	83°	63°

TEMPERATURE EXTREMES

Maximum Temp.	Annual No. of Days	Minimum Temp.	Annual No. of Days
90° and above	17	32° and below	133
32° and below	49	0° and below	13

NORMAL WEATHER CONDITIONS

Clear	Partly Cloudy	Cloudy
85	105	175

ANNUAL PRECIPITATION	Days	Inches
All Precipitation	126	35
Snowfall	NA	39

■■■■ TRANSPORTATION

All roads lead to Chicago. Well, not exactly, but bordered by suburbs to the west, north, and south, Chicago is well-fed by a network of bus, rapid rail, and commuter train lines, all of which merge and converge downtown. Getting around is relatively easy, and though most areas are quite walkable, the city is so spread out that people rely on public transportation and/or cars or bikes.

Streets are laid out on a grid; there's hardly a curve in the bunch. It's those darn angled streets—Lincoln, Clybourn, Archer, Clark, to name a few—that muddle things up. Once you're used to them and have your directional bearings, however, finding your way is easy enough. Addresses on major streets have a single directional prefix that designates location north or south of Madison Street and east or west of State Street (that great street, that's right). Addresses begin at Madison and State, increasing by 100 every eighth of a mile (which often means every block); thus 210 S. Canal Street is located approximately three standard city blocks south of Madison.

PUBLIC TRANSPORTATION

Chicago Transit Authority (CTA). Most of the "actor's Chicago" is accessible via public transportation. Theatres in the north end are easily reachable by both bus and the "L" (rapid transit line, also spelled "El"), and even many suburban theatres and facilities can be reached via commuter lines. Of course, the L, combining elevated and underground routes, generates its share of complaints, from stuffiness-induced motion sickness, to frozen fingers and faces that come from waiting too long on elevated platforms in wintertime. Long waits sometimes end with trains coming one after the other, and local trains are rerouted to express routes often enough that it's essential to pay close attention to announcements made over the public address system. (Newly transplanted New Yorkers will be gratified to know that in Chicago such messages are actually intelligible.) Though the trains look rather old and rickety, they do work, covering the city extensively and fairly efficiently. Most people consider the trains relatively safe, although many (especially women) switch to buses at night, when some platforms can be awfully isolated and deserted. Buses, though slower than the L, are also reasonably speedy and efficient (except, perhaps, in heavily-trafficked areas like the Loop); express buses help keep things moving. Be sure to contact the CTA for a system map, which includes a map of the L, bus route descriptions, and bus route first-run/last-run tables.

The CTA fleet includes buses, rail (subway and elevated), Metra commuter rail, and Pace suburban buses. *For information call:* 836-7000; 800-972-7000 (from suburbs); 836-4949 (TTY); 521-1154 (door-to-door service for seniors/disabled).

Maps and schedules are available at CTA Offices, Merchandise Mart, 350 N. Wells, 7th floor, Chicago, IL 60654, 664-7200.

Exact fare (dollar bills accepted) or a token is required; there is a basic fare for buses and the subway/elevated, with a surcharge during rush hours and for transfers and express routes. Transfers allow two additional rides within two hours, but not on the line of origin. (Be sure to ask for your transfer back from the conductor if you'll need it a second time.) Fares are reduced for children ages seven to eleven, students through high school, seniors, and the disabled; children under six ride free. Tokens sold in packages of ten offer a small savings and are available at banks, currency exchanges, Jewel and Dominick's supermarkets, and rapid transit stations. Fourteen-day, monthly, and Sunday/holiday unlimited passes are available at CTA rail terminals and the above locations, except rapid transit stations. CTA tokens, transfers, and passes are good on Pace buses; Metra commuter trains have separate fares.

The following is a list of terminals and additional transportation systems:
Amtrak, Union Station, 210 S. Canal Street, Chicago, IL, 558-1075.
Greyhound, 630 W. Harrison Street, Chicago, IL, 781-2900.

Indian Trails, Inc., 630 W. Harrison Street, Chicago, IL, 928-8606. These
buses operate between Chicago, Indiana, and Michigan.

TAXIS

Street hailing is easy in many areas of town, and rates are on the low
side. However, Chicago is spread out enough to make travelling by taxi
less than economical. Taxis are metered, with surcharges for each
additional passenger between the ages of twelve and sixty-five.

DRIVING

While cars aren't strictly necessary, many Chicago residents have them
anyway. Some like them for comfort and convenience, others for the status
they convey. Actors—especially women—may want cars for coming home
late, when some buses aren't running and safety is a concern. Combining
public and private transportation makes the most sense; unfortunately,
many car owners get lazy and bypass the generally very good public
system. Driving around the city is easy enough, although it seems there's
always a major construction project jamming things up on one main
thoroughfare or another. Though parking isn't quite the ordeal it is in
some cities, it does present certain challenges. The trick is having intimate
knowledge of frequently-visited neighborhoods (including one's own).
Taking a car into the Loop on business days, for example, is pure
madness; at night, however, traffic in that area is sparse, and parking easy.
And while Chicagoans don't fret as much as New Yorkers do about car
vandalism, the wise car owner knows which neighborhoods are safe for
street parking. Finally, since Chicago parking-ticket givers have grown
more vigilant of late, it's necessary to feed meters regularly and steer clear
of no-parking zones.

■■■■■■HOUSING AND COSTS OF LIVING

It's just not that hard to find decent, affordable housing here. Longtime
residents may notice prices rising, but anyone relocating from New
York or the Bay Area should feel like a kid in a candy store. Find
a neighborhood you like and walk around, keeping eyes open for "For
Rent" signs. Check the classified ads in *The Reader,* a free paper that
comes out Thursdays; check the bulletin boards at Equity and at Act I
Bookstore, which usually have some sublet and share announcements.
There are several no-fee-to-renter apartment locator services. Recommended
affordable neighborhoods include Lakeview, Bucktown, Wrigleyville,
Rogers Park (slightly less convenient, but you get more for your money),
and suburban Oak Park.

Artist in Residence, 6165 N. Winthrop Avenue, Chicago, IL 60660, 743-8900.
Two adjacent apartment buildings are rented (at rates just slightly
below market) solely to people active in the fine or applied arts. The
buildings also contain performance and rehearsal facilities.

INTERAREA SHELTER INDEXES	Renters	Owners
Chicago	101	101
(Philadelphia)	(100)	(100)

COSTS OF LIVING	
Total average annual expenditures	$32,349
Food at home	2,454
Telephone	559
Gas and motor oil	917
Public transportation	510
Personal care products and services	498

■■■■■■EMPLOYMENT

1989 Average Annual Pay
Chicago-Gary-Lake County: $25,702

1990 Average Unemployment Rates
Illinois: 6.2%
Chicago metropolitan statistical area: 5.9%

1990 Average Weekly Unemployment Benefits
Illinois: $169.94

■■■■■CRIME

You can check your machine gun and topcoat at the airport; though people
love to think about gangsters when they think about Chicago, a reality
check is in order. Sure, there's crime—of the organized, gang, and garden
varieties—but on a day-to-day basis, the average person doesn't worry about
running into Al Capone's grandson. Among cities in this book, Chicago's
murder rate is a little higher, its burglary rate a little lower, than average;
the city does, however, have the second highest rate of aggravated assault.

There are areas that get creepy at night, like parts of the North Side
that attract some real "types" after dark, and the Loop, which bustles

during the day and all but shuts down after business hours. Some people who happily ride the subway/L during the day avoid it at night. Though trains are cut down to a couple of cars (making them more populated) and fairly well guarded, some platforms are well below the level of the payment booth and can be scarily deserted.

1990 CRIME RATES[2]	Violent	Property
Total Crimes	72,120	231,367
Crimes per 100,000 People	2,842	8,311
Average 1 Crime per Every	35 people	12 people

■■■■■MISCELLANEA

NEWSPAPERS
Chicago Tribune (all day)
Chicago Sun-Times (morning)
Chicago Reader (weekly)
Chicago Daily Defender

LIBRARY
Central Library, Harold Washington Library Center, 400 S. State Street, Chicago, IL 60605, 747-4300.

POST OFFICE
Main Branch, 433 W. Van Buren Street, Chicago, IL, 765-3009 or 765-3210.

MUSEUMS
Museum of Broadcast Communications, 800 S. Wells Street, Chicago, IL 60607, 987-1500.

THE BUSINESS

Chicago has a reputation for producing ballsy, realer-than-real guerrilla theatre whose intense young mega-talents go on to be Hollywood successes via, perhaps, some maverick, wildly successful, seat-of-the-pants independent feature. Indeed, there's plenty of speculation about what it means to be a Chicago actor, so let's come down to earth for a moment: for starters, there's a lot more than head-bashing going on, even at houses like Remains Theatre and Steppenwolf, two companies most often credited with creating "Chicago style." The truth is, all sorts of theatre happens here. In fact, while many people praise the community for continuing to do the risky, boundary-pushing work that made its reputation, others complain Chicago theatre has grown stale, safe, complacent.

What continues without debate is the emphasis on acting, directing, and writing, rather than on lavish production and eye-catching spectacle. But while it might be said that theatre here belongs to the artists, national fame and fortune are not likely to be won in Chi, despite the bicoastal success of several local actors. Most theatre actors get paid, however, and many do well in the thriving commercial and respectable corporate and feature films markets. Of course, it isn't every actor who gets by without supplementary income, but plenty do earn their keep without having to rely on survival jobs. The sums they bring home may not be princely, but often are enough for life in Chicago.

Many who've done well here go on to try their luck in Hollywood or the Apple, leaving room for newcomers. This is a pretty friendly, mutually-supportive community in which actors tend to share information and help one another. That doesn't mean it's always easy to break in. While the Chicago actor pool increases steadily, the number of theatres does not. There's plenty of competition and a certain amount of politicking, making it necessary to do your homework: find out, for example, which theatres and agents are right for you, and market yourself appropriately.

RECOMMENDED READING

Jonathan Abarbanel, "Working in Chicago," in *The Back Stage Handbook for Performing Artists,* rev. ed., Sherry Eaker, comp. and ed. (New York: Back Stage Books, 1991). Anyone considering a move to Chicago should read this piece.

Act One Reports (Chicago: PerformInk). Updated approximately three times a year, this booklet provides contact information for Chicago-area agents, casting directors, union offices, production companies, ad agencies, support and technical services, hotlines, and Chicago and Midwest theatres. A must for new- and not-so-newcomers.

Don Kaufman, *Acting and Modeling Resource Guide to Chicago* (Chicago: Don Kaufman). Updated yearly, this guide contains lists of instructors, agents, casting directors, employment agencies, apartment referral services, health and exercise services, and transportation information.

Julia Corbett Westrich and Ronda Pierson Farrell, *The Chicago Talent Handbook* (Chicago: Chicago Review Press, 1985). Listings may need updating; otherwise this is a helpful introduction to the business for models, actors, and voice-over talent.

■■■■■PROFESSIONAL ASSOCIATIONS

TALENT UNIONS

Actors' Equity Association (AEA), 203 N. Wabash Avenue, 17th Floor,
  Chicago, IL 60601, 641-0393.
  Members: 1,470
American Federation of Television and Radio Artists (AFTRA),
  307 N. Michigan Avenue, Chicago, IL 60601, 372-8081.
  Members: 2,451
Screen Actors' Guild (SAG), same address and phone as AFTRA.
  Members: 2,568
American Guild of Musical Artists (AGMA), 343 S. Dearborn Street,
  13th Floor, Chicago, IL 60604, 922-2800.

■■■■■LOOKING FOR WORK

PUBLICATIONS

Act One Reports (see *Recommended Reading,* p. 23).
Audition News, Chicago Entertainment Co., 6272 W. North Avenue,
  Chicago, IL 60639, 637-4695. Available by subscription or at retail outlets,
  Audition News is published monthly. This trade magazine contains
  lists of agents, casting directors, and theatres; ads for photographers,
  classes, etc.; some news/press releases. It advertises few auditions, but
  is good for listings.
Chicago Reader, 11 E. Illinois, Chicago, IL 60611, 828-0350. This free
  weekly general-interest newspaper (available at retail outlets and
  streetcorner boxes around town, or at the above address) is also
  a source of audition information. It is published on Thursdays; check
  the "Wanted" section of the classifieds.
PerformInk, 2632 N. Lincoln, Chicago, IL 60614, 348-4658. The primary
  trade publication here, PerformInk is used less for audition information
  (though it is a source) than for keeping up-to-date with goings-on in
  the theatre community; it also runs ads for teachers, services, and so
  on. Published biweekly, it's available by subscription or can be picked
  up free-of-charge at agents' offices, theatre lobbies, the Act I
  Bookstore, and other outlets.

HOTLINES

The Equity and non-Equity hotlines are the most-utilized sources of
audition information.
Non-Equity, 976-CAST (2278). This has the most comprehensive non-
  Equity listings, and is a toll call.

Audition News, 637-2776. Also non-Equity, this is not as comprehensive, perhaps, as the above number, but is a free call.

Illinois Film Office, 427-FILM (3456). The IFO primarily announces calls for extras and stand-ins.

BULLETIN BOARDS AND BINDERS

Act I Bookstore (see "Bookstores," p. 33). The bulletin board carries some audition announcements (most of which also appear in *Performink*), as well as some actors' night announcements, theatre posters, and apartment sublets and shares.

TALENT BOOKS AND TALENT BANKS

AFTRA/SAG Talent Directory

TALENT SHOWCASES AND COMBINED AUDITIONS

Illinois Theatre Association; Indiana Theatre Association; Michigan Theatre Association; Mid-America Theatre Conference Auditions; National Dinner Theatre Association; Wisconsin Theatre Auditions. (For addresses, see Appendix B.)

League of Chicago Theatres, 67 E. Madison, Suite 2116, Chicago, IL 60603, 977-1730. This audition, showcasing union and nonunion ethnic minority and physically challenged actors, is held every year in spring or summer. The League keeps P&Rs on file throughout the year following participation.

◼◼◼◼◼◼TALENT AGENTS AND CASTING DIRECTORS

Traditionally, Chicago agents and talent work nonexclusively, meaning actors can list with several agencies. Though that still happens, signing with one agent is growing much more common. There's no best system, only that which works best for you and your agent(s); some actors multi-list for several months to a year in order to see how things go. If two or three agents are getting you auditions with any sort of frequency, and are negotiating contracts to your satisfaction, that system is working. Being signed with a single agent, on the other hand, implies you'll be given priority over talent merely listed with the agent. If you do sign with an agency, be certain it's one that handles all the areas of film and broadcast in which you want to work.

For the most part, agents aren't part of the theatre audition process, although some get occasional calls for Midwest—and sometimes New York—theatre, and for hard-to-cast roles at major local houses. It can be helpful, though it's not essential, for actors who don't have good Midwest theatre contacts to work with one of these agents. Actors who've reached a point at which negotiating contracts gets complicated might want to be with an Equity-franchised agent.

The list of local agents may be long enough to confuse the newcomer, but it's also short enough that an experienced Chicago actor could go through a current copy of *Act One Reports* or *Audition News* and explain who's who. Agents are relatively accessible—certainly more so than in New York or L.A.—though as the talent pool increases, accessibility decreases. Time was when most agencies held open registration hours each week, and getting listed was almost as simple as dropping off pictures, but times have changed. Open registrations are less common and no longer mean automatic listing. You can find out which agencies have open registrations by calling directly, or by checking both publications mentioned here. Actors attending open registrations should bring several P&Rs. Once listed, an actor may need to keep in touch with agents by sending postcards, offering theatre comps, and continuing to send P&Rs every six or eight months.

For a list of casting directors, turn to that handy copy of *Act One Reports*; again, an assist from an experienced local will help you get oriented. Actors may send P&Rs (and postcards, fliers, and so forth) to appropriate casting directors, but it's best not to drop by uninvited; there's a taboo against it here, and many casting directors don't appreciate that sort of surprise.

Though the system is not completely compartmentalized, several casting companies specialize, one handling mostly local commercials, another commercials and industrials, another extras; yet another may be under contract to a major film studio. Some out of town (including New York) theatres hold casting sessions here, and quite a few local theatres have casting directors on staff. You can send a P&R to them at the theatre; if the person also works as an independent, send a separate P&R to their office.

It's not easy, but some actors manage to work in film and broadcast without having agents. If you're not represented, be sure to send your materials to the casting directors and to stay in touch. However, some producers of corporate film and video bypass casting directors and go straight to agents. Either way, doing theatre is a good way to get seen; the stage is taken quite seriously here, and many agents and casting directors attend regularly. The funny thing is, some actors are so involved with their stage work—and earn enough money at it—that they don't bother to pursue commercials and corporate work. If you really make a mark in theatre, though, the casting directors will find you.

▬▬▬ THEATRE

Chicago experienced a theatre renaissance during the late '70s and early '80s. New theatres were built, companies were formed, playwrights created important works; Steppenwolf Theatre and several of its actors gained national attention for doing work that seemed unique and exciting. After a period of stagnation, Chicago theatre was reborn. Today, there's so much theatre happening that local newspapers' theatre listings are as lengthy as most cities' movie listings. The spring 1991 issue of *Act One Reports* lists well over a hundred Chicago-area theatres—and that's not including single-entity commercial productions and the small ensembles that will have formed since publication (it may, of course, include a few that are no longer with us). Some people estimate there are as many as two hundred Chicago-area theatres, representing a wide range of styles and sensibilities.

There are only two LORT theatres in the area, the Goodman and Northlight. Production Contracts have been rare (some of the mega-musicals come to town, and some national tours even originate here, but casts aren't made up entirely of locals) as the city's major presenting houses have remained dark. By mid-1991, however, there were indications of a general revitalization of the big houses. On the other hand, more and more of New York's hit plays are being presented by local commercial producers. Reversing the equation, several playwrights and producers with an eye on Off-Broadway start with a run here, where a show is less likely to die overnight, as it might in New York. Most of the small commercial producers, along with the majority of the not-for-profit Equity theatres, use the tiered Chicago Area Theatre (CAT) contract, similar to New York's Off-Broadway contract. Approximately thirty productions, companies, and theatres use the contract; there's also an extremely limited, rarely-used Equity Showcase code.

Here, the countless non-Equity companies are taken as seriously as their Equity counterparts. Professional non-Equity companies are reviewed in major papers alongside Equity productions, and some are leading organizations with full seasons and respectable subscriber bases. Less dependent on the bottom line, Non-Equity theatre is often credited with carrying on the tradition of innovative, rule-breaking work. A few companies pay reasonable stipends, though none, perhaps, offer enough for actors to live without supplementary income.

People may not immediately associate Chicago theatre with musicals, but the mega-hits do come through, the Goodman produces a musical each year, and the area has no fewer than four dinner theatres, some of which are huge, multistage operations producing shows with Broadway-sized casts. Midwest regional theatres, as well as a few from New York and California, come to hold auditions, although not as many as some folks would like. Still, a lot of actors have busy regional theatre careers using Chicago as home base.

People are fond of saying, "If you're good, you'll work in Chicago." Leaving aside the unspoken implication that the inverse is also true, the statement is a seductive one, and shouldn't be taken at face value. True, with so much theatre, it may seem there's always room for another good actor. But if you're an Equity woman, unpack your bags—you might find the going tough. It's the case everywhere that there are fewer roles for women, but if Chicago style exists, it's a pretty macho party: think Shepard; think Mamet. If you're an Equity man, come, but keep aside enough money for a return ticket—just in case. There are a lot of actors here, and even Chicago's stages can't support them all; even here, breaking in can be a long and arduous—and for some people, ultimately disappointing—task. Of course, there are always exceptions, and with any luck you'll be one of them. (Highly-skilled musical theatre actors—male and female—may have an easier time, at least initially.) As a general rule, however, Equity actors would be wise to investigate further before committing financially or emotionally to moving here.

There's enough decent-or-better nonunion theatre that non-Equity actors probably have an easier time of it. These actors can almost certainly get on the stage; it might not happen immediately, and with a wide range of quality, there's no predicting where on the food chain one will land. But at this point, non-Equity theatre is still pretty open, and people fortunate enough to play good roles in quality productions can get noticed. In fact, the theatre community, proud of its accomplishments, can be rather "Chicago-centric," and there's a tendency to favor people who come up through the ranks locally. That means non-Equity actors who've been seen on local stages may have an easier time than Equity newcomers getting cast on Equity stages.

Most theatres hold annual general auditions; the unofficial audition season is between May and July. Check the hotlines and *Chicago Reader;* each announcement usually includes a date and time when actors may begin calling to set up appointments. You can also call the theatres that interest you and inquire about dates and procedures. Equity theatres have both eligible and noneligible calls and, while some auditions are popular and fill up quickly, actors on waiting lists usually get seen. Noneligible auditions at the Cort, the Goodman Theatre (which does some casting in New York), and several other Equity theatres are by invitation only, based on P&R self-submissions; submission dates are announced annually on the hotline.

Since most Equity (and many non-Equity) per-show auditions aren't open, it's important to attend generals and to have some good, strong monologues to perform. Generals at the top theatres often are attended by casting and artistic directors from other theatres as well, so auditioners actually are seen by several people. The Equity office handles scheduling for many auditions; you can sign up by phone, fax, or in person. Cancellations must be made twenty-four hours in advance; failure to cancel can result in suspension from scheduling appointments for upcoming auditions. Eligible actors should be sure to read the Chicago National Contracts Audition Code, available at the Equity office.

■■■■■FILM AND TELEVISION

Though few film and even fewer TV projects originate here, work opportunities are increasing. But like everywhere else, there are far more actors than there are jobs. Even before the labor dispute of early 1991 that kicked several features from New York to Chicago, theatrical film production was showing an upward trend. Of course, principal casting is generally complete by the time a film arrives, leaving day player and small supporting roles to be cast locally, but Hollywood takes Chi actors a little more seriously than it does their counterparts in other location cities. And every so often, L.A. looks at Chicago actors for films that aren't coming here at all.

Only rarely does a TV series set up shop here or come on location; there have been some visits from the reality-based programming that seems to hop all over the map. Only a small handful of pilots come each year, but Chicago's ever-strengthening ties with L.A. mean pilot season is a busy time anyway, when local agents, casting directors, and actors are included in the casting process. L.A. casting people may not come here very often, but they see Chicago talent on tape for pilots and soaps. Of course, living in Chicago takes you out of the running for day player roles and bit parts on L.A.-based shows; in addition, if a principal role is narrowed down to an L.A. actor and an equally right, equally unknown out-of-towner, the former is more likely to get the job.

Since stardom, or even a consistent on-screen career, is all but unattainable here, many of the city's more established actors move on to New York or L.A., creating space for newcomers. But breaking into film and TV production here in the first place can be difficult. Younger actors may have it a little easier: they have more time to prove themselves on stage, and youth excuses them from being as polished as older newcomers who must compete against a pool of experienced talent whose work is already known. Still, this being a theatre town, casting directors know something about acting, and young people are expected to have training, if not a lot of experience. Whatever your age, agents and casting directors do see theatre, whence the leap to the small and big screens is most likely to be made.

■■■■■CORPORATE AND COMMERCIALS

Chicago has a more-than-respectable corporate market. Most of the union work is AFTRA, and there's also quite a bit of nonunion production. Industrials don't always hire casting directors, so it's helpful to have agents, although some corporations and production companies have staff members who handle casting in-house; these are listed in *Act One Reports*. Most corporate work requires a conservative look; eccentric types and intense character actors won't find as much work. Here as elsewhere, then, most industrials require the "typical" industrials actor, although, when the occasional dramatic script comes along, agents turn to those they think of as primarily theatre and/or theatrical film actors. People who do a lot of corporate work run the risk of being tagged "industrials actors" and, unless they also do stage work, may find they aren't considered for theatrical film.

When it comes to the advertising industry, Chicago is second only to Madison Avenue, and commercials are bread and butter for many actors. The SAG market is strong (Chicago's SAG commercial earnings are topped only by those in New York and Hollywood) and, though some of the nationals that come for location shoots do their casting on either coast, there's enough work originating locally to keep people busy. While a Midwestern P&G look is most popular here, extreme characters also do well in commercials. It's not unusual for actors to come to commercials via theatre, and talent agents and ad agency types have been known to haunt comedy and improv clubs searching for new blood.

Voice-over is big-time here; the market is as strong as the wind off Lake Michigan and, though v/o is always a tough nut to crack, the door is slightly ajar. But pursuing voice work means making a major commitment of time, effort, and money. As an unknown newcomer, you'd be wise to wait till you arrive to make a tape; ask agents to let you listen to the demos of some of their top people so you can learn what's in style.

CASTING DIVERSITY

Efforts by the League of Chicago Theatres and active union committees have contributed to growing awareness and understanding of nontraditional casting issues and concepts, and though examples of tokenism exist, the situation is probably better here than it is in many other cities. In general, non-Equity theatre has embraced the principals of diverse representation; Equity houses have been slower, though there are examples of color-blind and progressive casting, including that of actors with disabilities. The CAT contract mandates that producers ensure the hiring of ethnic minority actors and indeed, ethnic minority hiring has increased appreciably. There are some constituent-specific companies, including an Asian group still in the formative stages at the time of this writing. Too little attention is given to increasing opportunities for women actors, although several women have become directors of note.

There has been some progress in the commercial world, although many clients may be holding onto a narrow view of just what population constitutes the Midwest market. The bilingual voice-over market is expanding to keep up with the growing Spanish-speaking population. As the corporate world responds to an increasingly diverse work force, industrial film and video provide more opportunities for ethnic minority actors, though some continue to feel frustrated by limited opportunities resulting from preconceptions and misperceptions about race and ethnicity.

ADDITIONAL OPPORTUNITIES

Bailiwick Repertory Directors Festival, 3212 N. Broadway, Chicago, IL 60657, 883-1091. Yes, the focus is on directors, but the festival offers actors a good opportunity to be seen and to meet people. A general audition is held in July, but if you direct (or know a director) you can try to put something up yourself.

Columbia College, Department of Film and Video, 600 S. Michigan, Chicago, IL 60605, 663-1600. Actors interested in participating in student projects can post their names and phone numbers on the 8th floor bulletin board.

Music Theatre Workshop, 5647 N. Ashland, Chicago, IL 60660, 561-7100. This multi-arts organization utilizes actors who sing for outreach to area teenagers. Send a P&R to Michael Curtis, Production Coordinator.

TRAINING

Chicago actors aren't known to study as much as their New York counterparts. The reason may have less to do with lack of either interest or good teachers than with the fact that most Chicago actors spend more time on stage. Several directors, casting directors, and artistic directors offer instruction in a range of techniques and styles, from auditioning to voice and body work, from voice-over to Shakespeare, from on-camera to singing and dancing. Act One Studio (not affiliated with the bookstore, except in the creation of the *Reports*) offers classes in the workings of the biz; their seminars and private career consultations could provide introductory information to experienced actors who are new to Chicago. Actors Center is often recommended for courses in acting technique. Check local trade publications (see p. 24) for school and instructor advertisements.

CERTIFICATE/DEGREE PROGRAMS

DePaul University, The Theatre School, 2135 N. Kenmore Avenue, Chicago, IL 60614, 362-8374, 800-433-7285.

Northwestern University, Theatre Department, 1979 Sheridan Road, Evanston, IL 60208, 708-491-3210.

Roosevelt University, Department of Visual and Performing Arts,
430 S. Michigan Avenue, Chicago, IL 60605-9865, 341-3719.

University of Illinois at Chicago, Department of Communications and
Theatre, Box 4348, Chicago, IL 60680, 996-3187.

▬▬AFFORDABLE ARTS

Hot Tix Booths. Half-price or discounted day-of-performance tickets are
available at
- 24 S. State Street (Downtown);
- 1616 Sherman Avenue (Evanston);
- 1020 Lake Street (Oak Park).

Theatre Low-Price Policies. Several theatres have instituted low-price
policies: Remains Theatre (all tickets, $10); Steppenwolf Theatre
(half-price "Rush Tix" are sold fifteen minutes before curtain; arrive a
little earlier to get in line); The Goodman Theatre (half-price day-of-
performance "Tix at Six" are sold from 6 p.m. until curtain).

Actor Nights. It seems actors rarely pay full price—if they pay anything—
for theatre tickets. Free actor nights are announced on hotlines and
in *PerformInk;* it's sometimes necessary to show an Equity card or
a P&R. You can call theatres and ask if they're having an actor night
or if they have unsold seats to give away.

Women in Film Hotline, 236-3618. Most announcements are WIF-related,
but the line also has occasional information about free screenings.

▬▬RESOURCES

LIBRARIES

The Chicago Public Library, 400 S. State Street, Chicago, IL 60605.
- Art Information Center, 269-2858. This department has some film,
  TV, and radio scripts.
- Literature Information Center, 269-2880. The Center attempts to
  acquire all new titles in 20th-century English-language drama; its
  holdings include monologue and special collections.
- Music Information Center, 269-2886. The Center has musical theatre
  librettos.
- Special Collections Division, 269-2926. This contains the Chicago
  Theatre Arts and History collection, including the Goodman Theatre
  Archives.

Ray Lonergan Memorial Library, Actors' Equity Association, 203 N. Wabash,
Suite 1700, Chicago, IL 60601. The library contains more than 500 scripts
and theatre books.

BOOKSTORES

Act 1 Bookstore, 2632 N. Lincoln, Chicago , IL 60614, 348-6757.
Scenes Coffee House and Dramatist Bookstore, 3168 N. Clark, Chicago, IL
   60657, 525-1007.

■■■■■NETWORKING AND SOCIALIZING

Schmoozing, getting to know people, is part of the art here. Go to the
theatre, go to parties, talk to people. The wise actor will target the
theatres that interest him most and try to get involved even, perhaps,
before he auditions. Restaurants listed below are frequented by actor-
types; Sweet Home Chicago is especially popular.

Joel's Theatre Café, 3313 N. Clark, Chicago, IL 60657, 871-0896.
Scenes Coffee House and Dramatist Bookstore, 3168 N. Clark, Chicago, IL
   60657, 525-1007.
Sweet Home Chicago, 3270 N. Clark, Chicago, IL 60657, 327-3202.

[1]   Ivor S. Irvin, "Sonderkommando," *The Sun,* no. 186 (May 1991).
[2]   Rape is not included in Chicago calculations because "figures furnished [to the FBI]
      by the state-level UCR [Uniform Crime Report] program . . . were not in accordance
      with national UCR guidelines."

D   A   L

THE CITY

Big D. For a city that started out as a one-room trading post, Dallas certainly has grown. What some people call the Third Coast (odd, since there's no coastline) is home to the world's largest wholesale trade center and to numerous major corporations. Dallas also claims the titles of news media center for the Southwest and of third largest film production center in the nation. Still, while film and television production brings a lot of dollars to the area, there's far less civic support for the performing arts than there might be. Despite shoe-string budgets, however, the local film commissions work hard to attract production to the region. For actors, the bottom line is this: stardom is unlikely here, but it's possible to work and, in some cases, even make a living; quite a few people do so working in film and broadcast, and a very few in theatre.

Many people agree Dallas is a friendly town. Those who've never been here might imagine a city full of oil tycoons in business suits, bolo ties, and ten-gallon hats. Sure, these types are here, along with Southfork Ranch, rodeos, Billy Bob's honky tonk, and enough shopping centers and theme parks to last a lifetime. But there are also an annual film festival, quite a bit of theatre, and some fine museums. While one can't deny the presence of rednecks and nouveaux-riches, there are far more cultural sophisticates than

FAST FACTS

1990 CENSUS
1,006,877 (+11.3%)

COUNTIES
Dallas
Tarrant (Fort Worth)

TIME
Zone: Central
Telephone: 844-4444

AREA CODES
Dallas County: 214
Tarrant County: 817
UNLESS OTHERWISE NOTED, ALL PHONE NUMBERS
IN THIS CHAPTER USE THE 214 AREA CODE.

**DALLAS CONVENTION AND
VISITORS BUREAU**
Renaissance Tower
1201 Elm Street, Suite 2000
Dallas, TX 75270
746-6677

INFORMATION
West End Market Place
603 Munger
Dallas, TX

INFORMATION
Union Station
400 S. Houston Street
Dallas, TX
747-2355

outsiders have been led to believe. If anything, the Lone Star State's wonderful eccentricities are somewhat sanitized in Dallas. This is Texas, all right, but not quite Hollywood's version.

Despite some unusual architecture, Dallas' financial district, right in the center of town, looks much like that of any other large city. The rest of Big D, however, is made up of numerous residential districts with plenty of greenery, and is peppered with shopping centers, mini-malls, and smaller business and industrial areas.

RECOMMENDED READING

Larry McMurtry, *In a Narrow Grave* (New York: Touchstone Books, Simon & Schuster, Inc., 1989).

Carrie Shook and Robert L. Shook, *Only in Texas* (New York: Perigee Books, Putnam Publishing Group, 1989).

MOVIES

Giant (1956), *North Dallas Forty* (1979), *The Thin Blue Line* (1988)

■■■■■ POPULATION

The 1990 census shows Dallas' population has passed the one million mark. With some exceptions, the population remains fairly segregated: most non-Hispanic whites live north of Interstate 30 and the Trinity River, which divide the city roughly in half. Most blacks and Hispanics live south of I-30 and the River. There are, however, integrated enclaves here and there throughout the city.

■■■■■ CLIMATE

Ice storms in Dallas? They've been known to happen. Oh, sure, winters are short and relatively mild, but they're also unpredictable: there can be cold snaps, ice storms and, if you look, you *might,* on occasion, see some snow. Summers are hot, hot, hot and a little steamy. Wet or dry, the heat lasts a good six months, and air conditioners are, as they say, a way of life. Dallas gets its share of stormy weather, although it's far enough from the Gulf Coast to be spared the hurricanes; unfortunately, the city is near enough Kansas and Oklahoma to be on Tornado Alley. Air pollution isn't too bad, but is getting worse. Allergy sufferers may have real difficulty; some people have simply had to abandon this high-pollen area. *For weather information call:* 787-1700; 360-6000 Ext. 8888 (touchtone only).

NORMAL TEMPERATURES	Average Daily High	Average Daily Low
January	54°	34°
July	98°	75°

TEMPERATURE EXTREMES			
Maximum Temp.	Annual No. of Days	Minimum Temp.	Annual No. of Days
90° and above	96	32° and below	40
32° and below	3	0° and below	—

NORMAL WEATHER CONDITIONS		
Clear	Partly Cloudy	Cloudy
137	98	131

ANNUAL PRECIPITATION	Days	Inches
All Precipitation	78	32
Snowfall	NA	3

◼◼◼◼ TRANSPORTATION

Some Dallas residents say there isn't any public transportation. That's not exactly true, but there isn't much. (As one rather blunt resident put it, "DART sucks.") There's a decent enough bus system, but Dallas covers 378 square miles; that's a lot of land, and for most people, covering it means saddling up the ol' Pinto or Mustang (or Rabbit or Accord or Geo).

PUBLIC TRANSPORTATION

Dallas Area Rapid Transit (DART). While Dallas provides plenty of bus seats per capita, less than 20 percent of commuters actually utilize the system each day. The-downtown Hop-A-Buses, with names like Green Frog, Red Kangaroo, and Blue Bunny (now really, would Duke

Wayne ride a Blue Bunny?), are low-fare, convenient shuttles that loop around the downtown area on weekdays. *For information call:* 979-1111; 828-6800 for Handirides (door-to-door service for people with disabilities).

Schedules are available at DART Retail Sales Centers: Elm and Akard Streets; Main and Ervay Streets.

Based on a four-zone system, fares are comparatively low. Exact change is required, and transfers are free (ask for one when boarding). There are no area commuter trains, so drivers can park all day in Lot E at Reunion Arena and get free round-trip Hop-A-Bus transfers to get in and out of downtown.

The following is a list of terminals and additional transportation systems:
Amtrak, Union Station, 400 S. Houston (at Young), Dallas, TX, 653-1101.
McKinney Avenue Transit Authority, 855-5267. An electric trolley
connects the downtown Arts District with McKinney Avenue shops and restaurants.
Greyhound, 205 S. Lamar (at Commerce), Dallas, TX, 655-7000.

TAXIS

Taxis are metered, with a surcharge for each additional passenger. Hailing is best downtown, at hotels, and at airports. Taxis are also available by phone.

DRIVING

Most residents and visitors find it necessary to have a car. Dallas covers a lot of territory, and actors work throughout the Dallas-Fort Worth metroplex. While the downtown area is compact enough to be walkable, agents, production facilities, theatres, and casting directors are all over the place. The Dallas Communications Complex, where some of the area's film and commercial production happens, is located in Irving, about ten miles from central Dallas.

Until you really know your way around, downtown driving can be mind-boggling, so a good map is a necessity, and a compass won't hurt. Streets are laid out in a number of differently-angled grid systems. Through-streets angle off this way and that, changing direction and suddenly crossing over streets that ran parallel a couple of miles back. Highway driving isn't too bad; a number of freeways and a tollway spiderleg out from the center of town, while two others circle the city. Be sure to know both the name and number of any highway you'll be using; you may have been told to take Northwest Highway, but the signs say Loop 12. With so many highways and major surface roads, it's not hard to get around as long as you get good directions and have a detailed map.

■■■■■■■ HOUSING AND COSTS OF LIVING

Texas's oil boom years resulted in, among other things, a flurry of construction: all sorts of office buildings and apartment houses were built to accommodate the many people who flocked to the city. By the late 1980s, when the wells ran dry, a lot of real estate sat empty, and landlords started giving it away: you could drive around and see apartment houses bearing signs offering one, two, even three months' free rent along with a lease. At the time of this writing, the city is making a comeback. Apartment-hunters may not find months of rent-free living anymore, but should have no trouble finding decent, affordable places to live. Listings can be found in the Sunday edition of *The Dallas Morning News,* in *The Dallas Times-Herald,* and in free publications distributed at supermarkets. Some rentals are also posted on a bulletin board at STAGE (see *Other Associations,* p. 41). Recommended affordable areas are Lakewood, Oak Lawn (known as the artsy part of town), North Oak Cliff, and the apartment complexes of Northern Greenville.

INTERAREA SHELTER INDEXES	Renters	Owners
Dallas	68	76
(Philadelphia)	(100)	(100)

COSTS OF LIVING (DALLAS-FORT WORTH	
Total average annual expenditures	$33,736
Food at home	2,281
Telephone	698
Gas and motor oil	1,220
Public transportation	391
Personal care products and services	456

■■■■■■ EMPLOYMENT

1989 Average Annual Pay
Dallas, Fort Worth: $24,297

1990 Average Unemployment Rates
Texas: 6.2%
Dallas metropolitan statistical area: 5.1%

1990 Average Weekly Unemployment Benefits
Texas: $162.07

■■■■■CRIME

In April 1991 the *Dallas Times Herald,* reporting on a proposal to impose a nightly curfew on teenagers, quoted a city council member who referred to the "nightly carnage from street violence."[1] Indeed, it seems as though every day the news media report at least one shocking incident. Dallas virtually ties with Minneapolis for the highest incidence of rape among cities in this book for which statistics are available[2]; that rate is a full 35 percent higher than that of the city that follows. Dallas has the second highest rates of burglary and murder, outdistanced—by 75 percent at that—only by Washington, D.C. But the city is so spread out that people who live in safer neighborhoods, while concerned about increasing crime and violence, may be able to live as though it all happens somewhere else.

1990 CRIME RATES	Violent	Property
Total Crimes	24,550	133,272
Crimes per 100,000 People	2,438	13,236
Average 1 Crime per Every	41 people	8 people

■■■■■MISCELLANEA

NEWSPAPERS
The Dallas Morning News (morning)
Dallas Times Herald (all day)
Dallas Observer (weekly)
Dallas Post Tribune (weekly)
El Extra (weekly)

LIBRARY
Dallas Public Library, J. Erik Jonsson Central Library, 1515 Young Street (at Ervay), Dallas, TX 75201, 670-1400.

POST OFFICE
Main Branch, 401 DFW Turnpike, Dallas, TX 75260, 741-5508.

MUSEUM
National Museum of Communications, Dallas Communications Complex, 6305 N. O'Connor Road, Irving, TX 75039, 556-1234. This collection relates to the technology and history of human communications, and it includes a working radio station studio and classic TV and radio shows.

ADDITIONAL INFORMATION

Select Talk, 360-6000. This free service offers weather, news, and sports reports; legal, medical, and financial information; soap opera updates, jokes, trivia, horoscopes, and more. Touchtone codes are listed in the front section of the Yellow Pages.

THE BUSINESS

Texas has three production hot spots. Houston, popular for location shooting, has a small but vital stage community, with the Alley Theatre as flagship. The Austin-San Antonio market is showing steady growth in the film and broadcast markets. So while the Texas actor has several options, this chapter focuses on Dallas because it's still the place where most actors and performing arts professionals live and work. The Dallas area has more acting union members than the other two markets, the greatest percentage of the state's franchised talent agents, and an awful lot of theatres. Some Dallas-area actors have agents in Houston and/or Austin as well as in Dallas, and most try to stay abreast of what's going on in those cities.

Texas is a right-to-work state, which means nonunion talent can work for signatory producers without joining the unions. In Texas (more so than in Florida, another right-to-work state), unions and their members suffer because of this. The unions work hard to attract signatories and meet with some success, but this is Texas, where a "nobody's gonna tell me how to run my business" mentality prevails. While more producers are either becoming signatory or signing limited letters (per-production agreements with the unions), nonunion actors have far more opportunities to work here. In fact, many actors who are eligible to join the unions choose not to. Union members work, make no mistake, but the talent pool is large and includes many experienced union and nonunion actors. Eventually, most actors who become well-established in theatre and/or film and broadcast do join the unions; pay, prestige, and working conditions are better, and those who go on to L.A. or New York usually want to do so with their cards.

Most Dallas-area theatres cast locally, and people here don't go ga-ga over New York and L.A. résumés. Oh, they might be impressed, but not like they are in some cities. New York or Chicago credits might get you an audition at Dallas Theatre Center, for example, but they won't get you the job. On the other hand, a Dallasite who goes away and returns with N.Y. or L.A. credits may attract favorable notice.

RECOMMENDED READING

Dale Kassel, *Dallas Actors' Handbook* (Irving, Tex.: Handbook Publications). Updated approximately every year (or as needed), the *Handbook* lists agents, casting directors, theatres, photographers, teachers, and so forth. It also tells which corporate producers, production houses, and ad agencies accept P&Rs. It lists supply resources and includes a glossary of stage and screen terms.

Elaine Liner, "To Join or Not to Join," *Dallas Observer* (August 9, 1990).

Jerome Weeks, "Building Stages on the Prairie" and "Theatre Ideas for the Borrowing," *The Dallas Morning News* (August 18 and 19, 1991).

■ PROFESSIONAL ASSOCIATIONS

TALENT UNIONS

Actors' Equity Association (AEA), Liaison City.
   Members: 352 (Dallas/Fort Worth)
American Federation of Television and Radio Artists (AFTRA), 6060 North Central Expressway, Suite 302, LB 604, Dallas, TX 75206, 363-8300.
   Members: 565
Screen Actors' Guild (SAG), same address/phone as AFTRA.
   Members: 570
American Guild of Musical Artists (AGMA), 3915 Fairlakes Drive, Dallas, TX, 279-4720.

OTHER ASSOCIATIONS

Cross-Cultural Artists' Forum (call STAGE, below, for contact name/phone number). This grass-roots, completely voluntary organization is dedicated to the promotion of multicultural and nondiscriminatory representation in the performing arts. It maintains a list of ethnic and "exotic-look" actors to help producers locate such talent.
The Society for Theatrical Artists' Guidance and Enhancement (STAGE), 4633 Insurance Lane, Dallas, TX 75221, 559-3917. Ask almost anybody how a newcomer gets started in Dallas and they'll say, "Join STAGE." This not-for-profit organization offers numerous services to actors, including classes, talent showcases, a script library, callboard, casting file, newsletter, and group health insurance.

■ LOOKING FOR WORK

PUBLICATIONS

Centerstage. STAGE's monthly publication, sent to members, includes audition notices, STAGE class offerings, a "Now Playing" column, news and announcements, and a list of area theatres.
Dallas Observer. This free weekly paper has a few (primarily nonunion) audition notices.

HOTLINES
Actors' Equity Association (see *Talent Unions,* p. 41)

BULLETIN BOARDS AND BINDERS
STAGE (see *Other Associations,* p. 41). Members check the callboard every week or so between issues of the newsletter.

TALENT BOOKS AND TALENT BANKS
Cross-Cultural Artists' Forum (call STAGE for contact information). CCAF maintains a list of ethnic and exotic-look actors; updated frequently, it's distributed to theatres, agents, and casting directors.
The Official Southwest Talent Directory, 2908 McKinney Avenue, Dallas, TX 75204, 754-4729. This directory goes to agents and casting directors. You must have an agent or be a union member to be included.
STAGE (see *Other Associations,* p. 41). Members can keep their P&R on file at the STAGE office; casting directors and directors frequently use the file.

TALENT SHOWCASES AND COMBINED AUDITIONS
Southwest Theatre Association. (For address, see Appendix B.)
STAGE, Noon Preview and Stages '92 (see *Other Associations,* p. 41). Once a month for six months each year, STAGE sponsors a scene showcase in which five two-person scenes are presented to agents, producers, and casting directors. All STAGE members may audition; the audition alone allows you to be seen by a panel of casting directors. Auditions are announced in *Centerstage.* Each summer, STAGE also produces a festival of four previously unproduced plays. Members may audition. Auditions for Noon Preview and Stages are announced in *Centerstage.*

■■■■■■■TALENT AGENTS AND CASTING DIRECTORS

There's no freelancing or multiple listing in Texas; agents work with talent on a signed, exclusive basis only. To work in any area but theatre in Dallas, you absolutely need an agent; very few people can work steadily in film/broadcast without one. AFTRA/SAG can provide a list of franchised agents; STAGE and *Dallas Actors' Handbook* are additional sources of information. Even nonunion actors are better off with franchised agents, among whom there's an unwritten hierarchy: at the top are those agencies that work almost exclusively with the most experienced, busiest talent; below, there's a nice handful of (also franchised) agencies to choose from. Because of the right-to-work situation, most agents give union and nonunion people equal consideration, although it's not always easy to get signed with a franchised agent; the local talent pool is large enough and able enough that people who come to Dallas with union membership but little on-camera experience may have a tough time finding representation. Nonunion actors also have the option of working with licensed, nonfranchised agents. As always, however, when seeking representation by a nonfranchised agent, find out who's legit and busy by asking other actors, the folks at STAGE, and other contacts.

Some Dallas actors have agents in Houston, Austin-San Antonio, and/or Oklahoma City, although many productions in those markets draw on the larger Dallas talent pool anyway. To varying degrees, agents promote their actors in those other markets as well, so having your work on tape is an advantage.

Remember where you got lists of agents? Those are sources for lists of casting directors, too. It won't take long to discover who the current top casting directors are, and who specializes in what media. Actors can—and should—send promotional materials to casting directors, and check *Dallas Actors' Handbook* to find out which production companies and corporations keep in-house casting files. Since new casting directors often have general auditions or interviews, it's important to stay abreast of what's happening in town. Taking part in STAGE's Noon Preview or in graduation showcases at schools like KD Studio (see *Training,* p. 47), are good ways to be seen by casting directors, some of whom also attend theatre. Actors should stay in touch with casting directors who've expressed interest or called them for auditions.

THEATRE

Dallas was home to one of the country's first regional theatres, Theatre in the Round (established by Margo Jones, a matriarch of the regional movement). Today, the Dallas-Fort Worth metroplex boasts approximately fifty theatres, according to the April 1991 issue of *Centerstage,* and new companies and grass-roots ensembles sprout like dandelions. Presenting houses aside, there are roughly three generations of theatre here. The grandfolks are Theatre Three, Dallas Theatre Center, and Dallas Repertory Theatre (whose doors, at the time of this writing, are closed while the company searches for new permanent space)—Equity houses that have been around for years. The Theatre Center has a permanent company and, though they hold a general audition each year and outside casting is increasing, it's hard to get in.

Next is a group of theatres that haven't been on the scene quite as long but are well-established, like Addison Center Theatre, Stage West, Casa Mañana, and Open Stage. Some use SPT or Guest Artist contracts or LOAs, while others are non-Equity. Many of those non-Equity companies, by the way, are very well-respected. In fact, some actors prefer to put off joining Equity, for they fear that becoming a member would limit work opportunities. In the meantime, the proliferation of interesting new nonunion companies coupled with dwindling opportunities at Equity houses has been a cause of concern among union members. In an effort to address the issue, in December 1991, the national Equity Council approved on a year-long trial basis an umbrella plan that brings a number of nonunion theatres under the auspices of a single producer of record for the purpose of hiring Equity actors.

The youngest generation of theatres largely consists of the many small, mostly nonunion companies and the occasional offerings produced under the Equity Members Project Code. There's also a handful of community theatres; some use Guest Artist contracts from time to time.

Most auditions are announced in *Centerstage* and/or on the STAGE callboard. Getting an audition spot is rarely a problem, and only a couple of theatres go to New York to cast. Monologues may be requested for general auditions. Quite a few theatres from surrounding states send casting notices to STAGE; a few, particularly summer companies, come to Dallas to hold auditions.

Public support for theatre waxes and wanes; even those theatres that are most established get nowhere near the support the Dallas Cowboys get. Each of the mainstream theatres has a distinct audience but, in general, theatre subscribers tend to be older, and many companies are attempting to cultivate new, younger audiences. Many people in the theatre community feel that audiences just want to be entertained, and new plays and progressive or experimental works are often left to the younger, non-Equity companies, which do their own thing no matter what the reception. Ironically, when the more mainstream theatres do try something a little risky, they usually get an audience, and the area has had a few very successful Southwest—and even some national—premieres.

■■■■■FILM AND TELEVISION

With its mostly dependable weather, varied topography, and low costs, Texas is a popular location state. Dallas gets its share of film and TV production, but the work is sporadic. After a dry spell, the early '90s took off like gangbusters, with several productions based in the area. It doesn't hurt that Oliver Stone likes to work in Texas: most of his films spend at least part of their shooting time here. And many features set in other southern states are actually filmed in and around Dallas. While Houston and Austin-San Antonio are equally, if not more, popular locations, Dallas actors have the opportunity to audition for a number of projects shooting in those areas, although doing so usually means travelling. When films do come to town, locals get a lot of work. Very low-budget pictures aside, principal and secondary roles are cast in Los Angeles; locals usually get hired for day player roles and under fives. Slowly, slowly, however, things are changing as the always-strong credibility of Dallas's talent pool grows even stronger; there are some actors who consistently get good supporting roles.

For ten of the thirteen years "Dallas" was on the air, the first twelve episodes of every season were filmed locally. Dallas actors filled numerous small roles, and a few even had recurring parts. Life has gone on post-"Dallas" but, on the whole, episodic TV hasn't done well here. Still, several episodes of the various reality-based shows have filmed here, there's usually a pilot or so a year, and a couple of new series have come and quickly gone.

The 1991 SAG agreement claiming more widespread jurisdiction over extra players in some markets could bring runaway production to right-to-work Texas. SAG members would be wise to check with their local SAG office before accepting work as extras.

■■■■■CORPORATE AND COMMERCIALS

Since Dallas is a popular relocation area, many major corporations have opened headquarters here, resulting in increased corporate film and video production. There are actors who do quite well in this market, although some union members have suffered since 1988, when SAG applied Rule One[3] to industrials. As noted earlier, some local corporations are antiunion and others just don't want to be bothered. Still, production personnel at several of these companies want access to SAG talent, and frequently produce under limited letters (per-production agreements with the union); more and more frequent use of limited letters indicates the rift may be healing. All in all, there's plenty of both union and nonunion corporate work, enabling actors to make money while gaining experience on camera.

The commercial market is big here: approximately 75 percent of the earnings that go through the local AFTRA/SAG office are from commercial production. Enough advertising agencies are headquartered or have branch offices here that a lot of production originates locally, although plenty comes in from out of state as well. But union actors take note: this is a right-to-work state, and signatory employers hire as many nonunion actors as they do union.

Dallas remains a fairly conservative area and is probably not the best market for character types. The Spanish-language commercial market is strongest in the Austin-San Antonio area, although some casting and production is done in Dallas. Voice-over and narration is very big here; no matter what fluctuations are felt in other markets, there'll always be voice work. Newcomers need to remember that it's very hard to break into this market.

■■■■■ CASTING DIVERSITY

Like many places, Dallas is a little slow to understand and put into practice the concepts of cultural diversity and equal opportunity. Neighborhoods tend to be ethnically and culturally segregated, and segregation remains an issue in the artistic community as well as in the community at large. Some artistic and production personnel who have expressed interest in nontraditional casting appear not to understand what it really means, and the reasons they give for why it won't work reveal a subtle racism they may not even be aware of.

In February 1991, the Cross-Cultural Artists' Forum membership held a meeting to introduce themselves and their mission. That event helped increase awareness of multicultural issues and started a dialogue between CCAF and the performing arts community. In response to the complaint from theatre artistic directors that ethnic minority actors don't show up for auditions—even when a casting notice specifically mentions multicultural or nontraditional casting—CCAF developed several measures to help actors and theatres find each other.

There are quite a few constituent-specific theatres in the area. Teatro Dallas is a well-established company that produces Latino plays and consistently utilizes culturally diverse casts. A newer company, Gryphon Players, is committed to nontraditionally casting classic plays, and Callier Theatre of the Deaf utilizes both hearing and non-hearing actors in plays that are presented simultaneously in spoken and signed English. There are other ethnically-mixed or -specific theatre companies as well, including two black companies, Vivid Theatre Ensemble and Jubilee Theatre. Theatre Three has a "Voices Unsilenced" festival, concentrating on the non-Anglo experience, and is planning a multiracial company to tour schools with topical plays. Interestingly, women hold top administrative positions at a great number of area theatres, although their presence doesn't necessarily result in increased opportunities for women on stage.

Slow progress is being made in the areas of film and broadcast, and a handful of ethnic minority actors do well in those areas. Women are seen more frequently as on-screen announcers, but the voice-over market remains largely male. A couple of casting directors and agents really push for more culturally diverse and increased female representation, but they have an uphill climb. Characters described in casting breakdowns are assumed to be non-Hispanic white unless a specific ethnic minority is named. When there are commercial calls for ethnic minority actors, the actors are often lumped together: a breakdown might call for, say, a young working mom, an elderly grandmother, a middle-aged female executive (all of whom are assumed to be white), and a black woman— no age or description.

Slowly, theatre, casting, and production personnel, as well as clients and audiences, are showing increased understanding of nontraditional casting practices. And slowly, minority actors are throwing their hats in the mainstream rings. CCAF may help everybody speed things up a little.

■■■■■■ADDITIONAL OPPORTUNITIES

Student Film. Area film students sometimes run casting notices. In addition, actors may send P&Rs to: Southern Methodist University, Cinema Department, 202 Umphrey Lee, Dallas, TX 75275, 692-3076.

Texas Commission on the Arts, Company/Artist Roster, P.O. Box 13406, Austin, TX 78711, 800-252-9415. This is an approved list of Texas-based touring companies and individual artists for whom funds are reserved and disbursed. Companies and artists with high-quality presentations and previous touring experience may apply for inclusion by January 15 of each year.

Young Audiences of Greater Dallas, Attn: Program Director, 30 Highland Park Village, Suite 216, Dallas, TX 75205, 520-9988. This educational agency presents performing arts programs to schoolchildren. Auditions are held annually; for information, contact the program director in September.

■■■■■■TRAINING

For the most part, training is geared toward beginning and less-experienced actors; more seasoned actors may be able to find appropriate training if they do enough investigating. There are numerous schools and private teachers in the area, along with a handful of teachers who come in every so often from New York and Los Angeles. *Centerstage* and the STAGE bulletin board are good sources of information. Each month, STAGE offers relatively low-cost and oft-recommended workshops in acting, movement, on-camera technique, the business of acting, and more. Perhaps the best-known school in the area is KD Studio, an accredited institution offering a diploma in acting performance or an Associate of Applied Arts degree.

CERTIFICATE/DEGREE PROGRAMS

KD Studio, 2600 Stemmons Freeway, Suite 117, Dallas, TX 75207,
    638-0484.
Southern Methodist University, Meadows School of the Arts, Dallas, TX
    75275, 692-2558.
Texas Christian University, Theatre Department, 2800 University Drive,
    Box 32928, Fort Worth, TX 76129, 817-921-7625.
University of Dallas, Drama Department, 1845 E. Northgate Drive, Irving,
    TX 75062, 721-5061.
University of Texas at Arlington, P.O. Box 19088, Arlington, TX 76019,
    817-273-2119, 800-876-9120.
University of Texas at Dallas, P.O. Box 830688, Richardson, TX
    75083-0688, 214-690-2341.

■■■■■■AFFORDABLE ARTS

STAGE (see *Other Associations,* p. 41). More than two dozen area theatres
    offer discount admission to STAGE members; see "Performing Arts
    Directory" in any issue of *Centerstage.* In addition, announcements of
    free or discount tickets are posted on the STAGE bulletin board.
Shakespeare Festival of Dallas, Sammons Center for the Arts, 3630 Harry
    Hines Boulevard, Dallas, TX 75219, 559-2778. SFD presents three plays
    in Samuell-Grand Park during June and July each year. Admission is
    free to these open-air performances, although members and patrons
    receive early admission.
Fort Worth Shakespeare in the Park, 3113 S. University, Suite 310,
    Fort Worth, TX 76109, 923-6698. Admission is free to these outdoor
    summer productions at Trinity Park; it's best to arrive at about 6:30
    for an 8:30 curtain.
Ushering. This is another way to see free theatre; call theatres to inquire.

■■■■■RESOURCES

LIBRARIES

STAGE maintains a well-stocked lending library of books and scripts.
    When auditions are being held, theatres will send a copy of the script
    to STAGE; members may read the script in the office.

BOOKSTORES

While there aren't any theatre bookstores, stores like Shakespeare Books,
Bookstop, B. Dalton, and Taylor's have decent selections of plays, as
does the Dallas Public Library.

■ NETWORKING AND SOCIALIZING

Lower Greenville is an eclectic area where artist types tend to congregate; there are a couple of theatres in the neighborhood. Deep Ellum, at the east end of downtown, is another popular nighttime area; there are restaurants and bars, and in recent years, a few small theatre companies have taken up residence in this, the Greenwich Village of Dallas, Texas.

[1]   The curfew, affecting youths under age 17, was adopted in June 1990.

[2]   Figures are based on 1989 crime and population statistics for Minneapolis, and 1990 statistics for Dallas.

[3]   "No member of the Guild shall work for any producer who is not signatory to a Guild contract."

L O S   A N

"This is the city . . . Los Angeles, California. Pretty much like your town."[1] *Huh?* If anybody ever got it wrong, it was the guy who wrote that. In fact and in fantasy, L.A. is like no other place in the world, a land of myth, legend, and unbelievable truth. The object of envy and scorn, a dreamland filled with harsh realities, L.A. is a dizzying mix of the sublime, the ridiculous, and everything in-between.

"How can an outsider ever understand such an unwieldy place?" asks John Heminway. "In the end, L.A. seems dead easy to dismiss, near impossible to comprehend."[2] Hollywood, Beverly Hills, the Valley, Malibu, East Los Angeles, palm trees, gangs, surfers, smog, movie stars . . . the names and images are an indelible part of the American consciousness. To the uninitiated, L.A. can be a source of overwhelming confusion—and one of sun-warmed, breezy delight.

Look out the airplane window next time you fly in or out—the city seems to go on forever; indeed, what people call L.A. covers a vast area of land and an even wider range of experience. But the L.A. of actors and entertainers—from those struggling for recognition to movie stars with production deals—can seem like a city within a city. L.A. actors can find themselves so surrounded by industry folk that they forget the city is home to all kinds of people and lifestyles. Those who can afford to live in one of the many decent-to-excellent

FAST FACTS

1990 CENSUS
3,485,398 (+17.4%)

COUNTY
Los Angeles

TIME
Zone: Pacific
Telephone: 853-1212

AREA CODES
213 (Los Angeles: downtown and surrounding communities)
310 (Los Angeles: western, coastal, southern, and eastern portions)
818 (San Fernando and San Gabriel valleys)
UNLESS OTHERWISE NOTED, PHONE NUMBERS LISTED IN THIS CHAPTER USE EITHER THE 213 OR 310 AREA CODE.

DOWNTOWN LOS ANGELES VISITOR INFORMATION CENTER
695 S. Figueroa Street
Los Angeles, CA 90017
689-8822

HOLLYWOOD VISITOR INFORMATION CENTER
The Janes House
Janes Square
6541 Hollywood Boulevard
Hollywood, Ca 90028
461-4213

GELES

parts of town can be so well-insulated that the only reminder of hardship is the sight of housekeepers climbing the hills of Beverly and Bel Air on their way to work each morning.

For the actor between engagements, L.A.'s nearly always tolerable weather and miles of beach make the livin' seem very easy: your career may be going nowhere, but the surroundings are so seductive that all that the waiting doesn't seem so bad. In fact, L.A. can be breathtakingly beautiful, and just when you feel most discouraged, you'll catch sight of a red sun blazing to rest behind the Pacific, or find yourself in the hills above Hollywood on a foggy, eucalyptus-scented night, hanging suspended at the edge of the world.

On the other hand, some people can't stand the place. They hate the driving, the pollution, the *brightness* of it all. The people are too slow, their brains overbaked in the sun, they're uncultured and unaware of the world at large. A fair assessment? Maybe. Take all your preconceptions about who lives in L.A.—and hang on to them. The bleached-blond pretty boys and girls are here. The deal-making producer who wouldn't know good acting if she fell over it is here. But so are a lot of bright, creative, interesting folks; some people say you just have to look a lot harder to find them.

But be warned: there are plenty of lost souls in what David Ferrell, reporting in *The Los Angeles Times,* recently called "a place of great expectation (that) attracts tens of thousands of newcomers each year. Some come filled with visions of an almost quixotic land . . . and these dreamers are often disappointed to discover a harsh, competitive city much like any other." For some, Ferrell says, that city is a place of "tics and violent moods, ravaged by urban crowding, greed, crime, divorce."[3]

RECOMMENDED READING

John Miller, ed., *Los Angeles Stories: Great Writers on the City* (San Francisco: Chronicle Books, 1991).

David Rieff, *Los Angeles: Capital of the Third World* (New York: Simon and Schuster, 1991).

MOVIES

The Big Picture (1989), *Boyz N the Hood* (1991), *El Norte* (1984), *Shampoo* (1975)

▧▧▧ POPULATION

Los Angeles is growing fast. That 17.4 percent increase from 1980 shows quite a jump, but even more worthy of note are the astounding increases (in one case as great as 83.5 percent) in several nearby communities that are very much part of the Southern California landscape. The population of this second-largest metro area in the nation is about as ethnically diverse as can be. Proximity to the Mexican border and the Pacific Ocean bring large immigrant populations from Central and South America and the Far East. In addition, as the world capital of filmdom and the center of numerous other industries, L.A. attracts people from all over the country and around the globe.

▧▧▧ CLIMATE

If the thought of a fireplace glowing indoors when snow is piled high outdoors makes you feel all warm and cuddly, L.A. isn't for you. If the sight of crocuses bursting through the ground after a harsh winter gladdens your heart and puts a spring in your step, turn back. The only fires you'll find in L.A. are the terrible, destructive rages blown out of control each summer by hot Santa Ana winds, and as for flowers, well, you can see those all year round.

On the other hand, if you've got to be near an ocean, you could hardly pick a better one than the Pacific. And despite serious drought conditions (residents must save and ration water), there's plenty of greenery, from desert palm to mountain pine. Near the coast, ocean-scented breezes tease and delight. Summer air is dense, the dry heat heavy like satin; winter nights can be surprisingly chilly.

Local newspapers, in addition to reporting the weather, also publish daily air quality forecasts. Indeed, there are days when the smog is so bad you can feel it in your lungs. Despite "promising developments" resulting from the South Coast Air Quality Management District's efforts to clean up the skies by the year 2010, there's "a growing consensus that the goal cannot be met," for progress made is constantly undercut by an ever-increasing population that is expected to result in "35% more cars driving 47% more miles in 20 years."[4] *For weather information call:* 554-1212.

NORMAL TEMPERATURES	Average Daily High	Average Daily Low
January	67°	48°
July	84°	65°

TEMPERATURE EXTREMES

Maximum Temp.	Annual No. of Days
90° and above	22
32° and below	—

NORMAL WEATHER CONDITIONS

Clear	Partly Cloudy	Cloudy
186	106	73

ANNUAL PRECIPITATION

	Days	Inches
All Precipitation	35	15
Snowfall	NA	—

▮▮▮▮ TRANSPORTATION

Contrary to popular myth, people do walk in L.A. (and not just between the house and the garage), but the sprawl of freeways, cities, towns, and coastline that make up the L.A. area is so vast that more often than not it is necessary to cover a lot of ground. There are some exceptions, but for the most part L.A. is not the sort of place where you can dash out to the corner market, stroll to the neighborhood movie theatre, or exercise by walking to work. When you do walk, watch out—you can get ticketed for crossing against the light or in the middle of the street.

PUBLIC TRANSPORTATION

Southern California Rapid Transit District (RTD). While L.A. has one of the country's largest bus transit systems, most area residents never use it.[5] That's unfortunate, because the system's really not bad, and all the cars people drive instead have created an environmental disaster. In addition to local bus service, commuter routes utilize both freeways and surface roads. The Downtown Area Short Hop (DASH) shuttle system operates along two routes and is a good, low-cost alternative for getting around an area that can be a parking purgatory. The Metro Blue Line, a surface rail line in operation since mid-1990, runs from Downtown Los Angeles to Long Beach, connecting with bus routes at stops along the way. Despite controversy and some serious setbacks, construction of an additional commuter line and an intra-city subway line (scheduled for operation in 1993) continues.

The RTD fleet includes buses and light rail. *For information call:*
626-4455 (from Central L.A., Hollywood); 273-0910 (from West L.A.,
Beverly Hills, Culver City, Santa Monica); 800-252-0940 (TTY);
800-621-7828 (disabled rider services).

A "Rider's Kit" with maps and schedules is obtainable by writing to:
RTD Customer Relations, 425 S. Main Street, Los Angeles, CA 90013-1393.

Exact change is required. Transfers can be used twice: pay the regular
fare and a transfer charge on your first bus, and pay an additional transfer
charge on your third. Discounted RTD ticket books and monthly passes
can be purchased at Customer Centers and pass outlets; for locations,
contact the address or phone numbers shown above. Qualified students,
seniors, and disabled riders are eligible for discounted fares and/or
passes. For slightly higher-than-normal fares, the RTD has buses running
to Universal Studios, Disneyland, Long Beach, and other locations.

The following is a list of terminals and additional transportation systems:
Amtrak, Union Passenger Terminal, 800 N. Alameda Street, Los Angeles,
   CA 90012, 624-0171.
Greyhound, 1716 E. 7th Street, Los Angeles, CA, 620-1200.

TAXIS

You can grab a cab at airports, at train and bus stations, and at major
hotels, but not on the street, although they can be ordered by phone.
Taxis are metered.

DRIVING

A young woman once came to L.A. for pilot season. Unable to drive, she
took city buses everywhere, and made it to all her appointments on time
and without mishap. This was a very unusual young woman. Most people
would find it tough, if not impossible, to manage without a car. There's
no theatre district, the studios are scattered about town and the Valley,
and agents and casting directors are anywhere and everywhere. As an
actor, it doesn't matter what you drive, as long as it's sturdy and gets you
where you need to go; actors who don't have a lot of money buy
something cheap and drive it till it falls apart. (Still, there are those for
whom the vehicle they own defines their status in the industry. What fun
it was in the late '80s to see all the necktied, car-phoned young execs
tooling along Sunset in their shiny new Jeeps and Land Rovers that never
saw terrain more rugged than Mulholland Drive!)

Driving can be a real challenge. Distances are far, and traffic is often
stop-and-go, even on the multilane surface roads. Freeways are almost
always faster, although there are times during rush hour when it's a thrill
just to see the speedometer hit 35—not a good scene for the claustrophobic.

(Some actors make use of all that time spent behind the wheel: they vocalize, listen to dialect tapes, and so forth.) The vast system of freeways and surface streets isn't terribly hard to learn, but it's always a good idea, particularly during rush hours, to tune into radio traffic reports that warn drivers away from tie-ups and traffic jams that might otherwise ensnare them in inescapable, labyrinthine nightmares. Finding parking space isn't a problem in many areas; watch out, though, for Downtown, Westwood Village, and commercial Beverly Hills, to name just a few trouble spots. It's often possible to avoid the meters that line commercial streets by choosing spots about half a block down along the side streets.

■■■■■■■HOUSING AND COSTS OF LIVING

Since there's no central or most convenient place to live, L.A. offers a lot of choice, and housing isn't hard to find. The best thing to do is arrange before arrival for temporary quarters (you can rent a furnished apartment on a month-to month basis, or check the bulletin boards at the actors' unions for shares and sublets) and get to know the city. When you find an area you like, drive around and look for "For Rent" signs. (It might only be a slight exaggeration to say it's possible to drive around with your belongings in the car, see a building you like, and move in the next day.) Telling everybody you meet that you're looking is another good way to find housing.

If rents aren't exactly cheap, neither are they outrageous. Recommended affordable areas in the L.A. area include Los Feliz, parts of West Hollywood, and popular Beachwood Drive, just east of Hollywood (check the bulletin board at the Village Coffee Shop—see *Networking and Socializing*, p. 70). And don't assume that Beverly Hills and its even tonier neighbor, Bel Air, are completely out of the question; scan the want ads for mother-in-law apartments and cottages for rent.

The San Fernando Valley (just call it "the Valley") to the north, and the San Gabriel Valley to the northeast, offer further options. The Valley includes communities like Encino, Studio City, Sherman Oaks, Burbank, and Toluca Lake. Some folks hate the Valley, which is smoggier, hotter, and more suburban than L.A.; others find it more affordable, more liveable, and just as, if not more, convenient.

Living along the coast offers respite from the city, as well as some protection from smog and the worst of the summer's heat. It also means longer commutes, necessitating an even higher tolerance for driving. It's grown difficult to find a place in lovely-but-yuppified Santa Monica, while funkier Venice Beach (which certainly isn't for everybody) remains more accessible.

The following organization may be of help to housing-hunters:

Housing for Entertainment Professionals, Inc. (HEP), 817 Vine Street, Hollywood, CA 90038, 462-2161. HEP helps place entertainment professionals in low-cost housing; you must have earned 50 percent of your income from the entertainment field for five of the previous seven years to be eligible.

INTERAREA SHELTER INDEXES	Renters	Owners
Los Angeles County	141	148.5
Los Angeles Suburb	134	126
(Philadelphia)	(100)	(100)

COSTS OF LIVING	
Total average annual expenditures	$33,482
Food at home	2,739
Telephone	677
Gas and motor oil	996
Public transportation	468
Personal care products and services	499

■■■■ EMPLOYMENT

Fortunately, since even bit parts pay reasonably well, many actors manage to live off occasional film and TV work. Those who have survival jobs, however, often work evenings in order to keep their days free. As sprawling as L.A. is, it's not the kind of place where you can easily pop over to pick up sides during a lunch hour; getting to and from a couple of auditions can take up an entire day. And things can happen pretty quickly; it's not unheard of for an actor to get a 10 a.m. call for an audition at noon. Some people try to temp at the studios, where they can meet directors and casting personnel. Check *Drama-Logue* and bulletin boards at union offices for survival job notices.

1989 Average Annual Pay
L.A.-Anaheim-Riverside: $25,682

1990 Average Unemployment Rates
California: 5.6%
Los Angeles-Long Beach: 5.8%

1990 Average Weekly Unemployment Benefits
California: $131.36

CRIME

Between gang wars, freeway shootouts, and police brutality, L.A. has earned quite a reputation for violence. Well, while it's not quite the Old West, there are areas where crime and violence are tragic parts of the landscape. But L.A. is full of contrasts. If one's daily contact is with the pristine luxury of Beverly Hills, the perfectly-sculpted bodies of gyms and health clubs, and the obscene amounts of money spent on making movies, it can be easy to forget that people are living in poverty and despair just a few miles away. There are areas of the city—and L.A. is not alone in this—in which, when the nightly shooting starts, the kids dive under their beds. Downtown L.A. is not particularly safe at night, and gang violence has spread to some formerly-calm areas of the city and the Valley. Still, among cities in this book for which statistics are available, L.A.'s murder and reported rape rates are fairly low. Aggravated assault is at the high end of the scale but, surprisingly perhaps, L.A. ties with San Francisco for the lowest burglary rates.

1990 CRIME RATES	Violent	Property
Total Crimes	83,809	243,110
Crimes per 100,000 People	2,404	6,975
Average 1 Crime per Every	42 people	14 people

MISCELLANEA

NEWSPAPERS
Los Angeles Times (morning)
L.A. Weekly
La Opinion (morning)

LIBRARY
Central Library, 433 S. Spring Street, Los Angeles, CA 90013, 612-3200.

POST OFFICE
General Mail Facility, 7001 S. Central Avenue, Los Angeles, CA, 586-1467.

MUSEUMS
Hollywood Studio Museum, 2100 N. Highland Avenue, Hollywood, CA 90068, 874-2276. This is a barn transformed into a studio by C.B. De Mille himself.
Max Factor Museum, 1666 N. Highland Avenue, Hollywood, CA 90028, 463-6668.

THE BUSINESS

Sometimes, in this world capital of movie-making and television production, it seems as if everybody you meet is connected with the industry—and everybody else is writing a screenplay. There's more acting work in L.A. than anywhere else, and a lot of people who couldn't get work or agents in New York have moved to L.A. and found both. (Of course, for some people, that happens in the other direction.) On the other hand, many are called but few are chosen, and lots of people have been "sitting by the pool" for years, listening for a phone that never rings.

It's a tougher city than it may appear to be. The actor is an ingredient, a commodity useful only as long as it sells. There are people in positions of power who have little interest in, or knowledge of, acting: they're businesspeople creating products in an extremely consumer-oriented industry. Because it's an industry that always needs new products, some actors start working almost immediately, only to find their "new faces" become old ones pretty quickly. To minimize the chances of winding up the subject of whatever-happened-to speculation, some people advise, it's important to have solid acting training, the ability to reinvent oneself as necessary, good business acumen, and the energy and ability to create opportunities. Your pretty face might make you popular for a while, but somewhere down the line you'll probably have to back up good fortune with skill and ability.

The business operates on connections and personal recommendations, so use any resources you've got. If your Aunt Tillie used to babysit for a producer, call Till and ask her to get you an intro. Good shmoozing skills are an asset, and you're just as likely to get a job by meeting someone at a party as you are by auditioning. If you're considering simply trying out L.A. for a few months to see how you like it, that's fine; just bear in mind that relationships with agents and casting directors will be hard to establish if you're not staying put. Breaking in, which often involves a process of being seen again and again by industry personnel, can take a long time.

Remember that here, looks count. There are a lot of beautiful people, and most of them work hard at getting and staying that way. The business is especially hard on women, on whom there's terrible pressure to be thin, youthful, and pretty; make sure that's pressure you can live with. Finally, this is what one young actor heard upon arrival: "There are no rules here, and everybody has their own rules." You're on your own with that one.

RECOMMENDED READING

Pat Hilton, "Acting in Los Angeles," in *The Back Stage Handbook for Performing Artists,* rev. ed., Sherry Eaker, comp. and ed. (New York: Back Stage Books, 1991).

M.K. Lewis and Rosemary Lewis, *Your Film Acting Career: How to Break into the Movies and TV and Survive in Hollywood* (Santa Monica: Gorham House, 1989).

Karin Mani, ed., *The Working Actor's Guide L.A.: The Complete Resource for Performers and Other Industry Professionals* (Los Angeles: Paul Flattery Productions, 1991).

Rob Stevens, "L.A. Theatre," in *The Back Stage Handbook for Performing Artists,* rev. ed., Sherry Eaker, comp. and ed. (New York: Back Stage Books, 1991).

■■■■ PROFESSIONAL ASSOCIATIONS

TALENT UNIONS

Actors' Equity Association (AEA), 6430 Sunset Boulevard, Los Angeles, CA 90028, 462-2334.
Members: 7,995

American Federation of Television and Radio Artists (AFTRA), 6922 Hollywood Boulevard, 8th Floor, Hollywood, CA 90028-6128, 461-8111.
Members: 25,554

Screen Actors' Guild (SAG),[6] National Headquarters, 7065 Hollywood Boulevard, Hollywood, CA 90028-6005, 465-4600.
Members: 31,000

American Guild of Musical Artists (AGMA), 12650 Riverside Drive, Suite 205, North Hollywood, CA 91607, 877-0683 or 984-3950.

American Guild of Variety Artists (AGVA), 4741 Laurel Canyon Boulevard, North Hollywood, CA 91607, 818-508-9984.

OTHER ASSOCIATIONS

American Indian Registry for the Performing Arts, 1717 N. Highland Avenue, Suite 614, Hollywood, CA 90028-4403, 962-6594. This non-profit organization "functions as a central registry for North American Indians (including Canada and Alaska) in the performing arts," and works to promote employment and change stereotyped portrayals of Indian characters. Services include a monthly newsletter, talent directory, casting assistance, and workshops.

Association of Asian Pacific American Artists (AAPAA), 3518 Cahuenga Boulevard West, Suite 302, Los Angeles, CA 90068, 874-0786. AAPAA works to promote "balanced portrayals and realistic images of Asians, Asian Pacifics and Asian Americans in the mainstream media." Programs include a talent showcase and writers' workshops.

Nosotros, 1314 N. Wilton Place, Hollywood, CA 90028, 465-4167. This nonprofit organization works to enhance the image of the Hispanic actor. Activities include the Nosotros Theatre, talent showcases, workshops, and talent files.

Theatre League Alliance (Theatre L.A.), 644 S. Figueroa Street, Los Angeles, CA 90017, 614-0556. Theatre L.A. is an association of "theatres and independent producers dedicated to the development and growth of theatres throughout Los Angeles." Services to members include access to a theatre management library, JobBank (administration, design, and so on), and cooperative advertising. College theatre students are accepted as interns. (The Alliance is primarily of interest to actors who produce and/or manage theatre companies.)

Women in Theatre, P.O. Box 3718, Hollywood, CA 90078, 465-5567. This is an organization of professional female and male theatre artists "whose purpose it is to enhance our art form though education, interaction, and experience with one another." WIT provides seminars, networking activities, an annual magazine, workshops, and play readings. Member actors' P&Rs are kept on file for the use of member directors, playwrights, and other parties.

■■■■■■LOOKING FOR WORK

PUBLICATIONS

If you want to work in movies and television, it helps to know what's going on within those industries. Many actors read *Daily Variety, The Hollywood Reporter,* and *American Film* in order to keep up with who's who in the industry and stay well-informed about current and upcoming production. In addition, there's a handful of other weekly and biweekly trade papers available at newsstands and bookstores like Samuel French (see *Resources,* p. 70).

The Agencies, P.O. Box 44, Hollywood, CA 90078. Available by subscription or at Samuel French and Larry Edmunds Bookshops, this source is updated monthly. It lists information about every agency, including the names of agents and subagents, union franchise status, "types" represented, and so on, with a line or two per entry of useful commentary.

The CD Directory and *The Agency Guide,* Breakdown Services, Ltd., 1120 S. Robertson, 3rd Floor, Los Angeles, CA 90035, 276-9166. *The CD Directory* is published quarterly and The Agency Guide semi-annually. They are obtainable at French and Edmunds (see *Bookstores,* p. 70), although monthly updates for either are available by subscription only. Corresponding mailing labels are also available.

Drama-Logue, P.O. Box 38771, Los Angeles, CA 90038-0771, 464-5079. This weekly is available by subscription and at newsstands all over town. It contains reviews, articles, ads, and casting notices. *Drama-Logue* is probably most useful for 99-seat plan and non-Equity theatre; student film; and nonunion TV, video, and film auditions.

HOTLINES
Actors' Equity Association; SAG (see *Talent Unions*, p. 59)

BULLETIN BOARDS AND BINDERS
SAG; Equity. The Equity office keeps three big binders filled with current casting information for Chicago, New York, and L.A.'s 99-seat theatres.

TALENT BOOKS AND TALENT BANKS
Academy Players Directory, 8949 Wilshire Boulevard, 6th Floor, Beverly Hills, CA 90211-1972, 247-3058. The *Directory* is published by the Academy of Motion Picture Arts and Sciences. To be listed, you must be a member of a talent union or be signed with a franchised agent. Being in the *Directory* is a must for anyone who wants to work in film and television. Call for the filing period deadlines.

American Indian Registry for the Performing Arts (see *Other Associations,* p. 59). This is a nationwide directory of American Indian participants in the performing arts.

Nosotros (see *Other Associations,* p. 59). Nosotros maintains a member P&R file for use by casting and artistic personnel.

Women in Theatre (see *Other Associations,* p. 60). WIT maintains a P&R file of actors interested in participating in readings, and of actor-members for use by director and playwright members.

TALENT SHOWCASES AND COMBINED AUDITIONS
AFTRA Showcase, 467-8702. Held the first Tuesday of every month; actors perform scenes for agents and casting personnel. Registration is on a first-come, first-served basis; call the phone number above for sign-up information.

National Alliance of Musical Theatre Producers, 330 W. 45th Street, Lobby B, New York, NY 10036, 212-265-5376. This organization recently began sponsoring combined auditions in Los Angeles. Dates change from year to year. Read *Drama-Logue* for announcements.

Nosotros (see *Other Associations,* p. 59). Nosotros sponsors scene showcases to present members' work to the professional community.

SAG Seminars and Scene Showcases, 461-1023. Call the SAG office for schedule and registration details. SAG's Casting Committee-sponsored seminars consist of question-and-answer sessions with casting directors; some include cold readings. Scene showcases, jointly sponsored by SAG and the Casting Society of America, are presented twice each month.

■■■■■■■TALENT AGENTS AND CASTING DIRECTORS

Many people advise against coming to L.A. without an agent or at least some solid introductions. On the other hand, who doesn't know somebody who knows somebody who went to L.A. without any connections and got an agent the first day? For most people, reality lies somewhere in between. Certainly, L.A. agents are not noted for their openness to newcomers. Recommendations mean an awful lot, so turn to teachers, other actors, and anyone else who might be able to help.

Representation is on an exclusive, signed basis. Since many agents specialize, however, you might be signed with one for commercials and another for legit. There's no freelancing (at least, not officially). Agents are ranked A, B, C, and so on: A and B agents have more clout than their C-and-below colleagues. Depending on which agents are representing which hot and hotter actors, the rankings fluctuate and shift over the years; they certainly aren't fixed or official. To find out how agencies are ranked, talk to actors and industry personnel, and refer to some of the publications suggested in this chapter. In addition, SAG members can go to the national office and look at agents' client lists. An actor who can't find representation by an A or B agent might nevertheless be able to build a modest-to-decent résumé while working with a less influential agency. (Be advised that in TV things can happen awfully fast, so that an actor whose agent makes submissions by mail risks missing out on some auditions; before signing with an agent, then, find out—tactfully—if she uses a messenger service.)

You can do a mass mailing of P&Rs to agents. Commercial agents might invite you in to read copy; since legit agents may invite you to do a scene, it's good to have something prepared with a partner. Some agents rarely sign anybody they haven't seen on tape, so as camera-oriented as L.A. is, you're at an advantage if you have a sample of your work. Get whatever you can that has a professional look to it; commercials or a high-quality student film will do if they're all you've got. What won't do is anything amateur or homemade-looking, or a video of a stage production.

Almost everything is cast through independent, studio, and network casting directors, and for the most part, you have to be submitted by an agent to get auditions. Nonetheless, casting directors do call people directly, so it's important to make yourself known to them. Go ahead and send P&Rs; they'll probably sit in countless piles in countless corners of countless offices. Eventually, though, someone's going to open all those envelopes, and when they do, who knows? It just might be your lucky day.

Invite casting directors to come see you in the theatre. A currently popular way to be seen by casting directors is to participate in weekly showcases in which you and an assigned partner do cold readings; check *Drama-Logue* for ads and announcements. Some people consider the showcases unethical: after all, you pay to participate, and casting directors get paid to attend. As if that isn't enough, getting paid to see a bunch of actors do short scenes may undermine casting directors' incentive to attend theatre. Still, a lot of people find a showcase to be an effective way to be seen, especially since TV casting directors always need new people for the many small roles they cast every week.

Casting directors move around a lot, so it's important to stay on top of who's where. Some of the many helpful publications are noted in this chapter's reading lists. Stay in touch with casting directors: send postcards, offer comps to plays you're in. What you don't want to do is pester the casting director who got you that bit part on an episode of that sitcom by asking her to get you on the show again: once you've appeared, you can't be seen in another part on the same series. But do stay in touch; that casting director certainly will go on to other projects.

▇▇▇▇▇ THEATRE

Turn to the calendar sections of the Sunday *Times* or *L.A. Weekly:* you may be surprised to see that the theatre listings go on for pages. Okay, it's not New York, and if theatre's your one-and-only passion, this isn't the best place to be. But L.A. is full of actors who, wanting to work, needing to be seen, or simply loving the stage, have created a busy theatre scene.

In 1988, after much wrangling and a lot of controversy, Equity hammered out the Los Angeles 99-Seat Theatre Plan, which permits Equity members to appear for only expense reimbursement at theatres seating no more than ninety-nine people. The Plan allows actors to showcase themselves, get exposure and experience, and stay busy (after all, a lot of TV and film jobs only last a few days). Under the Plan, actors who belong to any 4-As (Associated Actors and Artistes of America) union receive a per-performance reimbursement; payment of nonunion actors is at the discretion of the producer. A number of Plan productions are by ensembles that were formed during or since the small theatre boom of the mid-1980s. Many of these artist-initiated companies, often supported by the collection of dues, don't do much outside casting, although some hold auditions for new members. (And the harder it gets to break into these companies and their shows, the more new companies and one-shot productions come into being. Hence, all that theatre!) Of course, with only two restrictions (no more than ninety-nine seats, no more than eighty performances), the Plan also can be used by commercial producers, some of whom sink lots of money into shows while paying their actors next to nothing.

There are no minimums or limits on the numbers of union or nonunion actors that may appear in a Plan production, so nonmembers may attend auditions and be cast as easily as Equity members. Non-Equity actors have additional options: there are some small non-Plan productions, as well as a number of community theaters in the area, some of which mix nonunion professionals with "hobby" actors. Some auditions for Plan and for nonunion theatre are by appointment; others utilize open calls. While monologues aren't as popular in L.A. as they are in New York, it's a good idea to have a few ready.

There are a half dozen or so LORT theatres from Los Angeles to San Diego and a handful of production houses, as well as a few Special Production houses (the closing in late 1991 of Los Angeles Theatre Center was a major—though hopefully temporary—loss). The Ahmanson (Production) and the Mark Taper Forum (LORT) each hold a general audition a year. There are also a few theatres operating under the HAT (Hollywood Area Theatre) contract, for houses with no more than 399 seats. It's not so easy to get cast in the LORT and Production houses, which utilize casting directors and agent submissions. The HAT theatres are somewhat more open. You can call any of these theatres to find out what's being produced in the upcoming season and inquire about general auditions.

Many theatres, including Plan, HAT, and LORT productions, hold per-show open calls. Since auditions can be crowded, it's wise to arrive and sign up early. Actors may be asked to do monologues or to read from the script; companies auditioning potential members may ask to see a prepared scene.

■■■■■FILM AND TELEVISION

You already know L.A. is the hub of the film and television industries. Everything is cast through submissions and recommendations, so a good agent is a real necessity. At the same time, being seen on stage and networking with casting directors and industry personnel is part of the process. (Casting directors have been known to call unagented actors directly.)

When an audition is scheduled, your agent will tell you where to pick up sides; if you don't have time to get them in advance, go to the audition early and look them over. You'll also find out if the audition will be taped (first and second readings often aren't); if so, you should pay extra attention to hair and makeup. In general, actors here pay more attention to appearance than they might in other cities. For women, the instruction "No makeup" really means *non-glamour* makeup. Men may be able to get away with auditioning in T-shirts and jeans, but women are expected to be well-dressed and coiffed. Many people carry extra clothes in the trunks of their cars.

Since most TV and many film projects don't allow for the kind of rehearsal time theatre actors are used to having, many directors and casting personnel want to see more than the mere suggestion of a character in an audition: they may not have the time (and in some cases, the imagination) to help you flesh things out. For TV especially, they need to see that you look like the role being cast. It's probably overstating the case just a little to say that if you're auditioning to play a biker, you'd better wear a torn T-shirt, pull up in a Harley, and spit on the floor; just remember that in most cases we're talking *Hollywood's version* of a biker (or secretary, or doctor, prostitute, and so on). In addition, pay attention to the sometimes not-so-subtle differences between types as they appear in theatrical film versus daytime or prime-time TV. Say you're auditioning to play that biker. Is it a soap-opera biker, a prime-time dramatic-series biker, or an adventure-movie biker? It's also wise to familiarize yourself with the work of as many directors as possible. Are you auditioning to play a New Yorker in a Spike Lee or a Woody Allen or a Mike Nichols film? A teenager in a John Hughes or John Waters film?

If you're thinking of coming to L.A. for pilot season, the period from January to May when new TV series are packaged and pitched, there are a few things you need to know. Two recent trends—that of producing pilots all year round, and the live presentation of scenes replacing taped episodes—have rendered the season less well-defined and have, to some degree, increased opportunities throughout the year. Pilot season remains a busy time, however, and unless you have an agent with a sister office in L.A., simply showing up here in January, when agent and casting directors have little time to meet new people, doesn't make much sense. You'd be better off coming several months in advance and getting your life in order: find a place to live, pick up a survival job if you need one, and learn the lay of the land.

Of course, series that are already on the air need new people all the time—except from late spring through summer, when they're on hiatus—and you can prepare to enter that ring as well by familiarizing yourself with all the series. Suppose you get a call on Monday to audition on Tuesday for a show that airs on Saturdays. If you've never seen the show, you won't know its style or the relationships of the characters. You don't have to sit and watch TV all day, every day; if you have a VCR, create your own reference library. Here's another reason for watching all the shows at least once or twice: you can decide which you're most right for and market yourself accordingly. Find out who produces and who casts "your" shows by checking *Drama-Logue, The CD Directory* updates, SAG's production schedules, and other sources.

Actors can also send P&Rs to soap-opera casting directors, and follow up with postcards, fliers, and so on. (Actors interested in doing extra work can call the "General Hospital" casting office to inquire about openings; some people, however, believe doing so is a surefire— if unofficial—way of getting oneself excluded from consideration for speaking roles on that show. Interested actors would be wise to do some further investigating.) Several publications, including *Ross Reports Television,* list contact names and addresses. AFTRA's "show sheet" lists current production, including casting personnel, and is printed in the union's quarterly newsletter; members may also get updates at the union office or by mail.

CORPORATE AND COMMERCIALS

In 1990, L.A. led the nation in SAG corporate earnings and was either first or second in AFTRA earnings for the same year. But while the area has a busy corporate market, doing industrials isn't something people do a lot of boasting about. After all, people come here to be movie stars, not to help Acme Corporation's sales reps increase their productivity. Industrials are, perhaps, the Hollywood equivalent of those embarrassing, not-so-classy relatives who just happen to be loaded; you may not like to talk about them, but you just can't refuse their invitations to dinner. Nevertheless, corporate production provides plenty of would-be movie stars with enough income to keep them going. Most production is cast through agents, although some actors make direct contact with producers and directors.

In 1990 SAG commercial earnings, Hollywood was second only to New York. L.A. being what it is, there's probably more emphasis on "pretty people" commercials; although there's work for character actors, some have found greater opportunity in New York. Remember that a lot of outdoor and beach-scene spots are shot here, and model types and actors in good physical shape have an advantage. And because actors travel by car, many keep wardrobe changes, makeup, and hairspray in their trunks—even extra stockings, fingernails, and fingernail glue. The voice-over market is very busy here, branching beyond the commercial and corporate worlds to include cartoon work. Most cartoon features and television series are produced here, creating a unique additional, highly lucrative market for voice actors.

There's a handful of leading commercial talent agencies (or full-service agencies with powerful commercial divisions), and serious commercial actors would be wise to seek representation by one of them. Some of the publications recommended in this chapter are helpful sources of information; as always, however, the best way to learn which agencies are currently hot is to talk to casting directors and other actors. If you've been working in another city, chances are your agents (or casting directors you've worked with) have some L.A. contacts; ask them to make recommendations—or better yet, phone calls—before you make the move. Once you're here, you'll want to stay in touch with local casting directors, letting them know you're alive, especially when you've booked a job. Though the vast majority of commercials are cast though agents, *Drama-Logue* does run a few (mostly nonunion) commercial casting calls.

CASTING DIVERSITY

Los Angeles is home to quite a number of organizations and theatre companies that help meet the needs and promote the visibility of actors from underrepresented groups. (See *Professional Associations*, p. 59.) The film and broadcast industries are slow to make changes, although improvements have been seen. Some producers still don't understand, and others balk at, the ideas of multiculturalism and nontraditional casting. Still, many of those who've spoken out in favor of change are prominent enough to have some real influence.

African American actors have had more success moving into the mainstream than actors from any other ethnic minority and, clearly, we're seeing the work of more (overwhelmingly male) black actors, directors, and producers in film and on television. But the growing visibility of black filmmakers doesn't mean all's equal for black actors; it's not, especially for black women.

Other minority groups continue to get the short shrift, for when people do decide to "mix things up," they often overlook Hispanics, Asians, and American Indians. While many members of the American Indian community are pleased about the content and success of the 1990 film hit *Dances With Wolves,* they nevertheless would like to see increased visibility of Indian actors in contemporary settings.

The movie industry is tough for women, especially those over forty. SAG statistics show enormous disparities between men's and women's earnings and work weeks. Yes, women work, but in Movieland they must contend with the fact that much of what's available is at best of little substance and at worst downright exploitive.

It remains especially difficult to create breakthroughs for performers with disabilities, although here, too, some improvement has been seen.

There have been a few television series and commercials in recent years utilizing hearing-impaired or physically disabled actors. And recently, most casting directors have become aware that they should bring in actors with disabilities to audition for disabled characters; some casting directors bring in actors with disabilities for other roles as well.

ADDITIONAL OPPORTUNITIES

The Actors Jam, The Highland Grounds Coffee House, 742 N. Highland Avenue, Hollywood, CA, 466-1507. Actor Scott Colomby initiated this weekly event in which actors present scenes and monologues from mostly classical works. The informal setup allows actors to brush up their Shakespeare (or Wilde, or Pinter) before a friendly audience of coffeehouse patrons. Tuesdays at 8:00.

Disneyland. Located in Anaheim, Orange County, the Magic Kingdom is the original Disney theme park. Disneyland hires actors to sing, dance, and dress up as Disney characters.

Game Shows. And you thought all those contestants were high school teachers from Des Moines! Some may be, but many are actors, and you, too, can have a chance to spin the wheel or respond in the form of a question. *Drama-Logue* runs game-show casting notices.

STUDENT FILM

If you don't have any of your work on tape, student-made films could be your chance. If a sample of your work (as opposed to just experience) is your goal, concentrate on graduate student projects. Whatever you do, ask for a copy of the film; even if it's never completed, get some of your scenes. Casting notices appear in *Drama-Logue,* with separate columns for grad and undergrad projects, and those for which an agreement with SAG has been signed. You can also send P&Rs to:

American Film Institute/SAG Conservatory. SAG Conservatory members' P&Rs are kept on file at AFI. Since the Conservatory has a limited membership, it's best to apply in September. For an application, contact: SAG Conservatory, 2021 N. Western, Mayer Library Building, Room 104, Los Angeles, CA 90027, 856-7736.

Art Center College of Design, Model's Office, 1700 Lida Street, Pasadena, CA 91103, 818-584-5035.

Columbia College, Cinema Department, 925 N. La Brea Avenue, Los Angeles, CA 90038, 851-0550.

U.C.L.A. Actors Group, c/o Film and Television Department, 405 Hilgard Avenue, Los Angeles, CA 90024, 825-5761. Every other academic quarter, audition notices are mailed to everyone who has sent a P&R.

TRAINING

Image is everything; actors are filed and categorized. To increase opportunities, it's necessary to show range, which means continually developing skills. There are about a zillion acting schools, classes, and private teachers here, making it possible to find training in just about any specialty or discipline, from method acting to monologues, from stand-up to stunt work. Acting World Books, which publishes *The Agencies,* also puts out the *Acting Coaches and Teachers Directory.* Actors who've studied in New York often complain that L.A. is bereft of decent training, although there are highly-respected and even revered acting teachers, some of whom are quite well-known. Still, many actors prefer to get solid training in New York before moving to L.A.

Actors short on experience before the camera might consider taking cold-reading and/or "acting for the camera" classes. But actors enrolling simply in order to meet the casting director-instructors would be wise to find additional reasons to be in such classes. At the very least, on-camera classes can provide actors with opportunities to find out what makeup, hair, and clothing styles work best—and that's nothing to sneeze at.

CERTIFICATE/DEGREE PROGRAMS

American Academy of Dramatic Arts, 2550 Paloma Street, Pasadena, CA
    91107, 818-798-0777.
California State University, Dominguez Hills, 1000 Victoria, Carson, CA
    90747, 516-3588.
California State University, Long Beach, Department of Theatre Arts,
    1250 Bellflower Boulevard, Long Beach, CA 90840-2701, 985-5357.
California State University, Los Angeles, 5151 State University Drive,
    Los Angeles, CA 90032, 343-4110.
Loyola Marymount University, Theatre and Dance Program, 7101 W. 80th
    Street, Los Angeles, CA 90045, 338-2837.
University of California, Los Angeles, Theatre Department, 405 Hilgard
    Avenue, Los Angeles, CA 90024-1622, 206-0426.
University of Southern California, Division of Drama, Drama Center,
    Los Angeles, CA 90089-0791, 740-1285.

AFFORDABLE ARTS

EQUITY; SAG (see *Talent Unions,* p. 59). Check foyer bulletin boards
    for announcements of free and discount theatre tickets.
SAG Hollywood Film Society. Society members view first-run movies at a
    discount; call the SAG office or check the local SAG newsletter for
    application information.

TV Show Tapings. For free tickets, contact
- Audience Associates, 467-4697;
- Audiences Unlimited, 100 Universal City Plaza Building., Suite 153, Universal City, CA 91608, 818-506-0043;
- KABC-TV (Channel 7), 4151 Prospect Avenue, Hollywood, CA 90027, 520-1222;
- Paramount Promotional Services, 860 N. Gower Street, Hollywood, CA 90038, 956-5575.

RESOURCES

LIBRARIES

American Film Institute Library, 2021 N. Western, Los Angeles, CA 90027, 856-7600, 856-7655 (reference). Open to the general public, this reference library has books on film and television, unpublished scripts, and more.

Marjorie C. Branson Memorial Theatre Management Library (see Theatre League Alliance listing in *Other Associations,* p. 60), 614-0556. Open to Theatre L.A. members, the library contains books on theatre management (no scripts), including funding, marketing, administration, and public relations.

BOOKSTORES

Larry Edmunds Cinema and Theatre Bookshop, 6658 Hollywood Boulevard, Hollywood, CA 90028, 463-3273. This store specializes in books and magazines dealing with the film and television industries. They also have theatre books, as well as TV and movie photos.

Samuel French Theatre and Film Bookshops, 7623 Sunset Boulevard, Los Angeles, CA 90046, 876-0570. Also at 11963 Ventura Boulevard, Studio City, CA 91604, 818-762-0535.

NETWORKING AND SOCIALIZING

Don't worry about doing lunch and taking meetings. Just live your life, meet people, go to parties if you're invited, or throw some of your own. In L.A., more than in New York, actors, agents, and casting directors socialize, and schmoozing is a natural part of the party scene. Health clubs, gyms, and sport clubs provide great ways to meet actors and industry folk: the woman on the treadmill next to yours might turn out to be the director you read for yesterday.

There are many, many restaurants frequented by actors and industry-types. When you're feeling flush and want to mix it up with the glitterati and paparazzi, try Spago, Morton's, the City Restaurant. Here are a few other ideas, for when you're feeling more down-to-earth:

The Moustache Café, 8155 Melrose, Hollywood, CA 90046, 651-2111.
   As the man with the dreamy accent said, "All ze actors know ze Moustache."
Residuals, 11042 Ventura Boulevard, Studio City, CA, 818-761-8301. This low-key restaurant-bar is well-loved by actors. Showing a residual check for less than $1.00 gets you a $5.00 bar tab.
Village Coffee Shop, 2695 N. Beachwood, Los Angeles, CA, 467-5397.
   Commonly known as the Beachwood Café, this is a popular gathering place for neighborhood writers and actors.

[1]   Spoken by Joe Friday (actor Jack Webb) at the opening of the "Dragnet" television series.
[2]   John Heminway, "L.A. Is It," episode of "Travels" series (Kingfish Video Productions, Inc., in association with 13WNET, 1991).
[3]   David Ferrell, "Window on the Psyche of L.A.," *The Los Angeles Times* (April 27, 1991).
[4]   *The Los Angeles Times* (April 28, 1991).
[5]   Los Angeles is *not* listed in Table 20, "Metropolitan Areas with Over 10% of Workers Using Public Transportation" (Source: U.S. Bureau of Census, 1986), of the *1990 Transit Fact Book* (Washington. D.C.: American Public Transit Association).
[6]   SAG will be moving sometime in late 1992 or early 1993; the new address was unavailable at the time of publication.

M   I   A

Known far and wide as a resort, winter hideaway, and retirement mecca, South Florida is far more than a tropical playland. Miami is its urban center, and though it may not resemble most American cities, a city it is, with its share of commerce, culture, and crises, urban renewal and urban decay.

The area known as Greater Miami extends approximately forty-five miles along the southeast coast of Florida from Florida City on up to the Broward County line and includes the resort cities of Miami Beach and Bal Harbor, sophisticated Coral Gables, eclectic Coconut Grove, race tracks, jai alai frontons, and no fewer than fourteen public golf courses. Tourism is a major industry, and though visitors come from all over, the region is especially popular with northeastern Americans and Canadians seeking respite from harsh winters, and with Europeans and South Americans.

It's a relatively young city, and what was once just a big town is now a city still growing. Miami is quirky: a many-flavored stew, perhaps, rather than a melting pot. Where else would you find a chain of Spy Stores and an American Police Museum and Hall of Fame? Says *Miami Herald* reporter Edna Buchanan in her memoir *The Corpse Had a Familiar Face,* "Everything is exaggerated in Miami, the clouds, the colors too bright to be real, the heat, and the violence. Ugly is far uglier in Miami, but beautiful is breathtaking, it hooks you for life."[1]

FAST FACTS

1990 CENSUS
358,548 (+3.4%)

COUNTIES
Dade (Miami)
Broward (Fort Lauderdale)
Palm Beach (West Palm Beach)

TIME
Zone: Eastern
Telephone: 324-8811

AREA CODES
305 (Dade, Broward Counties)
407 (Palm Beach County)
THE AREA CODE FOR ALL PHONE NUMBERS IN THIS CHAPTER IS 305 UNLESS OTHERWISE NOTED.

GREATER MIAMI CONVENTION AND VISITORS BUREAU
701 Brickell Avenue, Suite 2700
Miami, FL 33131
539-3063
800-283-2707

MIAMI BEACH VISITOR INFORMATION CENTER
1920 Meridian Avenue
Miami Beach, FL 33139
672-1270

South Florida has a good share of professional actors who spend part of the year here and part in New York and other colder climates. Some find Florida's quality of life so attractive that they relocate permanently. No doubt, even the struggling actor struggles a little less furiously in Florida.

RECOMMENDED READING

Edna Buchanan, *The Corpse Had a Familiar Face: Covering Miami, America's Hottest Beat* (New York: Random House, 1987). These memoirs of the Pulitzer Prize-winning *Miami Herald* police reporter are not for the faint-hearted.

Joan Didion, *Miami* (New York: Simon and Schuster, 1987). This effective nonfiction work explores the politics and culture clashes underlying daily life in Miami.

MOVIES

Cocoon (1985), *Flight of the Navigator* (1986), *A Hole in the Head* (1959)

POPULATION

Miami is the largest city in the state, and while stereotypes abound about who actually lives here, not everyone is either an expatriate Cuban or a Jewish retiree, though there are plenty of each. 1990 census figures show nearly two thirds of Miami's population (and nearly half of Dade County's) to be of white or non-white Hispanic origin, and in March 1991 the *Miami Herald* reported expected record numbers of Cuban exiles entering the city. And though some Spanish speakers and English speakers get along without ever learning each others' languages, bilingualism no doubt enhances the experience of anyone spending time in the region.

CLIMATE

Is there any state in the U.S. with as famous a climate—except maybe Alaska? The mere mention of Miami Beach, Bal Harbor, the Keys, evokes visions of swaying palms, orange juice, winter tans, sunglasses, speedboats, and tropical storms. Winter? It lasts about twenty minutes. Still, there are those who insist Miami has four seasons: hot, less hot, hot again, then really hot. That "fourth" season is, of course, summer, which also tends to be humid and rainy. The heat can blast you like a furnace, but then you can always hit the beach, so who cares? The winter months see some drop in temperature; evenings can be cool, but leave the down parka back in Wisconsin. *For weather and surf information call:* 661-5065.

NORMAL TEMPERATURES	Average Daily High	Average Daily Low
January	75°	59°
August	89°	76°

TEMPERATURE EXTREMES	
Maximum Temp.	Annual No. of Days
90° and above	52
32° and below	—

NORMAL WEATHER CONDITIONS		
Clear	Partly Cloudy	Cloudy
76	174	115

ANNUAL PRECIPITATION	Days	Inches
All Precipitation	129	58
Snowfall	NA	—

▮▮▮▮ TRANSPORTATION

Mobility is an important consideration for South Florida actors, who live anywhere in the region from South Miami to Jupiter. Not only do they work within that area, they travel all over the state for auditions and jobs. Of course there's public transportation, but things are so spread out that it would be nearly impossible to rely on mass transit alone—not to mention bike or foot. Even within Miami, it's just not easy to get around without wheels.

PUBLIC TRANSPORTATION
Metro-Dade Transit Agency. Since actors' lives tend to be less than routine, public transportation has limited appeal. Metrobus, Metrorail, and Tri-Rail work best for people whose home and work are located near

bus and rail lines. Within downtown Miami, the elevated Metromover is convenient and inexpensive. Beach buses connect points along Miami Beach with numerous points on the mainland, and connect with Metromover and Metrorail. Utilize bus schedules to minimize waiting time. (Since Greater Miami covers nearly 2,000 square miles, you could wait an awfully long time for a bus! Or maybe it only seems long: when the sun is strong, a bus shelter quickly turns into a toaster oven.) While ridership has actually increased recently, Metro-Dade Transit, like many municipal transportation systems, has suffered financial distress that's resulted in service cuts.

The fleet includes buses, elevated rail, and motorized cars. *For information call:* 638-6700; 638-7266 (TDD); 638-6448 (Special Transportation curb-to-curb service).

Maps and schedules are available at visitor information centers (see p. 72) or by calling 654-6586.

Exact change is required, with a surcharge for transfers. Discount token packages and monthly passes are also available. Metromover, a fleet of individual motorized cars running along an elevated track around downtown Miami, is very inexpensive; transfers from Metrorail to Metromover are free at Government Center Station. Reduced fares and passes are available for qualified student, senior, and disabled riders.

The following is a list of terminals and additional transportation systems:
Amtrak, Miami Station, 8303 N.W. 37th Avenue, Miami, FL 33147, 835-1222.
Tri-Rail, 305 S. Andrews Avenue, Suite 200, Fort Lauderdale, FL 33301, 800-TRI-RAIL (874-7245). This is a commuter rail system connecting Dade, Palm Beach, and Broward counties. A pamphlet, *Way to Go,* details route connections to various points of interest; it is available at the mailing address above, local Chambers of Commerce, and other outlets.
Greyhound, 374-7222. There are five terminals located throughout the Greater Miami area. The main terminal is at 4111 N.W. 27th Street, Miami, FL 33142.

TAXIS

Taxis are metered, and since this isn't a compact metropolitan area, distances can be far and fares high. In most areas, it's just not the kind of town where you step off the curb and hail a cab; they are, however, available by telephone.

DRIVING

Living in Dade County may mean greater access to agents and auditions, but there are times when one must throw a suitcase into the car and drive up to Orlando, Tampa, or Jacksonville. Within Greater Miami itself, it's an unfortunate, polluting fact that an actor needs a car—and it should be a car that can stand having some miles put on it. Most agents, casting directors, advertising agencies, and a lot of location work are in South Florida. Still, you could find yourself driving for a good hour or more to an audition or theatre, or making treks to the studios in Orlando and to theatres in central Florida.

Getting around Miami is easy enough, once you understand the way the system of streets and avenues works. The city is divided into four unequal quadrants, with Flagler Street dividing north from south, and Miami Avenue separating east from west. What's confusing at first is that both the streets (which run east-west) and the avenues (north-south) are numbered, so make sure you know if you're looking for a street or an avenue, and pay attention to the quadrant-identifying prefix. And just so life isn't too easy, some streets and avenues also have names (*i.e.,* S.W. Bird Road is also S.W. 40th Street), but street signs aren't always marked with both; be sure, then, to get thorough directions until you're familiar with the city. I-95 is the main artery linking most destinations throughout the region—if you can get there, you can get just about anywhere.

Parking isn't much of a problem, except downtown and in certain other congested areas. Many spaces are metered, but there are plenty that aren't. The Miami Parking System, a self-supporting department of the City of Miami, manages lots and garages downtown and in outlying areas.

◼◼◼ HOUSING AND COSTS OF LIVING

Decent, affordable housing is readily available in South Florida, and there's no particular area in which an actor ought to live. Oh, North Miami may be a little more convenient than South, and those who live in Miami Beach always need extra time to cross over onto the mainland (and have to factor in extra time for raised drawbridges). The closer you live to I-95, the less commuting time you'll need, but really, South Florida actors can and do live anywhere they like, from Key Biscayne to North Miami to Fort Lauderdale, from Boca Raton to West Palm Beach to Jupiter.

INTERAREA SHELTER INDEXES	Renters	Owners
Miami	95	92
(Philadelphia)	(100)	(100)

COSTS OF LIVING

Total average annual expenditures	$31,108
Food at home	2,165
Telephone	688
Gas and motor oil	867
Public transportation	392
Personal care products and services	397

◼◼◼◼◼EMPLOYMENT

1989 Average Annual Pay
Miami-Fort Lauderdale: $21,918

1990 Average Unemployment Rates
Florida: 5.9%
Miami-Hialeah metropolitan statistical area: 6.7%

1990 Average Weekly Unemployment Benefits
Florida: $146.59

◼◼◼◼◼CRIME

"Miami Vice" did great things for the region's entertainment industry, and terrible things for its general reputation. Let it be said: not everyone living in Miami is a drug lord, drug runner, or drug user. The area does, however, remain "a crucial battle zone in the nation's war on drugs,"[2] and the problem is not to be minimized. Of cities in this book for which statistics are available, Miami has the highest incidence of burglary and of aggravated assault, and the third highest murder rate; the rate of reported rape, however, is just about in the middle. In general, residents don't walk around terrified that they're going to be caught in the middle of a gun battle between unsavory thugs and handsome men in pale suits, although there are areas that are less safe than others, and some residents of Miami Beach—particularly the elderly—feel less at ease than they used to.

1990 CRIME RATES	Violent	Property
Total Crimes	15,607	52,871
Crimes per 100,000 People	4,359	14,768
Average 1 Crime per Every	23 people	7 people

■■■■■MISCELLANEA

NEWSPAPERS
The Miami Herald (morning)
El Nuevo Herald (morning)
Sun-Sentinal (morning)
New Times (weekly)

LIBRARY
Main Branch, 101 W. Flagler Street, Miami, FL 33130, 375-2665.

POST OFFICE
General Mail Facility, 2200 N.W. 72nd Avenue, Miami Fl, 470-0222.

THE BUSINESS

In Florida, writes theatre critic and columnist Caroline Jack, life and art
don't imitate each other, "they both imitate the weather . . . [mimicking]
the daily subtropical pattern: rapid expansion fed by intense sun, leading
to turbulence and sudden, concentrated squalls."[3] What that means to
the actor is that things change rapidly and sometimes unexpectedly.
The film and broadcast industries grow, then falter, while theatre takes a
nosedive, then does a rebound—and everybody holds their breath.

Florida is the only region covered in this book in which there is no
single all-important urban center of production. This chapter focuses on
South Florida because, despite the openings of the Disney/MGM and
Universal studios in Orlando, the bulk of performing arts and commercial
enterprises are located along that stretch of Atlantic coast between the
southernmost part of Miami and West Palm Beach some one hundred
miles away. There's work to be had all over the state, but most actors still
live in South Florida. Late 1990 membership figures show far more Equity
actors in South Florida than in either Orlando or the Gulf Coast region.
Florida actors do travel, however, and even those who only work in
theatre have a venue that extends from Miami to Jupiter.

While the majority of Florida agents and casting directors are located
in Greater Miami, more and more are setting up shop in and around
Orlando. Many actors have an Orlando agent as well, and some keep an
Orlando-area phone number with voice mail, or an 800-number beeper.
Others do a phone number "swap" with an Orlando-based actor: both
actors' names go on both actors' answering machines—just be sure to
hook up with someone who'll be responsible about conveying messages.

Ultimately, the actor who's considering relocating to Florida may need to assess his own strengths and interests. If commercials are his forte, South Florida is the place to be; there are also more theatres in the area. If he's primarily interested in episodic television, it might be better to be nearer the studios, although as yet there probably isn't enough work to keep him busy.

RECOMMENDED READING
Carolyn Jack, "Florida Forecast: Actors Find a Healthy Climate for Theatre," and George Capewell and Tori Rodman, "Film & TV Production Shines," *Back Stage* (November 22, 1991). These articles provide realistic overviews of the Sunshine State's performing arts industries.

■■■■■■ PROFESSIONAL ASSOCIATIONS

TALENT UNIONS
Actors' Equity Association (AEA), Liaison City.
    Members: 437 (S. Florida)
American Federation of Television and Radio Artists (AFTRA),
    20401 N.W. 2nd Avenue, Suite 102, Miami, FL 33169, 652-4842.
    Members: 704 (Miami local)
Screen Actors' Guild (SAG), 2299 Douglas Road, No. 200, Miami, FL
    33145, 444-7677.
    Members: 2,925 (all Florida)

OTHER ASSOCIATIONS
Florida Professional Theatres Association (FPTA), P.O. Box 3805, West Palm Beach, FL 33402, 407-848-6231. In 1991 FPTA established a membership category for individual theatre professionals. Benefits include bimonthly newsletter, quarterly *Call-board,* workshop and theatre admission discounts, and inclusion in a P&R bank.
Professional Actors Association of Florida (PAAF), P.O. Box 610366, Miami Beach, FL 33161-0366, 932-1427. PAAF is a "not-for-profit organization dedicated to enhancing the employment of the Florida based actor." Activities include workshops, outreach to the production community, a member talent directory, and a car pool hotline. Membership requirements include an aggregate two-year performing union membership, Florida residency six months a year, and three principal speaking parts under union contracts within the previous two years. Nonmembers may participate in workshops and showcases by audition.

LOOKING FOR WORK

PUBLICATIONS

FPTA Call-board (see *Other Associations,* p. 79). Published quarterly and
sent to FPTA members, *Callboard* contains audition and job notices.

These newspapers run audition notices; most are for non-Equity theatre:

- *Sun-Sentinal,* Friday's "Showtime" section
- *The Miami Herald,* Friday "Weekend" section
- *New Times,* published on Wednesdays

HOTLINES

Actors' Equity Association (see *Talent Unions,* p. 79)

BULLETIN BOARDS AND BINDERS

Actors' Equity Association. The Equity bulletin board is located in the
AFTRA office (see *Talent Unions,* p. 79).

TALENT BOOKS AND TALENT BANKS

AFTRA. The union office keeps members' voice-over tapes on file.

FPTA (see *Other Associations,* p. 79). Members' P&Rs are included in
the FPTA talent file.

PAAF (see *Other Associations,* p. 79). The directory of PAAF members
is sent to producers, directors, and other personnel across the country;
there are plans to supplement the directory with voice-over and
on-camera reels.

TALENT SHOWCASES AND COMBINED AUDITIONS

Southeastern Theatre Conference; National Dinner Theatre Association.
(For addresses, see Appendix B.)

Florida Professional Theatres Association (see *Other Associations,* p. 79).
FPTA's annual auditions, held in late summer/early fall, are attended
by member theatres and occasional commercial/corporate film producers.
Non-Equity actors must be FPTA members; Equity members are
encouraged, though not required, to join.

Professional Actors Association of Florida (see *Other Associations,* p. 79).
PAAF's annual showcase presents scenes, monologues, and songs.
Members and nonmembers may audition to be included; auditions are
held monthly in conjunction with workshops, and an annual open call
is announced on the Equity hotline and in newspapers.

TALENT AGENTS AND CASTING DIRECTORS

Since few agents work with actors on an exclusive basis, the agent-actor
relationship is a little like a free-for-all. Exceptions aside (some agents

have a handful of signed clients, and Talent Network works only with signed talent), an actor may list with as many agents as he likes—or as will have him. This is a mixed blessing: obviously, the better-represented one is, the better the chances of being sent out; on the other hand, two agents sometimes call an actor for the same audition, resulting in a rather sticky situation. At other times, a casting director will call the actor directly, and then ask which agent the booking should go through; if that seems odd, remember the agent may be needed to negotiate the contract. By the way, people here use the word "casting" as a noun, in place of "audition" or "casting session."

For work in all media other than theatre, you need agent representation. Anyone—union member or not—can get a list of franchised agencies from AFTRA or SAG (AFTRA's quarterly newsletter include complete lists of franchised agents). Send P&Rs to the agencies, then call to ask for appointments. AFTRA, SAG, and AGVA members should have no trouble getting interviews with agents, though union membership is no guarantee of representation. Agents are fairly receptive to newcomers, though actors may have to remind agents they're alive, calling once or twice a week to ask if anything's come up. Headshot-postcards aren't yet all the rage, and so might make effective marketing tools.

Area agents and casting directors are great supporters of local talent and feel that if the pool isn't as deep as those in New York and L.A., it's equally worthy. They stress the need for good, trained actors. Some actors, however, complain that agents rarely go to see theatre, and even resent when actors work on stage because of potential conflicts with shooting schedules.

THEATRE

Florida theatre isn't concentrated in any single city: there are houses all over, from Miami to Tampa to Jacksonville to Tallahassee. Still, the majority of actors live in South Florida, from Miami through Fort Lauderdale and on up to West Palm Beach. (And while Equity's 1990 contract with Walt Disney World certainly means increased employment in that part of the state, remember that Disney performers are jobbed in from all over the country.) South Florida has a good number of theatres, although at least three have gone under in recent years—quite a blow for the region's many dedicated theatre actors.

The region has several large presenting houses. The local theatre scene is led by the partially state-funded LORT theatres the Coconut Grove Playhouse and the Caldwell Theatre Company, which cast primarily in New York. Not surprisingly, this frustrates locals, many of whom have lived and worked in the Apple. Theatre Club of the Palm

Beaches is gaining prominence, and the Jupiter Theatre and the Royal Palm are highly-visible dinner theatres. Rounding out the scene are a handful of both commercial and nonprofit SPT theatres, like the Actor's Playhouse, The Public Theatre of Greater Fort Lauderdale, and Brian C. Smith's Off-Broadway Theater on 26th Street; companies using LOA and Guest Artist contracts, like the Ann White Theatre and Acme Acting Company; and nonunion companies like Teatro Avante, the Red Barn Theatre, and New Theatre.

Equity theatres hold annual general auditions, and many announce per-show auditions on that union's hotline. The Florida Professional Theatres Association's annual general auditions are attended by Equity and non-Equity theatres from all over the state (see *Talent Showcases and Combined Auditions,* p. 80). That there's a core of actors who work repeatedly on South Florida's stages doesn't make it impossible for the newcomer to break in, although in the absence of a local trade paper, newcomers will have to do a lot of legwork. Equity members can listen to that union's hotline for the annual list of Equity theatres, then call the theatres to ask about upcoming seasons and auditions; others can read *The Miami Herald* and *Sun-Sentinal,* which announce theatre seasons. When you see (or hear of) something you're right for, call the theatre and ask about auditioning.

Equity theatre is not the best arena for new plays; old chestnuts and recent Broadway and Off-Broadway successes are more popular with the largely retirement-age audiences. However, while musicals and lighter fare are surer shots than more controversial works, remember that many of the retirees bring with them cosmopolitan sensibilities and sophistication, and even a lifetime of theatregoing.

Non-Equity theatre may offer greater opportunity for experimentation and innovation; it may, in fact, offer greater work opportunities, although those opportunities may be hard to track down, at least initially. Newspapers are a good resource, not only for casting notices, but for theatre listings. The annual FPTA audition, attended by both Equity and non-Equity theatres, is a good way to be seen. In addition, most Equity theatres use SPT Contracts, and so hire non-Equity actors.

There's a strong Latino theatre community here, existing quite separately from English-language theatre. Once a purely Cuban domain, it now includes actors from other parts of the Caribbean and from Central and South America. The work is primarily vaudeville, political satire, and comedy, and it's difficult, even for bilingual actors, to break in. There are, however, a few companies producing in Spanish or in Spanish and English that are independent of the traditional Spanish-language theatre community. Equity has no jurisdiction over entirely-Spanish-language companies.

█████FILM AND TELEVISION

Five years of "Miami Vice" really put South Florida on the map, and things have been good since then. A lot of people got their SAG cards doing "Vice," and Miami is still considered a good place to get into that union. The Florida branch, in fact, which includes a small percentage of members in other southeastern states, now has the third largest SAG membership in the country, having surpassed Chicago. In general, the unions are pretty strong here, facing less antiunion sentiment than in some other right-to-work states.

"Miami Vice" is no longer, but the region is seeing continued growth in the film and television industries. Many European production companies shoot in South Florida, and quite a few network TV shows pass through for an episode or two, and sometimes more. At the time of this writing, a nice little handful of TV series call Central Florida home. Of course, feature films and TV shows are still cast primarily in New York and L.A., and there are other inequities: a local actor gets paid scale, while an unknown from L.A. gets better pay, per diem, and maybe even above-the-title billing. But local agents and casting directors are real champions of Florida talent, which is gaining enough credibility that more and more roles are being cast locally. And with so much film production in the area, there's always extra work, most of which is non-SAG. Interested actors should send P&Rs to casting directors, along with a note expressing availability for extra work.

The million-dollar questions are: Is the entire film industry moving to Florida? Should actors bypass (or leave) South Florida for Central Florida in order to be nearer the Orlando studios? A few years after the openings of the Disney/MGM Studios and Universal Studios, the answers to these questions are no and maybe. It's true that a new market has been created, one that should continue to grow, though not, as it's turning out, at the rate some people expected. Industry insiders in both Florida and California predict that Hollywood (along with New York) will ever remain the corporate and (ahem) spiritual center of the film and TV industries.

As for the Central-versus-South Florida debate, South Florida still has the largest talent pool in the state, and many actors manage to work both markets. The studios have certainly brought work to Central Florida, but most of what comes in is prepackaged. Of the remainder, the relatively low-budget TV series that are based in Orlando have been good about hiring Florida actors for guest roles. Orlando casting directors generally turn to Miami agents only when they have trouble casting a role, but Miami-based actors with Orlando agents do work on these shows. Moving to Orlando certainly is an option, but you don't *have* to live there in order to work there, although it helps. Thus far, if you include commercials and industrials, there's still more going on in South Florida. Wherever you choose to live, get agents, know who the top casting directors are in both areas, keep a voice-mail service—and make sure you don't mind long commutes. What the future holds, only time will tell, but while work is increasing in Central Florida, it's increasing in the south as well. Actors would be wise to do additional research before relocating to the Orlando area.

■■■■■CORPORATE AND COMMERCIALS

Florida showed quite respectable SAG industrials earnings in 1990 (AFTRA figures were unavailable) and, indeed, corporate production appears to be increasing. As yet, however, few South Florida actors make a living in this market, which includes both union (AFTRA and SAG) and nonunion film and video. Most industrials cast corporate spokemen and women; there isn't a great deal of work for character actors. But the region's popularity means there's also a great deal of trade show and convention work. For both live and film/video productions, few producers hire independent casting directors; the more common practice is to go directly to agents, who sometimes hold casting sessions right in their offices.

South Florida actors have it really good in commercials, including both on-camera and voice-over work. When it gets cold up north, things get busy down south, and in this market, there's no Central-South debate: Miami wins, hands down. This has long been considered a popular location site, with its friendly climate and unique settings like Key Biscayne and Miami Beach's Art Deco District. Locals get cast as principals reasonably often, and there's enough locally-generated on-camera, voice-over, and print work to make a very strong market. "Real people" types who also look good in bathing suits have an advantage here, where so much advertising is shot in and around the water.

There's a tremendous Spanish-language TV and radio commercial market. Not all the work is local; a great deal comes from ad agencies in New York and South and Central America, and hiring is often done locally. Some talent agencies, like Green and Green, have entire departments representing Hispanic actors.

Actors (speaking any language) can try sending P&Rs, voice-over tapes, and other representative materials to production houses and advertising agencies. AFTRA can help with ad agency contact information. Actors should also ask friends and colleagues for advice; word of mouth is an essential tool of the trade here.

◼◼◼◼◼CASTING DIVERSITY

Hispanic actors who are not part of that tight-knit Latin theatre community don't have a lot of opportunity to work on stage. Hispanic Equity members may get some work in the mainstream theatres, but they aren't often cast in major roles. There may be a little more opportunity on the stage for black actors, although there aren't as many living in the region. The non-Equity Teatro Avante produces in both Spanish and English, utilizing multiracial casts, and the Vinnette Carroll Theatre presents work that focus on the African American experience.

Agents say there's a real need for black actors in film and broadcast. But while a few do quite well in film and television, there isn't enough work for most to make a living. The same goes for Asian actors; when the occasional call comes in, the industry notices there aren't very many in the community. Hispanics in the region do fairly well in film, TV, and commercials, though inequities remain. No small number of Hispanics have adopted Anglo stage names; others are relegated to portraying one stereotype after another. There has been some improvement for women in the voice-over and music markets. Change is coming to Florida, as it is everywhere else; this being the South, it might be coming a little more slowly.

◼◼◼◼◼ADDITIONAL OPPORTUNITIES

Condo Tours. A number of the region's many condominium complexes provide residents with entertainment. Independent theatre companies can try booking their packaged shows into condo theatres.

Cruise Lines. South Florida is the departure point for a number of cruises to the Caribbean, South America, and beyond, and that means work for Florida performers. Most of the lines hold auditions in New York, but they cast in Florida as well.

Disneyworld. As it is in Anaheim, so shall it be in Orlando: if you're right for Disney and Disney's right for you, the Magic Kingdom can be a source of steady, long-term work. Just make sure you're young and energetic.

Student Film. University of Miami, School of Communication, Motion Picture Program, Production Facilities Manager, P.O. Box 248127, Coral Gables, FL 33124, 284-3795. Send P&Rs.

◼◼◼◼◼TRAINING

Many area theatres have a school or training program attached. The most well-known, perhaps, is the Burt Reynolds Institute for Theatre Training, commonly called BRITT. Designed for the less-experienced actor, the program allows students to play small roles at the associated Tecquestah Theatre; as compensation they receive Equity Membership Candidate points, and have the opportunity to work with name actors, although the theatre no longer has the star power it once had.

PAAF's Monday night workshops (see *Other Associations,* p. 79), open to members and nonmembers by audition, offer a place to work on skills while meeting working actors. FPTA sponsors workshops in a variety of performance skills. And while there are a number of private teachers here, the selection and variety aren't as great as they are in some regions. For this reason, some actors spend summers studying in New York.

CERTIFICATE/DEGREE PROGRAMS

University of Miami, Department of Theatre Arts, P.O. Box 248273, Coral
    Gables, FL 33124, 284-6439.

AFFORDABLE ARTS

Courtesy Discounts. FPTA members receive discounts at participating
    member theatres.
Equity Comps. With the exception of the presenting houses, most Equity
    theatres will provide complimentary tickets for Equity actors.
    Sometimes there are announcements on the hotline; you can also call
    the theatre the day of performance and ask if a seat is available.

RESOURCES

LIBRARY

Gary Drane Collection, Barry University Library, 11300 N.E. 2nd Avenue,
    Miami Shores, FL 33161, 899-3760. This private reference library,
    created as the result of the bequest of an Equity councillor, holds a
    substantial collection that includes scripts and scores. Visitors must
    show an Equity card for admittance.

BOOKSTORES

No area bookstores specialize in the performing arts, but since actors find out theatre seasons well in advance, they have time to order scripts from New York. In addition, the following stores have pretty good selections of plays:
Book and Books, 296 Aragon Avenue, Coral Gables, FL 33134, 442-4408.
Bookworks, 6935 Red Road, Coral Gables, FL 33143, 661-5080.
The Grove Bookworm, 3025 Fuller Street, Coconut Grove, FL, 443-6411.

◼◼◼◼NETWORKING AND SOCIALIZING

The actor's world is pretty decentralized: there's no trade paper, no non-Equity hotline, no theatre district. The newcomer, then, has got to find ways to meet other actors. AFTRA and SAG members can take advantage of union-sponsored activities. Actors may join FPTA; those who qualify can join PAAF, and those who don't may audition to participate in that organization's weekly workshops.

Artsbar, 300 S. Dixie Highway, West Palm Beach, FL 33401, 407-832-0944.
   Improv is featured on Sunday nights.
Back Stage, 1061 E. Indiantown Road, Jupiter, FL 33477, 407-747-9533.

---

[1]   Edna Buchanan, *The Corpse Had a Familiar Face* (New York: Random House, 1987). Thanks to Emily Listfield in "The Reporter Has a Familiar Face," *American Way* (April 15, 1991), for the Edna Buchanan quotation.
[2]   *The Miami Herald* (March 28, 1991).
[3]   Caroline Jack, "Florida Stages," *Back Stage* (February 22, 1991).

MINNEAPOL

Minneapolis, it's said, is the nation's easternmost western city, St. Paul its westernmost eastern. With the Mississippi River serving as a rather unfussy dividing line, the Twin Cities are merged everywhere, perhaps, but at the ego. St. Paul, east of the great river, is the more sedate, old-fashioned, and sometimes-overlooked elder sibling; here are old families, old money, and several long-established ethnic enclaves. Younger, more glamorous Minneapolis, largely west of the river, is the trendy, cosmopolitan kid.

FAST FACTS

1990 CENSUS
Minneapolis: 368,383 (−0.7%)
St. Paul: 272,235 (+0.7%)

COUNTIES
Hennepin (Minneapolis)
Ramsey (St. Paul)

TIME
Zone: Central
Telephone: 546-TIME
633-3333

AREA CODE
612

VISITOR INFORMATION
Twin Cities Tourism
Attractions Association

Minneapolis Convention and
Visitors Association

1219 Marquette Avenue
3rd Floor
Minneapolis, MN 55403
338-6427
800-328-1461

Folks also say this is the hardest place to get people to come to, and the hardest to get them to leave. After all, the unconverted may think, who wants to go to that cold, cold place way up north? But cold can be dealt with, say those who love it here, and you won't find any other area more committed to winter activities. Anyway, doesn't it sound delightful to live on Snowflake Drive or Snowy Owl Lane? Winter, in any case, may have everything to do with the area's unusually healthy cultural life. Surprised? It's a long season: people need to get out of their houses, and even here, life doesn't begin and end with ice fishing. Harsh winters aside, life is easier here than in many of our nation's cities. The pace is slower, attitudes a little more laid-back. The people, the majority of whom are of Scandinavian heritage, are friendly if not effusive, tolerant if reserved.

If the area isn't a major film and broadcast center, its standing in the American theatre scene is more than respectable. The high regard with which the country views Twin Cities theatre has drawn theatre folk from all over the map. If the Cities' theatre star has dimmed slightly of late, it seems there are enough people sufficiently devoted to life among the lakes that there will always be an active, energetic theatre community.

RECOMMENDED READING

Paul Deblinger, *Culpepper's Minneapolis and St. Paul* (Minneapolis: Culpepper Press, 1990). Though some listings need updating, this comprehensive guide is unusual in that it includes listings of arts organizations and film societies along with other performing-arts-related information.

Sinclair Lewis, *Main Street* (New York: Harcourt Brace Jovanovich, Inc., 1920).

MOVIES

Patti Rocks (1988), *The Personals* (1983), *Purple Rain* (1984)

■■■■■CLIMATE

Winter may be long and harsh and, yes, this may be one of the colder spots in the country, but look on the bright side: winter doesn't last forever—it just seems that way. Although the Twin Cities can experience blizzards and freezing rains, sometimes it's cold winds and low temperatures, rather than constant precipitation, that keep snow on the ground from November to April. And though some people struggle with winter depression, there's enough of the frozen stuff to keep sports-loving Twin Citians occupied with ice skating, cross-country skiing, and sledding—and all practically in their own back yards. There are usually a few weeks each year when the temperature never makes it above zero degrees, and the wind can drive the thermometer even lower. But though things may slow down a bit, nothing comes to a complete halt. Skyway systems—covered walkways connecting extensive parts of the downtown districts in both cities—offer year-round protection from the elements.

Temperatures can vary greatly from season to season, going from –30 degrees in winter to over 100 degrees during the summer. Autumn is a lovely time here; spring, which is relatively short, can be awfully wet, bringing plagues of mosquitoes. Summer days range from gently hot to uncomfortably humid, steamy in the rain. Tornadoes and floods, though not common, aren't unheard of. *For weather information call:* 452-2323; 725-6090.

NORMAL TEMPERATURES	Average Daily High	Average Daily Low
January	20°	2°
July	83°	63°

TEMPERATURE EXTREMES			
Maximum Temp.	Annual No. of Days	Minimum Temp.	Annual No. of Days
90° and above	15	32° and below	156
32° and below	79	0° and below	33

NORMAL WEATHER CONDITIONS		
Clear	Partly Cloudy	Cloudy
97	101	167

ANNUAL PRECIPITATION	Days	Inches
All Precipitation	114	27
Snowfall	NA	49

■■■■■ TRANSPORTATION

Though the Twin Cities are rather spread out, getting around is rarely a problem. The basic street pattern is a due north-south, east-west grid; entire sections of both cities, however, list slightly one way or another, and several diagonal streets slice this way and that, making a detailed map essential. The bus system is excellent, and traffic generally manageable. With plenty of bike trails and no hills to speak of, bicycling can be a great way to travel except, of course, in harsh winter weather. Theatre-only actors can manage without a car, since all but two of the area's major theatres are reachable by bus, and people carpool to those two suburban houses. However, with production houses located throughout the Twin Cities and surrounding suburbs, most actors who do film and broadcast consider a car a necessity.

PUBLIC TRANSPORTATION

Metropolitan Transit Commission (MTC). Twin Cities buses are known to be clean, dependable, and efficient. Folks who live in the Twin Cities or the nearest suburbs can manage very well on public transportation, but even though service drops off dramatically past the nearest ring of suburbs, commuters in the farther 'burbs can rely on good rush hour connections. In this area of mostly manageable traffic, buses tend to arrive on or close to schedule, and breakdowns are dealt with promptly. Heating and air conditioning systems function well, which is important in frigid winter and sultry summer. Of course, you still have to wait outside, but shelters at most stops offer some respite from nature's cruelty. *For information call:* 827-7733; 341-0140 (TTY); 349-7480 (reduced fare certification for people with disabilities); 827-1700 Metro Mobility (door-to-door service for seniors and the disabled).

Maps and schedules are available at banks, department stores, 7-Eleven stores, and the following MTC Transit Store locations:
- 719 Marquette Avenue (Minneapolis)
- American National Bank Skyway, 101 E. Fifth Street (St. Paul)

Regular adult fares are divided among zones and into peak (Monday-Friday rush hours) and off-peak travel times; express buses cost extra. Transfers, issued upon request when boarding, can be used up to three times, though not to complete round trips. Students up to age seventeen, seniors, and people with disabilities qualify for reduced fares. Children under six ride free with a fare-paying adult. Fares in Minneapolis' downtown zone are especially low. SuperSaver options include reduced-price token packages, tickets, and monthly passes, which can be purchased by mail, at Transit Stores, and in stores and banks throughout the metro area.

The following is a list of terminals and additional transportation systems:
Amtrak, Midway Station, 730 Transfer Road, St. Paul, MN 55114, 339-2382. *Greyhound,*
- 29 N. 9th Street, Minneapolis, MN, 371-3311;
- 25 W. 7th Street, St. Paul, MN, 371-3311.

TAXIS

While there are a number of taxi companies in the Twin Cities, cabs generally aren't found cruising the streets. Instead, they can be found at taxi stands or ordered by phone—and they come promptly.

DRIVING

Twin Citians' favorite driving joke is that there are two seasons here: winter and road repair. When the spring thaw comes, road crews set to work building, rebuilding, and repairing. But while road work slows things down, the area rarely experiences the terrible congestion of many other metro areas. During rush hours, 35W can get pretty jammed, as can 94 and 12, the major arteries connecting the downtown districts of Minneapolis and St. Paul.

Parking downtown, while not impossible, is difficult. On-street parking is metered, and parking ramps and lots, though plentiful, can be expensive; allow extra time to find available space in one of the lower-priced lots. A vehicle with front-wheel drive is an absolute necessity here. During snow emergencies, cars must be moved for street plowing; to avoid having your car impounded, pay attention to street signs and temporary parking bans. For twenty-four-hour snow emergency information, call 348-SNOW (7669).

◼◼◼◼◼ HOUSING AND COSTS OF LIVING

Costs of living are relatively low in the Twin Cities, and a high vacancy rate means housing is both plentiful and affordable. It's not hard to find apartments, duplexes, and even houses in pleasant neighborhoods, several of which, plentiful with trees, have a suburban feeling. Many actors live in south Minneapolis, where almost every house is within walking distance of at least one of the city's twenty-two lakes. And the gorgeous homes around some of the lakes aren't completely out of the question: persistent hunting might turn up a carriage house converted into a rental unit. Of course, actors live all over the Twin Cities and in the surrounding suburbs, many of which are just a short commute from one downtown or the other. Recommended areas are Bryn Mawr, Uptown (don't get confused—it's in south Minneapolis), Stevens Court, Kenwood, Oak Park, Whittier, the Wedge, and Seward.

Winter heating costs can be astronomical, so be sure heating is either included in the rent or factored into the monthly budget. Housing-hunters usually check the classifieds in the *Star Tribune* or in free publications available in supermarkets. Co-op Supermarket bulletin boards, particularly in the Wedge Co-op on Lyndale and Franklin in Minneapolis, are good sources, and there are several free-to-renter apartment-locator services.

Though property taxes are high, a surprising number of actors own homes. A theatre-loving pair of real estate agents have helped many actors make the leap to ownership. They are:

John and Carlyn Chrisney, Edina Realty, 3270 West Lake Street,
   Minneapolis, MN 55416, 925-7781.

INTERAREA SHELTER INDEXES	Renters	Owners
Minneapolis	92	86
St. Paul	n/a	n/a
(Philadelphia)	(100)	(100)

COSTS OF LIVING

Total average annual expenditures	$31,140
Food at home	2,167
Telephone	492
Gas and motor oil	1,042
Public transportation	415
Personal care products and services	422

■■■■■■EMPLOYMENT

The annual State Fair, located at the fairgrounds in St. Paul, provides dependable supplementary employment for many area actors who work as salespeople, product demonstrators, and so on.

1989 Average Annual Pay
Minneapolis-St. Paul: $24,372

1990 Average Unemployment Rates
Minnesota: 4.8%
Minneapolis-St. Paul metropolitan statistical area: 4.3%

1990 Average Weekly Unemployment Benefits
Minnesota: $188.69

■■■■■■CRIME

While newcomers from tougher towns find the Twin Cities pretty tame, longtime residents are aware of increasing crime and violence including gang- and drug-related activity, and even drive-by shootings. Among cities in this book, FBI statistics reveal that while St. Paul and Minneapolis, respectively, have the first and third lowest murder rates, they're beat out only by Dallas for highest incidence of rape in cities for which statistics are available. Minneapolis' burglary rates are at the high end of the scale, while St. Paul's lie more comfortingly toward the middle. Fortunately, it's not hard to sense which parts of town require greater caution and care.

Since some theatre neighborhoods get pretty quiet and a little scary at night, actors often escort one another to their cars post-performance.

1990 CRIME RATES[1]	Violent	Property	
Total Crimes	5,367	37,092	(Minneapolis)
	2,764	19,671	(St. Paul)
Crimes per 100,000 People	1,541	10,647	(Minneapolis)
	1,015	7,225	(St. Paul)
Average 1 Crime per Every	65 people	9 people	(Minneapolis)
	98 people	14 people	(St. Paul)

■■■■■■MISCELLANEA

NEWSPAPERS
Star Tribune (morning)
St. Paul Pioneer Press Dispatch (all day)
City Pages (free weekly)
Twin Cities Reader (free weekly)

LIBRARIES
Minneapolis Public Library and Information Center, 300 Nicollet Mall, Minneapolis, MN 55401, 372-6500.
St. Paul Public Library, Main Branch, 90 W. 4th Street, St. Paul, MN 55102, 292-6311.

POST OFFICE
Main Branch, 1st Street and Marquette, Minneapolis, MN 55401, 349-9100.
Main Office Station, 180 E. Kellog Boulevard, St. Paul, MN 55101, 293-3021.

ADDITIONAL INFORMATION
City Line, 654-6060. This free telephone service supplies news and weather forecasts, health, legal, and employment information, and more.

THE BUSINESS

Twin Citians are quick to say that this is a great place for theatre, great because the community patronizes its stages and respects the noble profession, great because of generous public and private funding. Without a doubt, this is an artsy, culturally-lively community in which locals are proud that the "metropolitan area has more nonprofit arts activity than New York City on a per capita/annual budget basis."[2]

But is this a great place for actors? That is the question, one that has no easy answer. Plenty of theatres plus less competition equals an attractive region, but despite a mutually supportive acting community, breaking in isn't always easy. Many actors do well in the healthy corporate film and video market, and the commercial industry isn't bad either, though it suffers from the recession blues. But actors whose main interest is theatrical film and television would be wise to look elsewhere; ditto those hoping for fame and glory. Actors settle down here for the lifestyle as much as for the work. They may not be exempt from typical actors' problems, but those who break in find they have the opportunity to do good work while leading stable, if unglamorous, lives. Without the great gulf that often exists between actors and casting and artistic personnel, meaningful contacts can be made, and the aggravation factor is relatively low.

RECOMMENDED READING

Misha Berson, "A Tale of Two Cities," *The Seattle Times/Seattle Post-Intelligencer* (May 26, 1991).

William B. Collins, "It's a warm climate for the theater: Plays and playwrights prosper on the stages of Minneapolis and St. Paul," *The Philadelphia Inquirer* (February 5, 1989).

Beth Lane, ed., *Twin Cities Reports* (Chicago: PerformInk). Published twice yearly, this guide lists agents, casting directors, ad agencies, and more.

▮▮▮▮ PROFESSIONAL ASSOCIATIONS

TALENT UNIONS

Actors' Equity Association (AEA), Liaison City.
    Members: 329
American Federation of Television and Radio Artists (AFTRA),
    15 S. 9th Street, No. 400 Frisco Building, Minneapolis, MN 55402,
    371-9120.
    Members: 925
Screen Actors Guild (SAG). There is no SAG office; AFTRA acts as caretaker.
    Members: included in Chicago total

OTHER ASSOCIATIONS

Lipservice, 400 1st Avenue N., Minneapolis, MN 55401, 338-LIPS (5477).
    This is a guild for some of the Twin Cities' busiest voice-over talent.
    New members, brought in by invitation only, are rare.

LOOKING FOR WORK

PUBLICATIONS

Spotlight, 3120 Hennepin Avenue S., Suite 404, Minneapolis, MN 55408,
   823-3719. This monthly publication carries theatre, music, and film
   industry news; a theatre directory; feature articles and interviews; and
   a few casting notices. It is distributed free at theatres and other Twin
   Cities locations.

Star Tribune. The Sunday edition's classified section includes casting
   notices and is the primary source of casting information.

Twin Cities Reports (see *Recommended Reading,* p. 95)

HOTLINES

Actors' Equity Association (see *Talent Unions,* p. 95). The Equity hotline
   announces auditions for productions in the Great Lakes states, as well
   as in the Twin Cities.

Film Board Production Hotline, 333-0436. Announces who's casting films
   shooting in the area; sometimes coordinates the collection of P&Rs.

Minneapolis Association of Community Theatres (MACT), 521-5692.
   Though geared toward community theatre, this hotline announces
   some professional non-Equity auditions.

BULLETIN BOARDS AND BINDERS

AFTRA/SAG (see *Talent Unions,* p. 95). Equity audition information is
   compiled in a binder at the AFTRA office; the same information is on
   the Equity hotline.

TALENT BOOKS AND TALENT BANKS

AFTRA/SAG Directory. This is a joint project with the Film Board.

TALENT SHOWCASES AND COMBINED AUDITIONS

Mid-America Theatre Conference; National Dinner Theatre Association;
   Wisconsin Theatre Auditions. (For addresses, see Appendix B.)

TALENT AGENTS AND CASTING DIRECTORS

Once upon a time, not so long ago, a New York actor planning a trip to
the Twin Cities wanted to set up appointments with talent agents. List in
hand, telephone at the ready, the actor hesitated: after years in New York,
he knew the experience of being treated like a nobody. He took a deep
breath and started calling. To his surprise, Twin Cities agents were not at
all like those he'd encountered in the Big Apple. They were friendly and
welcoming, and happily made appointments to meet him.

Though the local talent pool has grown since then and it's no longer quite so easy to get representation, agents remain reasonably receptive and accessible. There was a time when getting listed with agents was almost as easy as walking in and dropping off P&Rs. Today there's a growing trend toward exclusivity (Creative Casting works only on that basis, except with actors who are here temporarily), and agents have been known to turn people away altogether. Still, the trained, experienced actor, especially one with a strong theatre background, shouldn't have trouble setting up interviews and getting listed with an agency or two (although agents and casting directors don't handle theatre). Someone whose résumé is relatively bare will have a tougher time, unless she has a standout commercial look. Anyone can get a list of franchised agents from the AFTRA office; there are also a couple of busy, legitimate nonfranchised agents in the area. The *Twin Cities Reports* has a complete list of agencies. Send agents P&Rs, and follow up with phone calls.

Being listed doesn't always mean getting auditions, so newcomers might need to stay persistently, politely in touch with agents. Some actors worry that agents here don't promote even their exclusive talent with enough vigor. If that's true, it may be because the market is small enough that casting directors know who's out there; they consult their own files and call the agents of the actors they want to see. Of course, agents can and do offer additional suggestions, but it's important that the casting directors know you're alive. Newcomers can ask their agent(s) to set up go-sees in order to meet the casting directors. You can also can send P&Rs to CDS or, better yet, drop by in person and introduce yourself (but don't expect to hang around for a lengthy chitchat); send another P&R every several months, and send postcards or arrange for comps when you're in a show. Nonunion actors are usually called directly by casting directors, so it's especially important that they make themselves known.

■■■■■THEATRE

The '70s and '80s were theatre boom years, when numerous and varied companies were formed, and playwrights flourished. Though new companies continue to be born, the growth is tapering off; there have been some major losses, leaving significant gaps, and more than a few directors, actors, and playwrights have relocated to (or spend a great deal of time in) Seattle and other regions.

But if the theatre is in a holding pattern, it remains very much alive. The Guthrie Theatre is the area's most prestigious institution and is, in fact, one of only two LORT A theatres in the entire Midwest. Another important fixture is the Playwrights' Center, which has gained national prominence as a nurturer of plays and playwrights. The Chanhassen

Dinner Theatre, with four stages, may be the busiest dinner theatre in the country, and holds the record for longest-running-show-with-original-cast, *I Do, I Do,* playing since 1970. At fifty-plus years old, the crowd-pleasing Old Log claims status as the country's oldest theatre in continuous use (but so does Philadelphia's Walnut Street Theatre; and does it really matter?). Children's Theatre Company, which operates under a special agreement with Equity, has been producing since 1965.

SPT Contract theatres come in a variety of sizes and styles, and several have quite a strong presence. A few companies have gone under in recent years, while some newcomers are finding fairly stable footing. Among the more well-established companies are Penumbra, Mixed Blood, Illusion Theatre, and Cricket Theatre. The Equity Members Project Code is used with some frequency by actors who want to self-produce. There are some nice small-to-medium presenting spaces, though availability can be a problem. The non-Equity scene, made up of theatres like Brave New Workshop, Theatre de la Jeune Lune, and Theatre in the Round, offer actors the opportunity to work in a range of theatrical styles.

Chanhassen and the touring company Troupe America are the most consistent producers of musicals; several other companies offer musicals on an irregular basis, among them Minnesota Opera and Hey City Stage (formerly Dudley Riggs' ETC Theatre). Some nonunion companies do musicals, and there's often a commercially-produced musical or two on the boards. National tours stop here, but they rarely do any casting. Theatres from other regions come to audition from time to time, and several summer companies come on a regular basis.

Most audition information comes from the Sunday newspaper and the Equity hotline. It's usually easy enough to get an appointment, although some auditions fill up early, so it's wise not to wait until the last minute to call. But since quite a few theatres only announce general (as opposed to per-play) auditions, *if any,* it's essential that actors stay on top of things. When you think you're right for something, call and ask to audition. Newcomers can call theatres to introduce themselves, and ask to do monologues or read for shows currently casting. The Guthrie is the only theatre that does a lot of casting out of town, though in recent years more locals have been brought into the company; still, it's the hardest Twin Cities nut to crack. It's also the best-paying, though a couple of other houses pay living wages.

Actors here are mutually supportive and share information with one another. Theatres, on the other hand, are rather territorial, the positive side of which is loyalty to actors. Many actors work again and again at a single theatre, getting the opportunity to stretch in roles they might not otherwise play. However, once an actor becomes associated with a particular theatre, she may have trouble getting cast elsewhere; even actors who've worked quite steadily can remain unknown to some directors. Making the transition to "actor-at-large" can be rough, though persistence and the passage of time usually help.

Equity actors who have credits in cities with good theatre reputations will be taken seriously here. Women, however, may have an especially tough time trying to get cast in the few roles that are available at theatres where the same people work again and again. What's more, women who work at both Equity and non-Equity theatres before they join the union sometimes find the work drops off once they cash in their EMC points and get a card. Non-Equity newcomers probably have an easier time finding work initially; in fact, this can be a great place for a young actor to cut her teeth playing a variety of roles. Several non-Equity companies do admirable work, though few pay much.

Union or not, most actors who find fairly steady and challenging work, whether at a single theatre or on a freelance basis, are quite satisfied with what they're able to do here. It's certainly not impossible for newcomers to break in, but it usually requires patience, persistence, and good networking skills. A great way to meet people and get exposure is to participate in the Playwrights' Center's Monday night readings and/or summer PlayLabs. Audition at their generals, and attend Monday night readings, where you can network with directors, playwrights, and other actors.

■■■■■FILM AND TELEVISION

The efforts of Minnesota's eager and aggressive Film Board have been instrumental in bringing increased production to the area. The upswing should continue, as more filmmakers discover the local talent pool and crew base, and if the shakily-funded Board can continue the courtship. Still, work is sporadic, and actors interested in doing film and TV work aren't going to find much here. Although some outside producers hire local casting directors, others send CDs from L.A., so it's helpful to be with an agent (or agents) for this kind of work.

When films come, extra and day player roles get cast; sometimes, actors in this smaller pool have the chance to audition for supporting roles they might not be seen for in L.A. or New York. Agents get the breakdowns from L.A. and, though they send pictures, and tapes are sometimes requested, not much comes of it. Kids are the exception: casting people turn to the Twin Cities when they're looking for children hoping, perhaps, to find kids they perceive as "realer" than the little pros on either coast. Extra calls are announced in the newspaper; you can also let casting directors know you're available. There's a small-but-active screenwriting community; some actors participate in screenplay readings and even productions (see *Additional Opportunities*, p. 102).

TV pilot work is rare and, despite some series location scouting, there's very little actual production. Exceptions are reality-based programming and the local public TV station, the latter of which has produced some dramatic programs for both local and national markets. Soap opera searches are unusual. In general, however, the Twin Cities have become a satellite search market for kids and hard-to-cast roles.

CORPORATE AND COMMERCIALS

Active corporate and commercial markets are what allow several Twin Cities actors to make those monthly house payments. The many corporations headquartered in the area help make this one of the largest corporate production markets in the country. In addition, the Armed Forces Radio and Television Services generates a lot of employment for young men who are willing to get military haircuts, although they won't hire an actor more than once every several years.

All union work is under AFTRA contract, and despite a general decline in production in recent years, actual (union) earnings have remained steady. (At the same time, a trend toward increased in-house production parallels dramatic growth in the nonunion market.) Still, the decrease in union production has been a rude awakening for many AFTRA members who, in the past, rarely had to do much hustling for work in this market. Now, as competition increases, the actor who's skilled at self-promotion might have an advantage. (A word of warning, however, to transplants from either coast: leave some of your intensity behind; your energy will serve you well, but coming on like gangbusters probably won't.) Though many corporations and production houses go directly to agents, the use of independent casting directors is growing.

The commercial market remains fairly active, despite a recent economic downturn. This is a popular region for food-related advertising, from packaged products to restaurants. The local and regional AFTRA markets are strongest, and the area gets a small share of SAG nationals. The nonunion commercial market, while growing, remains small.

The voice-over market remains healthy and strong, although some casting for local spots is done in Chicago and L.A. For many years, a handful or two of people had the local market all but sewn up; more recently, the door has opened enough to make room for several newcomers. Changes in style have meant increased opportunities for female and character voices, although the traditional velvet-tongued announcer is certainly still heard. A trend toward holding auditions (as opposed to hearing tapes) has made things easier for newcomers, although v/o is never easy to break into. For both on- and off-camera commercial work, it's important to have an agent and be known to the independent casting directors.

The words "wholesome," "generic," and "whitebread" are often used to describe the most popular look for the corporate and commercial markets. Those who work the most, according to one local director, look like people you'd see in shopping malls, people you wouldn't even notice. Non-Hispanic white, "middle-American"-looking, male baby boomers and grey-haired, over-forty corporate spokesmen do best in industrials; commercials utilize a wider range of ages and types. Whites with dark, non-Northern European features are sometimes considered too ethnic or exotic-looking for this market, although some actors who fall into this category, as well as some ethnic minority actors, do very nicely in the commercial and corporate markets.

CASTING DIVERSITY

The Twin Cities have a larger non-Hispanic white population than any other area in this book, although ethnic minority populations have grown dramatically since the 1980 census was taken. Relatively small ethnic minority populations mean smaller talent pools, and representation is a little slower in coming than in areas with more diverse populations. (Some producers and directors who come to the Twin Cities because a script calls for a "Midwestern" look, associate "Midwestern" with "white.") Most talent agents represent minority actors and make some attempts to integrate casting calls. Clearly, though, there's room for more assertiveness on the part of agents, casting directors, directors, and ethnic minority actors; some of the latter may fear making waves in a place in which their numbers are small and much of the racial tension either remains below the surface or is expressed in isolated incidents.

Women in the Twin Cities work much less frequently than men, and even those who work a lot discover employment takes a real dive once they stop looking like young mommies.

Still, some advertisers and major corporations here produce for markets outside the Twin Cities area, providing more opportunities for women and ethnic minority actors. At least one local industrial producer has made a real effort to increase minority hiring. There are, in fact, some black actors who do very well in these markets, and there's a small, growing Spanish voice-over market. At present, most of the roles that come along for ethnic minority actors are specifically written as such, although it's not unheard-of for such actors to be cast in roles in which race is neither germane nor specified. In order to have greater access to work in the film and broadcast markets, however, some ethnic minority actors have agents in Chicago as well as in the Twin Cities.

The situation in theatre, while far from ideal, is certainly better. There's been increased hiring of African American actors, who make up the largest minority group in the acting community. At some theatres, ethnic minority actors usually get cast in minor roles, although there are those who've had the opportunity to play leads. There are a few constituent-specific theatres like Penumbra Theatre Company and Northern Sign Theatre, as well as a few that do a decent job of diverse casting. A significant presence in the community is Mixed Blood Theatre, which mounts culturally-diverse productions using color-blind and color-inspired casting. The company also produces variety evenings which have included the presentation of, among other things, American Indian dance companies.

ADDITIONAL OPPORTUNITIES

Gustino's, The Marriott Hotel, 30 S. 7th Street, Minneapolis, MN 55407, 349-4075. Though the turnover among singing waiters here is low, auditions are held every once in a while; P&Rs are accepted.

Minnesota Renaissance Festival, 3525 W. 145th Street, Shakopee, MN 55379, 445-7361. Auditions, held in early summer, are announced in newspapers and posted at colleges; non-Equity only.

The Playwrights' Center, 2301 Franklin Avenue E., Minneapolis, MN 55406, 332-7481. An important institution in the Twin Cities, the Center holds readings every Monday night, except during production of the summer Midwest PlayLabs. Appearing in readings, and especially in the PlayLabs, is a great way to meet people in the biz here. Go to readings, talk to people, leave a P&R. Check newspaper listings or call the Center for schedules and locations.

Science Museum of Minnesota, 30 E. 10th Street, St. Paul, MN 55101, 221-9488. A small resident company performs one-act plays on science-related themes. Most acting positions are full-time, non-Equity only. The company accepts P&Rs, but auditions, when necessary, are announced in the *Star Tribune* and the *Pioneer Press Dispatch,* and notices are sent to area theatres.

Screenwriters' Workshop, 1624 Harmon Place, Suite 210, Minneapolis, MN 55403. Public screenplay readings are held four times a year; only highly-skilled and experienced voice actors should send résumés to Larry Russo at the above address. SW also produces tapings of screenplays-in-progress. A waiver agreement with AFTRA means union as well as nonunion actors may participate. Auditions are held as needed; you may also send a P&R to "Screenlabs" at the above address.

TRAINING

Actors who've come here from places like New York and Chicago may be disappointed in the lack of diverse training opportunities. Some theatres, like the Guthrie, offer courses; the Guthrie also is affiliated with the training program at the University of Minnesota. Though there isn't a lot in the way of acting classes for the working professional, there are on-camera classes, dance studios, and singing teachers, and AFTRA is planning an ongoing series of workshops. Some courses are advertised in the *Star Tribune;* asking other actors is another good way to find teachers.

CERTIFICATE/DEGREE PROGRAMS

Hamline University, Theatre Department, 1536 Hewitt Avenue, St. Paul, MN 55104, 641-2296.

Macalester College, Dramatic Arts, 1600 Grand Avenue, St. Paul, MN 55105, 696-6340.

University of Minnesota, Department of Theatre Arts, Meadowbrook Hall, Room 208, 412 22nd Avenue S., Minneapolis, MN 55455-0424, 625-0770.

AFFORDABLE ARTS

Discount Tickets. Prices at many theatres are low to begin with, and some offer discounted day-of-performance tickets. Company members don't always have comps to give out, but they often extend company discounts to friends and colleagues.

Guthrie Rush, 725 Vineland Place, Minneapolis, MN 55403, 347-1127. Low-price tickets are sold fifteen minutes before curtain; a full-season coupon book can be purchased, allowing rush tickets to be reserved two days in advance.

Minneapolis Park and Recreation Board, 310 4th Avenue S., Minneapolis, MN 55415, 348-2226. Each summer several companies, including the Minnesota Shakespeare Company, present plays in Twin Cities parks. Admission is free; bring a blanket for lawn seating. Schedules are available from the Board, or check newspaper entertainment listings.

RESOURCES

BOOKSTORES

Border's Book Shop, 3001 Hennepin Avenue, Minneapolis, MN 55408, 825-0336. This store has a good selection of plays.

The Hungry Mind Bookstore, 1648 Grand Avenue, St. Paul, MN 55105,
699-0587. The Hungry Mind is said to have the best selection of plays
and related books in the area.
Odegard's stores in St. Paul and Edina have good selections of scripts
and carry *Twin Cities Reports.*

■■■■■■NETWORKING AND SOCIALIZING

When the weather allows, actors from several theatres gather for softball
games in Minneapolis' Kenwood Park. If you're not on a team and not
too shy, go and introduce yourself—the natives are friendly. For food and
drink, the once-legendary Jimmy Hegg's is only a memory, but theatre
folk find solace at:

Loring Café/Loring Bohemian Bar, 1624 Harmon Place, Minneapolis, MN
55403, 332-1617.
Lyle's Bar and Restaurant, 2021 Hennepin Avenue, Minneapolis, MN
55405, 870-8183.
Oliver's, 2007 Lyndale Avenue S., Minneapolis, MN 55405, 871-5591.

---

[1]   1990 crime statistics for Minneapolis were unavailable; shown are 1989 figures, with
analyses based on 1989 population.
[2]   *The Metropolitan Council of Chambers of Commerce Official New Residents Guide*
(Minneapolis: Toma Publishing, 1989-90).

NEW YORK

THE CITY

Even people who've never been to New York City feel they know it. Books and movies—indeed, our national mythology—have made familiar Times Square's neon madness, commuters sardined into subway cars, the bright lights and broken hearts of Broadway; cabbies, cops, muggers, maniacs; the fabulous excesses of the wealthy; urban decay, degradation, despair; Columbus Circle, Coney Island, Spanish Harlem, Soho, Greenwich Village.

While to many outsiders "New York City" means no more and no less than Manhattan, in fact the city is comprised of five boroughs: The Bronx, Brooklyn, Manhattan, Queens, and Staten Island. Manhattan is, if you will, the control center; jam-packed onto this thirty-four square miles of island are City Hall, Wall Street, and Central Park; the theatre, diamond, and garment districts; the publishing, advertising, and art industries; and so on and on and on. Where else but in New York can you get the best, the most current, the most obscure whatever-it-is you're looking for? Having so much so close at hand renders the New Yorker's life rather easy—up to a point. There's hardly a Manhattanite who doesn't have a twenty-four-hour grocery, a Chinese restaurant, a video store, pharmacy, pizza parlor, movie theatre, and several dry-cleaners within walking distance of his apartment.

The irony is that in this city that has it all, anything and everything can seem so frustratingly out of reach. So what if you've got three dry-cleaners on the block if none of them can do pleats properly? Who cares if you have some of the most fabulous

FAST FACTS
1990 CENSUS
7,322,564 (+3.5%)
COUNTIES
Bronx (Bronx)
Kings (Brooklyn)
New York (Manhattan)
Queens (Queens)
Richmond (Staten Island)
TIME
Zone: Eastern
Telephone: 976-1616
AREA CODES
212, 917¹ (Manhattan)
718 (Bronx, Brooklyn, Queens, Staten Island)
ALL PHONE NUMBERS IN THIS CHAPTER USE THE 212 AREA CODE UNLESS OTHERWISE NOTED.
VISITOR INFORMATION
New York Convention and Visitors Bureau
2 Columbus Circle
(59th Street and Broadway)
New York, NY 10019
397-8222

resources in the world right at your fingertips if getting at them requires
wading through miles of red tape? What good is it being surrounded
by movies and nightclubs and restaurants galore if you feel lonely and
isolated? Oh, New York is a thrilling place alright; it's stimulating
and enriching. It's also intense, overwhelming, and not always a hell of
a lot of fun.

New York isn't the only place to be a performer, but for many, it's
the place. The city is jammed with would-be, has-been, up-and-coming,
might-be, part-time, top-of-the-heap, lost-in-the-crowd actors, with actors
on stage, back stage, at auditions, in rehearsal, taking classes, waiting
tables. A lot of people here love the arts—after all, so many are directly
involved—but the city has been in dire financial straits for some time,
and arts organizations struggle to stay alive in what is supposed to be the
culture capital of the nation. Between decreasing opportunities (even
in the best of times there aren't enough jobs to go around), intense
competition (in both quantity and quality), and simple day-to-day living,
the unknown actor has many hills to climb. In this city, thick skin,
patience, and high self-esteem (not to mention a rich uncle) can be more
valuable than an impressive résumé and a great headshot. Pursuing the
toughest of professions in the toughest of towns may be a little crazy,
but after all, this is *New York*.

RECOMMENDED READING

Jennifer Cecil, *The Newcomer's Handbook for New York City* (New York:
    Jennifer Cecil, T.L.C. and Co., 1990).
Michael Cunningham, *A Home at the End of the World* (New York: Farrar,
    Straus & Giroux, 1990). This beautifully written novel captures aspects
    of life in contemporary New York.
Allan Ishac, *50 Places to Find Peace and Quiet in New York: A Guide to
    Urban Sanctuaries* (New York: Avon Books, 1990

MOVIES

After Hours (1985), *The Brother from Another Planet* (1984), *Crossing
Delancey* (1988), *Do the Right Thing* (1989)

■■■■■POPULATION

The most populated city in the nation may well have the most diverse
collection of people of any city on the planet. From Chinatown to Little
Italy, Little Athens to Little India; from Chasidic to Haitian, Korean to
Cuban enclaves, if you wanted to locate a representative of any religion,
race, nation, language, lifestyle, philosophy, or profession, no doubt
you could do it in New York.

CLIMATE

Though New York has one of the most temperate climates on the Eastern Seaboard, the weather is almost always an issue, exacerbated by an overabundance of cars and people, noise and air pollution. Still, nothing stops New Yorkers from carrying on with their daily activities, so snow, strong winds, and stultifying humidity are obstacles met head on. Winters are cold, but the severest spells and snowfalls don't usually last too long. In well-traversed parts of the city, including most of Manhattan, a gorgeous white snowfall quickly turns to gray slush. Fall and spring can be lovely, though the latter never seems to last long enough. For many, summer is the killer: one learns to live with a permanent layer of sweat. Even New Yorkers who never take take it easy wind down just a notch on ozone-alert days. To escape the stifling heat and humidity, people flock to area parks and beaches; those who can, clear out every weekend, if not for the entire season. *For weather information call:* 976-1212.

NORMAL TEMPERATURES	Average Daily High	Average Daily Low
January	38°	26°
July	85°	68°

TEMPERATURE EXTREMES			
Maximum Temp.	Annual No. of Days	Minimum Temp.	Annual No. of Days
90° and above	17	32° and below	80
32° and below	21	0° and below	—

NORMAL WEATHER CONDITIONS		
Clear	Partly Cloudy	Cloudy
107	127	132

ANNUAL PRECIPITATION	Days	Inches
All Precipitation	121	44
Snowfall	NA	28

TRANSPORTATION

Despite delays and myriad other frustrations, New York is really quite accessible. It's the only U.S. city in which over half of commuters use public transportation. As a matter of fact, "one of every three people who take mass transit in the U.S. does so in New York City."[2] Between subways (which carry more than 3.5 million riders a day), buses, and ferries, the system runs some 4.8 million trips per day and covers all but the farther reaches of each of the five boroughs. Traffic is horrendous, but somehow keeps moving—well, most of the time. And while New Yorkers rely on their subways, buses, taxis, commuter trains, limos and private cars, Manhattan, compact and with few hills, is extremely walkable, not to mention (for the helmeted and stout-hearted), skate- and bike-able.

PUBLIC TRANSPORTATION

Metropolitan Transit Authority (MTA); *New York City Transit Authority* (NYCTA). Although New Yorkers love to complain about their subways and buses—undercooled in the summer, overheated in the winter, too slow (but they provide a ready excuse for tardiness!), dirty, unreliable, dangerous—the system actually is rather miraculous. In recent years, the MTA has spent millions on a subway improvement (and accompanying public relations) campaign, with some results: cars are free of graffiti, air-conditioning is more reliable, and (keep your fingers crossed) there are fewer delays and breakdowns. System (and sometimes neighborhood) maps are posted on station walls, and there's usually at least one subway map posted in each car. Crime is not nearly as rampant on the subways as popular legend would have one believe, but some people prefer buses, finding them cleaner and safer. Contending with traffic, however, makes buses much slower.

The fleet includes buses and rapid rail (subway and elevated). *For information call:* 718-330-1234.

Maps and schedules are available on some buses and at subway token booths and the Columbus Circle Visitors Center, 2 Columbus Circle.

Entry to the subway is via token; for buses a token or exact change is needed. Farecards will be introduced in late 1993, at which time the Transit Authority will begin phasing out tokens; the conversion won't be complete until later in the decade. Tokens, sold in most subway stations, are also available at some banks, museums, MacDonald's restaurants, and check-cashing stores. Bus fare includes one free transfer (ask for a transfer or "Add-a-ride" when you board) between uptown-downtown and crosstown lines. Seniors and people with disabilities ride for half fare; students ride free during school hours, and children forty-four inches or shorter ride free. Subway station entrances are marked with red and green bulbs. When the green bulb is lit, there's a token clerk on duty; a red bulb means you should read the instructions printed just above the entrance stairway.

The following is a list of terminals and additional transportation systems:

Grand Central Station, 42nd Street at Park Avenue, New York, NY.
Metro North: 532-4900.

Pennsylvania Station, 34th Street between 7th and 8th Avenues, New
York, NY. Long Island Railroad: 718-454-5477. Amtrak: 800-523-8720.

Port Authority Trans-Hudson (PATH train), 800-234-PATH (7284).
Connects points in New Jersey and Manhattan.

Port Authority Bus Terminal, 8th Avenue at 41st Street, New York, NY
10036, 564-8484. Greyhound: 971-6363. New Jersey Transit:
800-626-7433.

TAXIS

This is a taxi town. Street hailing is easy— except, of course, on Saturday
nights, rainy days, and whenever you really, really need one. Avoid
taking cabs through midtown during the day if you're in a hurry; you'll
make better time underground or on foot. Taxis are metered, with a
surcharge between 8 p.m. and 6 a.m. There aren't any more of those big
old wonderful Checker cabs, and you can't call for a yellow cab by phone
anymore, though unmetered car services are available; be sure to confirm
the price of the trip when you call. Unlicensed cabs, while not permitted
to make pickups in the city, sometimes do. They're unmetered and
unregulated, so you're probably safest sticking with the yellows.

DRIVING

Most people who live and work in Manhattan can get along without
cars; many prefer it that way. In fact, a lot of car owners in nearby areas
use public transportation when they come to Manhattan. Street parking
is always unpredictable, and garages and lots, though plentiful, are
expensive—some unbelievably so. If you park on the street, be sure to
read the street signs: you may have to move your car by 8 a.m. to avoid
being ticketed and even towed. This "Alternate-Side Parking" system
allows the Sanitation Department to clean the streets. When parking, many
people pull out their radios/tape players and either lock them in the trunk
or carry them along; some car owners suggest leaving absolutely nothing
in the car, and many post "no radio, no nothing" signs in the windows.

▮▮▮▮HOUSING AND COSTS OF LIVING

For pure convenience, Manhattan is the place for actors; those in the
other boroughs and in nearby counties and states must commute in for
most auditions, performances, and classes. But Manhattan can be intense,
and housing generally is more costly. Many people, particularly those

with families, prefer parts of the Bronx, Brooklyn, Queens, Staten Island, Long Island, Westchester County, and New Jersey, where the atmosphere is more suburban and housing costs are often lower. Recommended areas include Prospect Park, Brooklyn Heights, and Park Slope in Brooklyn; Long Island City and Sunnyside in Queens; Washington Heights, Greenwich Village, Chelsea, Soho, Tribeca, and the Upper West Side in Manhattan; Hoboken in New Jersey. Keep in mind that within any of New York's neighborhoods, conditions and prices can vary dramatically, sometimes from one block to the next.

The time to think about housing is before you arrive; put the word out to any New Yorkers you know that you're looking for a place to live. Complaints about the difficulty of finding a decent, affordable home are justified, although people find ways to make it work. Many live with roommates; younger students and new arrivals sometimes live three or four to a one- or two-bedroom apartment. Rental agencies charge commission, but may save you money in the long run. Serious hunters post "apartment wanted" fliers on telephone poles, pester building superintendents, and generally let it be known they're looking. For newspaper listings, the Sunday *New York Times* (buy it Saturday night) and the *Village Voice* (buy it at the crack of dawn Wednesday) are musts; competition is heavy, so start phoning right away. When signing a lease, don't be surprised if, in addition to the usual deposits, you have to pay "key" money to the super or previous tenant. Performers who do a lot of travelling often do a lot of subletting; there are legal and illegal sublets, and people live in both. Check bulletin boards at acting and dance schools, SAG, AFTRA, and Equity, and if you know any area university students or alumni, ask them to take you to student housing offices.

INTERAREA SHELTER INDEXES	Renters	Owners
New York City[3]	122	182
NY-Connecticut suburbs	137	168
New Jersey suburbs	132	152
(Philadelphia)	(100)	(100)

COSTS OF LIVING

Total average annual expenditures	$31,412
Food at home	2,477
Telephone	718
Gas and motor oil	755
Public transportation	673
Personal care products and services	387

▌▌EMPLOYMENT

Contrary to popular myth, not every New York waiter is an actor. Many of those who are, however, work at restaurants in the theatre district, where some of the customers they meet are in the business. But actors find a variety of ways to support themselves: they teach, run small businesses, work in childcare, in offices (especially through temp services), as tele-marketers, shoe models, department store demonstrators, bouncers, party-line operators, and so on. Some survival job notices are posted on the SAG bulletin board.

1989 Average Annual Pay
New York-Northern New Jersey-Long Island: $29,208

1990 Average Unemployment Rates
New York State: 5.2%
New York metropolitan statistical area: 6.2%

1990 Average Weekly Unemployment Benefits
New York State: $180.85

▌▌CRIME

New York crime tends to frighten outsiders more than it does most New Yorkers. More crimes are committed here, but with a population of over seven million, the city has neither the best nor the worst statistics in the country. In fact, of the cities in this book for which statistics are available, New York has the lowest incidence of reported rape, the fourth lowest of burglary, and is smack in the middle when it comes to murder. There are some especially unsafe areas, and it's important to be aware and use good judgment, but in many areas, the day-to-day reality isn't quite what legend would have it be. Certainly, crime and violence are not to be ignored, and newcomers need to learn the lay of the land until the automatic antennae kick in. Living in a building with twenty-four-hour security, though expensive, helps many people feel safer. Stay away from street con games, like three-card monte and the shell game; their only purpose is to part you from your money. Just say no to people who offer to get you a cab when you emerge, luggage in hand, from a train station or bus; some will graciously accept a tip, while others will grab the money from your wallet. Many people who ride the subway during the day, especially women and the elderly, switch to buses and taxis at night. Stay out of empty subway cars and the closed end of a deserted platform; at night, wait for your train in the designated lit area near the token booth, and try to ride in the car where the conductor is.

1990 CRIME RATES	Violent	Property⁴
Total Crimes	174,541	535,680
Crimes per 100,000 People	2,384	7,316
Average 1 Crime per Every	42 people	14 people

■■■■■■■MISCELLANEA

NEWSPAPERS
The New York Times (morning)
El Diario/La Prensa (morning)
Amsterdam News (weekly)
The Village Voice (weekly)

LIBRARIES
Central Research Library, 5th Avenue and 42nd Street, New York, NY
10017, 661-7220.
Library and Museum of the Performing Arts at Lincoln Center,
111 Amsterdam Avenue, New York, NY 10023, 799-2200 Ext. 241.

POST OFFICE
Main Branch, James A. Farley Building, 8th Avenue at 33rd Street,
New York, NY, 967-8585.

MUSEUMS
American Museum of the Moving Image, 35th Avenue at 36th Street,
Astoria, NY 11106, 718-784-4520.
The Museum of Television and Radio, 25 W. 52nd Street, New York, NY
10022, 752-7684 (information); 752-4690 (offices).
Songwriters Hall of Fame Museum, 950 8th Avenue, New York, NY 10019,
319-1444.

RELIGIOUS ORGANIZATIONS
St. Malachy's Church, The Actor's Chapel, 239 W. 49th Street, New York,
NY 10036, 489-1340. Roman Catholic.
Congregation Ezrath Israel, The Actors' Temple, 339 W. 47th Street,
New York, NY 10036, 245-6975. Jewish, Conservative.

THE BUSINESS

New York: two little words so full of meaning. To many performing
artists, the name suggests the realest stage there is, the pinnacle, the place

where dreams are realized or dashed to the ground. For most, reality lies somewhere in between. The majority of New York actors work now and then, some quite often, others only rarely. Some earn enough money that they can survive between acting jobs; more depend on survival jobs, many developing skills and interests that will keep them going emotionally and creatively, as well as financially.

Let's get one thing straight at the outset: most New York actors don't work steadily and don't make anything approaching a decent living from acting work. There's a lot of competition (it's not at all unusual for hundreds of actors to audition for a single role) and actors spend a lot of time doing readings and workshops, taking classes, and creating their own opportunities. Even those who work fairly steadily have a lot of time to fill between jobs.

Part of the New York actor's job is meeting people and making connections that might lead to getting agents, auditions, and job offers. Connections are very important, so call on old college friends, relatives, and friends of friends who may know somebody who knows somebody whose daughter is a casting director. The newcomer without connections can throw his hat in the ring by talking to actors at auditions (which often involve hours of waiting, allowing plenty of time to chat) and in classes.

What's great about being an actor in New York is that there's always something to get involved in. But making the leap to actor-as-income-earner can be tough, and in an expensive, intense city like New York, there's the danger of burnout and desperation. The effects of recession certainly haven't helped matters. As theatres downscale production (presenting small-cast plays), rely on star power (to draw audiences), and close down altogether, acting opportunities decrease. Since being seen on stage can have everything to do with getting agents and being considered for screen roles, the situation can also affect the actor's chances of working in film and television. Of course, there are people who practically walk off the bus and right into a career; the hope of that happening is what keeps the newcomers coming. Then there are those whose patience and persistence through the lean years eventually pay off; the hope of *that* happening is what keeps them going.

RECOMMENDED READING

K. Callan, *The New York Agent Book* (Studio City, Calif.: Sweden Press, 1988). New York Agents give advice on getting started, changing agents, and other aspects of the business.

Peter Glenn, *New York Casting and Survival Guide . . . and Datebook* (New York: Peter Glenn Publications). Updated annually, this popular guide lists everything from accompanists, bookstores, and chiropractors to talent agencies, vocal coaches, and wardrobe outlets. It includes a daily planner, and more.

Chuck Lawliss, *The New York Theatre Sourcebook* (New York: Simon and Schuster, 1990). This contains histories and descriptions of area theatres and theatre companies, plus seating plans, theatre terminology, and trivia.

Jim Monos, *Professional Actor Training in New York City* (Shelter Island, NY: Broadway Press, 1990).

NYC Geographical Casting and Agency Guide (New York: Pro-Labels). Updated quarterly, this guide lists casting directors and talent and advertising agencies by location; it also includes maps.

■■■■PROFESSIONAL ASSOCIATIONS

TALENT UNIONS

Associated Actors and Artistes of America, 165 West 46th Street, New York, NY 10036, 869-0358. The "Four As" is the national regulatory association for the talent unions listed below:

Actors' Equity Association (AEA), 1650 Broadway, New York, NY 10036, 869-8530.
   Members: 15,010

American Federation of Television and Radio Artists (AFTRA), 260 Madison Avenue, 7th Floor, New York, NY 10016, 532-0800.
   Members: 21,558

Screen Actors Guild (SAG), 1515 Broadway, 44th Floor, New York, NY 10036, 944-1030.
   Members: 22,943

American Guild of Musical Artists (AGMA), 1727 Broadway, New York, NY 10019, 265-3687.

American Guild of Variety Artists (AGVA), 184 Fifth Avenue, 6th Floor, New York, NY 10010, 675-1003.

Hebrew Actors Union, 31 E. 7th Street, New York, NY 10003, 674-1923.

Italian Actors Union, 184 Fifth Avenue, 6th Floor, New York, NY 10010, 675-1003.

OTHER ASSOCIATIONS

Hispanic Organization of Latin Actors (HOLA), 250 West 65th Street, New York, NY 10023 595-8286. HOLA is an "arts service organization committed to exploring . . . avenues for projecting Hispanic artists and their culture into the mainstream . . . ." Services include a newsletter, talent directory, workshops, and a theatre festival.

Manhattan Association of Cabarets and Clubs (MAC), 465-2662. MAC is a professional association of cabaret, jazz, and comedy club owners, performers, booking agents, and critics whose purpose is to promote and publicize cabaret, comedy, and jazz. Annual awards presentation honors outstanding cabaret and comedy artists.

Pentacle, 104 Franklin Street, New York, NY 10013, 226-2000. This organization provides support services (i.e., publicity, accounting, booking) for dance and performance artists.

Performers Against Racism on the Theatrical Stage (PARTS), 132 W. 43rd Street, 2nd Floor, New York, NY 10036. This organization's purpose is to end discriminatory hiring practices on the stage, help ethnic minority actors gain access to work opportunities, and lend support to minority actors.

SERVICE ORGANIZATIONS

Career Transition for Dancers, 1727 Broadway, 2nd Floor, New York, NY 10019, 581-7043. CTD provides vocational counseling to help dancers identify and put to use skills and interests other than dancing.

For Performers, 484 W. 43 Street, #42A, New York, NY 10036, 564-2485. Support groups are offered at no charge "for performers in vocational crisis." For Performers also offers an "ongoing hospitality program" for former group members.

Performers with Disabilities. The purpose of this tri-union committee is the increased employment of performers with disabilities and the promotion of nonstereotyped imagery. Contact the Equal Employment Opportunity offices at Equity or AFTRA or the Affirmative Action administrator at SAG.

■■■■■LOOKING FOR WORK

PUBLICATIONS

In addition to running casting notices and articles of interest to performing artists, New York trade papers run ads for survival jobs, actor-related services (such as photographers and teachers), and more.

Back Stage, 330 West 42nd Street, 16th Floor, New York, NY 10036, 947-0020. *Back Stage* is the oldest and best-established of the trades and is probably the primary source of audition information for a lot of actors. Published each Thursday, the paper is available at newsstands or by mail subscription; better to buy it on Thursday if you can, or you'll miss out on Friday's auditions.

New York Casting, 135 E. 65th Street, 4th Floor, New York, NY 10021, 472-6585. *NYC* is the newest kid on the block, geared primarily toward people in transition into the professional performing arts world. Published biweekly, it includes—in addition to casting notices—lists of agents, casting directors, production houses, and theatre companies. It is available at newsstands or by mail subscription, and is also distributed free to dance schools, unions, and other performers' organizations.

NYC Geographical Casting and Agency Guide (see *Recommended Reading,* p. 106).

Performer Cues, 1501 Broadway, New York, NY 10036, 997-1701. Established in 1990, *Performer Cues* comes out on Tuesdays and is available at newsstands or by mail subscription. In addition to casting notices, it includes weekly lists of agents, casting directors, and more.

Ross Reports Television, Television Index, Inc., 40-29 27th Street, Long Island City, NY 11101, 718-937-3990. This booklet, updated monthly, provides contact and/or casting information for New York and Los Angeles television shows, New York commercial producers, West Coast production studios, and New York talent agents and casting directors. It is a real help to agent-seekers.

The Theatrical Calendar, Celebrity Service International, Inc., 1780 Broadway, Suite 300, New York, NY 10019, 245-1460. This biweekly publication lists current and future Broadway and Off-Broadway activities; it includes some theatres outside New York.

HOTLINES

Equity Chorus (see *Talent Unions,* p. 114). This line has information on Equity chorus calls only.

BULLETIN BOARDS AND BINDERS

Equity Lounge; SAG

TALENT BOOKS AND TALENT BANKS

All sorts of directories and talent banks are advertised in New York. Before paying to be included in one, *make sure* it's a reputable enterprise that's actually utilized by casting personnel. Call some casting directors and ask if they know of and use the service you're considering.

Directory of Hispanic Talent (see HOLA under *Other Associations,* p. 114), 595-8286. This talent directory lists HOLA actor members.

Players' Guide, 165 W. 46th Street, New York, NY 10036, 869-3570. The *Players' Guide* has been around for years; it is for SAG, AEA, and/or AFTRA members only.

Non-Traditional Casting Project, Box 6443, Grand Central Station, New York, NY 10163-6021, 682-5790. NTCP, which "works to increase the participation of ethnic, female and special constituency artists . . . (and) champions the artistic benefits of multiracial participation in the theatre," maintains a national talent file of ethnic minority and disabled actors, directors, and choreographers. Send a P&R.

TALENT SHOWCASES AND COMBINED AUDITIONS

National Dinner Theatre Association; StrawHat Auditions. (For addresses, see Appendix B.)

Summer Theatre Group. Still in the planning stages at the time of this writing, Summer Theatre Group is intended as an Equity summer stock audition, brought to you by the folks who produce the StrawHat Auditions. Watch the trades for announcements.

■■■■TALENT AGENTS AND CASTING DIRECTORS

With well over a hundred talent agencies (and more than half as many casting companies) in the New York area, it might be surprising that many actors have a hard time getting even one to represent them, which should tell you how much competition there is. Still, there are as many stories in the naked city as there are actors, and some are about people who get agents with little or no effort. Finding representation often requires staying in touch with every agent who's ever expressed interest, in the hope that over time, working relationships will develop.

Agents and casting directors get hundreds of P&Rs, postcards, and announcements from actors each week, delivered by mail or dropped off in person. It's not surprising, then, that many agents post signs (which some people choose to ignore) saying "Do not knock or come in" on their doors. People do get called in on the basis of self-submission—eventually, all those envelopes get opened—but the odds are slim. Being seen in a good role in a good production is a better way to get an interview; a recommendation is even better, so ask friends, relatives, and colleagues if they can help. If you have no connections, go ahead and deliver those P&Rs, choosing the method that most suits your personality: shy people may be more comfortable submitting by mail, while good talkers might go in person. If you choose the latter, be sure to avoid busy times like Monday mornings, Fridays, and pilot season (see the "Los Angeles" chapter). Some actors do research (such as reading the *Ross Reports* and talking to working actors) to find out which agents are most right for them and vice versa, making the search for representation more manageable and realistic. Vigilant telephone receptionists can make follow-up calls rather daunting; if you feel intimidated, practice before dialing. And don't let New York agents' reputation for inaccessibility stop you from getting out there. Just try to remember that these agents are overworked, underpaid, and inundated with actor submissions.

Agents work on both exclusive and freelance bases; the latter often means you've been acknowledged, your picture has been filed, and you may or may not be submitted for auditions. You might be represented by one agency for all markets (the larger agencies usually have at least one subagent handling each market, i.e., theatre, film and television, industrials, commercials, and voice-overs), freelance with several agencies, or be represented by one for legit and another for commercial work.

Once you're working with agents, see if they can set up meetings with casting directors. Again, there are plenty of stories of rapid success and even overnight sensations, but most people have to work at building a career. This means being seen again and again by casting directors until you're a familiar face and a somewhat known quantity. By all means, send or drop off P&Rs, staying in touch via postcards, announcements, and invitations to see you on stage. Let casting directors know if you change agents. Independent casting directors, ad agency, soap opera, prime-time, and network casting directors are listed in the *Ross Reports*. The trade papers also run periodic lists of agents, CDs, and personal managers.

Many casting directors teach audition, on-camera, and general acting technique, and there are schools that offer classes in which a different casting director teaches each week. These practices are somewhat controversial, because actors tend to enroll only in order to meet the teachers. Another option is to participate in showcases in which several pairs of actors pitch in money to produce an evening of scenes, allowing agents and casting directors to see several actors in a single presentation. While some of these showcases are valuable, others are rip-offs, so try to get recommendations before putting up any money (and stay away from anything whose cost seems unreasonable), or organize a presentation yourself. SAG and AFTRA members can participate in those union's programs that enable actors to meet agents and casting directors; watch for announcements in newsletters.

THEATRE

New York's theatre scene has a definite structure, with all sorts of wild cards and exceptions thrown in to keep things interesting. In general, then: Broadway refers to the commercial theatres located in the Times Square (or Broadway) area, and to productions presented in those theatres under an Equity contract. Off-Broadway refers to 100- to 499-seat not-for-profit theatres that are outside the Broadway area, and to productions presented in those theatres under an Equity contract or agreement. Off-Off-Broadway describes limited-run, not-for-profit theatrical presentations in houses with no more than 99 seats. Some are in theatres that produce on an ongoing or seasonal basis, either

nonunion or under Equity's Funded Non-Profit Theatre Code. Others
are showcases, often artist-initiated, in which actors work for little or no
pay, sometimes sharing production costs and working under a range of
conditions. Showcases allow actors to work and, hopefully, be seen by
directors, agents, and casting personnel; Equity members may appear only
in those productions that utilize the union's New York Showcase Code.
To all the above add commercial nonunion theatre, comedy, performance
art, movement theatre, cabaret, and dance, and you've got a sense of the
many disciplines that coexist and sometimes merge in this big pot that
is the New York stage.

Many actors are shocked the first time they attend an open audition
or interview and find that hundreds of actors have already arrived. The
turnout for many open calls is so great that people arrive hours ahead of
time to sign up. When a casting notice asks you to call for an appointment,
start calling as soon as the designated time arrives. When an audition
spans two or three days, try to attend the first.

An audition required by Equity is facilitated by a monitor who
maintains a sign-up sheet. Actors sign up for the time slot of their choice,
then either wait or return at the appropriate time. Though the monitor
arrives to begin sign-ups an hour in advance of the audition, actors
frequently get in line an hour or two earlier. Detailed information on
eligibility and procedures is available at the Audition Center at Actors'
Equity. For Equity-required chorus calls, a sign-up list is posted one week
in advance of the audition. (For complete information, see *Chorus Call
Procedures,* available at Actors' Equity.) At nonunion and non-required
calls, there may or may not be a monitor; very often, the first person
to arrive starts a sign-up sheet that the auditors, arriving later, may or may
not honor. Actors returning after their names have been called should
ask to be worked in.

Though open calls are monologue assembly lines, actors do get
cast in summer stock, nonunion regional theatre, touring companies,
live industrials, and at dinner theatres, theme parks, and on cruise ships,
as well as in New York showcases and Broadway choruses. Chorus
work aside, only rarely does an actor get cast in Equity legit theatre via
open calls. Nevertheless, open calls provide unagented, unconnected
actors with their only opportunities to audition for some shows
and theatres. For Equity theatre, agents and casting directors are very
much part of the casting process, and people submitted by agents or
requested by production personnel have an advantage; these auditions
are by appointment, and actors almost always read from the script.
But no matter how one gets to an audition, there's a lot of competition,
and it includes plenty of people who already have impressive New
York credits.

FILM AND TELEVISION

Most feature films and television shows are cast on both coasts, so New York actors are seen for L.A.-based projects as well as for those that originate and/or shoot here. Almost without exception, auditioning for feature film and television roles requires agent submissions and/or being known by casting directors; only when a role is very difficult to cast will a notice appear in the trades. (Non-SAG independent projects do appear in the trades. Though many are legitimate low-budget projects, some are not, and you should begin work only if a satisfactory contract has been signed and everything appears to be aboveboard.) Each week, *Performer Cues* lists film and TV shows in production and preproduction, including the names and addresses of casting personnel; actors can try dropping off their P&Rs at casting offices. SAG members also can obtain the production schedule at the New York office.

Most prime-time television shows are produced in Los Angeles, but New York agents submit actors (by tape and in person) for principal TV roles throughout the year, especially during pilot season. Of course, extra work and the kind of small roles that sustain many L.A. actors are available only on the few prime-time series and episodes that shoot here at any given time. Daytime dramas are also sources of employment; at the time of this writing, six soaps are produced locally. Each has a casting director for principal and recurring roles, and one or more who handle extras and under-fives. Actors can submit P&Rs and stay in touch via postcards; though principal roles are almost always cast through agent submission, many actors make money by doing extra work and under-fives.

SAG members can do extra work in signatory films and television shows (and in commercials); some actors earn a nice living doing extra work. There's often work for nonunion extras, though the pay, if any, is usually quite low. Casting companies that specialize in providing extras place notices for both specific projects and general registrations in the trades; of course, you can send P&Rs any time (check the *Ross Reports* for contact information), and stay in touch via headshot postcards.

CORPORATE AND COMMERCIALS

New York may have the country's busiest corporate market, encompassing live, film, and video industrials. There's plenty of union activity (which, in the film/video area, is probably pretty evenly split between AFTRA and SAG), as well as a lively nonunion market.

Industrials are often cast through agents, although casting notices for live industrials also appear in the trades, seeking everything from spokespeople to celebrity look-alikes to tap dancers to dramatic actors.

On-camera work, however, is rarely advertised. Instead, producers hire independent casting directors or else go directly to agents. It's essential, then, to work with agents who specialize in this market, although it may not be easy for inexperienced actors to find representation. (Actors short on experience might try to get work—and sample tapes—in nearby markets like New Jersey and Connecticut.) Actors can also market themselves directly, finding lists of industrial production houses and corporations with in-house facilities in the *Ross Reports* and in the trades; the unions maintain lists of signatory producers. Be warned, however, that producers and directors are busy, busy people who may not be interested in receiving unsolicited submissions—and they really don't have time to take your phone calls. Once an actor has completed a job, though, it's certainly wise to keep politely in touch by mail, since it's not at all uncommon for producers and directors to make direct calls to actors whose work they know. Actors interested in industrials need to market themselves appropriately. Though there are jobs for character and blue-collar types, the bulk of on-camera work is for corporate/white-collar characters and narrators. The same is generally true for live industrials, although these sometimes utilize musical comedy performers, dancers, and specialty artists.

The *Standard Directory of Advertising Agencies* lists more than 900 agencies in New York City. Though only a small percentage of those agencies produce television and radio commercials, there's no doubt that this is the hub of the nation's advertising industry. Commercials are cast almost entirely through agent submissions; the good news is that commercial representation is a little easier to come by than legit. Most commercials are SAG, but you don't have to be a member in order to audition. Just be cautious about working on nonunion commercials and with nonfranchised commercial agents, some of whom pay very slowly— if at all. Actors interested in doing extra work can mail P&Rs directly to production houses and ad agency in-house casting personnel (as well as to independent casting directors who specialize in providing extras); contact information for those that accept submissions are listed in the *Ross Reports*. If you know a particular commercial is being cast, and you think you're right for it (and can move fast), drop a P&R off at the production house; attach a note politely requesting an audition.

◼◼◼◼CASTING DIVERSITY

New York's population is diverse enough and its political and social atmospheres so highly-charged that most people in the performing arts are at least aware of nontraditional casting concepts. In fact, controversies surrounding two Broadway productions of the early '90s have brought the issue to national attention and may serve to bring about greater awareness and even parity.

Several constituent-specific organizations, support groups, and Off- and Off-Off-Broadway theatre companies like Theatre by the Blind, American Indian Community House, Pan-Asian Repertory, Split Britches, American Jewish Theatre, the Negro Ensemble Company, The National Theatre Workshop of the Handicapped, and Repertorio Español help keep New York theatre diverse. A few artistic directors, most notably the late Joseph Papp, founder of the New York Shakespeare Festival, have made a real commitment to color-blind, culturally diverse casting.

But Broadway has a lot of catching up to do and, in this rather compact metropolis, headquarters of the national Non-Traditional Casting Project (see *Talent Books and Talent Banks,* p. 116), much progress is yet to be made. Take a look at any issue of the trade papers; most of the available roles are for men, and it's not unusual to find several notices for all-male productions. More and more casting notices call for ethnic minority (primarily black) actors; others state an intention to cast multiculturally, although some ethnic minority actors consider most such statements mere lip service. Of course, since there is more total production here than there is anywhere else except Los Angeles, there are more opportunities for actors from traditionally overlooked groups; unfortunately, there's also a lot more competition and, even in this comparatively enlightened city, racism, sexism, and ignorance continue to flourish.

ADDITIONAL OPPORTUNITIES

Plays for Living, 49 W. 27th Street, Room 930, New York, NY 10001-6936, 689-1616. Original stage and video plays addressing compelling social problems are performed for such organizations as schools, youth groups, counseling services, and corporations. Union and nonunion actors may submit P&Rs.

READINGS

With so many theatres, and so many plays in development or under consideration for production, plays can go through countless readings, backers' auditions, and other presentations ranging from extremely informal to rehearsed and costumed. Usually, actors are invited by the director or playwright; occasionally, auditions are held. Actors are rarely paid for their work in readings, but even some of the most established actors take part when they can. Participation never guarantees a role if a play is produced, but can be a great way to meet people and get one's face and work known. For information, contact playwrights' organizations and theatre companies that specialize in script development.

STUDENT FILM

Students at area film schools use professional actors in their film projects. Actors usually receive meals and a tape of the finished product, if there is one. SAG members need to be sure the student producer/director has applied for a SAG waiver; in this way, you comply with union regulations and ensure that if the film is distributed, you'll be paid for your work. Casting notices run nearly every week in *Back Stage;* some are posted on the SAG bulletin board.

TRAINING

New York must have at least one teacher of every performance-related discipline imaginable. Here, one can study dance, movement, body work, singing, voice production, diction, improvisation, musical theatre, comedy, cabaret, soap opera acting, commercial auditioning, film acting, career management, and, oh yes, plain old acting. For every such discipline there are teachers of every *style* and *technique* imaginable, offering classes representing a wide range of methods, approaches, and philosophies.

The city can boast some of the most renowned acting, dance, and music schools and teachers in the country. There are the old, established acting institutions like The Neighborhood Playhouse, The Actors' Studio, Juilliard, The American Academy of Dramatic Art, and H.B. Studios; the smaller private and/or nonprofit schools; and countless individual teachers and coaches of every kind, as well as college and university degree programs. Plenty of schools specialize in on-camera auditioning and acting technique, some providing actors with opportunities to meet casting directors (see *Talent Agents and Casting Directors,* p. 117). A few schools focus on career strategies, teaching classes in the business of being an actor. The trade papers run ads for many schools and private teachers. Respected fellow actors are great sources of information.

Many institutional theatres have training institutes, internships and/or "junior rep" or lab programs. Some actors enroll in classes, or sign on as interns or volunteers, hoping their involvement will lead to auditions and job offers. It certainly happens, but before you pay for classes or volunteer your time, remember there are absolutely no guarantees.

CERTIFICATE/DEGREE PROGRAMS

The American Academy of Dramatic Arts, 120 Madison Avenue, New York, NY 10016, 686-9244.

American Musical and Dramatic Academy, 2109 Broadway, New York,
    NY 10023, 787-5300.
Brooklyn College of the City University of New York, Department of
    Theatre, Bedford Avenue and Avenue H, Brooklyn, NY 11210,
    718-780-5666.
Circle in the Square Theatre School, 1633 Broadway, New York, NY
    10019-6795, 307-2732.
City College of New York, Department of Theatre and Dance, Shepard Hall
    No. 229, 138th Street and Convent Avenue, New York, NY 10031,
    690-6666.
Fordham University, Theatre Arts Department, 113 W. 60th Street, New
    York, NY 10023, 841-5267.
The Juilliard School, Drama Division, 60 Lincoln Center Plaza, New York,
    NY 10023-6588, 799-5000 Ext. 251.
Marymount Manhattan College, Department of Fine and Performing Arts,
    221 E. 71st Street, New York, NY 10021, 517-0475 Ext. 88.
National Shakespeare Conservatory, 591 Broadway, New York, NY 10012,
    219-9874.
New York University, Undergraduate Drama, Tisch School of the Arts,
    721 Broadway, 13th Floor, New York, NY 10003, 998-1850.
Pace University, Theatre and Fine Arts Department, 41 Park Row,
    12th Floor, New York, NY 10038, 346-1352.

■■■■■AFFORDABLE ARTS

TDF Vouchers, Theatre Development Fund, 1501 Broadway, New York,
    NY 10036, Attn: Applications, 221-0013. TDF sells vouchers that entitle
    you to reduced admission to Off-Off-Broadway, dance, and music
    performances.
TKTS Booths, 354-5800. Half-price day-of-performance tickets are sold at
    the following locations:
  • Duffy Square (a.k.a. Actors' Square), 47th and Broadway
  • 2 World Trade Center
  • Borough Hall Park, Brooklyn
  • Bryant Park, 42nd Street and 5th Avenue (music and dance only)
New York Shakespeare Festival Quicktix, The Public Theater, 425 Lafayette
    Street, 598-7150. Starting at 6 p.m., the Public offers half-price day-of-
    performance tickets; arrive early for popular shows.
New York Shakespeare Festival's Shakespeare in the Park, Delacorte
    Theater, Central Park, 861-7277. NYSF presents free summer theatre in
    Central Park. Bring something to sit on, some friends, a picnic, and
    make a day of it. Be sure to get there early; you'll wait for hours to

pick up vouchers that entitle you to tickets distributed in the early evening. Call for further details.

Equity Audition Center. Day-of-performance Broadway and Off-Broadway tickets are sometimes donated for distribution to Equity members on a first-come, first-served basis.

Showcases. Equity members get free admission to Equity Showcase productions if unsold seats are available. Members must show an Equity card. A list of current productions is posted in the member lounge.

Twofers. These coupons are good for the purchase of two tickets for the price of one when presented at Broadway box offices. Color-coded for each show, they can be found in various restaurants and stores—just keep your eyes open.

SAG Screening Club, 1515 Broadway, 44th Fl., New York, NY 10036, 944-1030. A low annual membership fee allows club members to see a number of first-run films throughout the season.

NYC Visitors Bureau, 2 Columbus Circle, New York, NY 10019, 397-8222. The Bureau distributes free day-of-taping tickets to TV shows.

Ushering. Many Off-Broadway theatres use volunteer ushers; simply call the theatre office when there's a show you'd like to see.

Audience Extras, 109 W. 26th Street, New York, NY 10001, 989-9550. An annual fee entitles members to free tickets (plus a small service charge) to shows and movie previews.

■■■■■■■ RESOURCES

LIBRARIES

The Museum of Television and Radio, 25 W. 52nd Street, New York, NY 10022, 752-4690. Radio and television programs are available for on-site listening and viewing in the Museum library.

The Performing Arts Research Center at Lincoln Center, 111 Amsterdam Avenue, New York, NY, 870-1670. Reserve and circulating collections include scripts, recordings, sheet music, theatre and dance books, videos, periodicals (including trade papers), reference and archival materials, and more.

BOOKSTORES

The Actor's Heritage, 262 W. 44th Street,New York, NY 10036, 944-7490.

Applause Theatre/Cinema Books, 211 W. 71st Street, New York, NY 10023. 496-7511.

The Drama Book Shop, 723 7th Avenue, 2nd Floor, New York, NY 10036. 944-0595.

Theatrebooks, 1600 Broadway, 10th Floor, New York, NY 10019,
    757-2834.
Shakespeare and Co. Booksellers, (2259 Broadway) and *B. Dalton*
    (6th Avenue and 8th Street) carry good selections of plays and
    performing-arts-related books.

PUBLISHERS[5]

Drama Book Publishers, 260 Fifth Avenue, New York, NY 10001,
    725-5377. This company publishes theatre-related books; catalogue
    available.
Dramatist's Play Service, 440 Park Avenue S., New York, NY 10016,
    683-8960.
Samuel French, 45 W. 25th Street, New York, NY 10010, 206-8990.
Theatre Arts Books, 29 West 35th Street, New York, NY 10001, 244-3336.
    Theatre Arts publishes theatre-related books, but not plays.

■■■■■■NETWORKING AND SOCIALIZING

Theatre auditions can involve hours of waiting. It's frustrating, but actors
use the time to catch up with old friends, make new ones, and share
news and information. Equity actors can meet and mingle at the Equity
lounge. Actors connect in classes, and participating in readings and
showcases can be a great way to meet and be seen by directors, casting
directors, and other actors.

AFTER THE SHOW

Sardi's is the place where Broadway babies have celebrated (or
eulogized) opening nights since 1921. Of course, there are restaurants
and nightspots throughout the Broadway area, including those on
Restaurant Row (46th Street between 8th and 9th Avenues) and Theatre
Row (42nd Street between 9th and 10th Avenues). There are many
favorites, like Le Madeleine, Marvin Gardens, Film Center Café, and the
glamorous Orso. Here are a few others:
Curtain Up, 402 W. 43rd Street, New York, NY 10036, 564-7272.
Joe Allen, 326 W. 46th Street, New York, NY 10036, 581-6464. Joe Allen
    has been a Broadway favorite for years and years.
Sam's Restaurant, 263 W. 45th Street, New York, NY 10036, 719-5416.
Sardi's, 234 W. 44th Street, New York, NY 10036, 221-8440.

PIANO BARS AND CABARETS

Singers meet, gather, do a couple of tunes, maybe book an act. Several
places have informal piano bars as well as cabaret rooms for featured
performers. Many run casting notices in the trades. This is a partial list:

Don't Tell Mama, 343 W. 46th Street, New York, NY 10036, 757-0788.
The Duplex, 61 Christopher Street, New York, NY 10014, 989-3015, 255-5438.
Eighty-Eight's, 228 W. 10th Street, New York, NY 10014, 924-0088.
Mimi's Restaurant, 984 2nd Avenue, New York, NY 10022, 688-4692.
Rose's Turn, 55 Grove Street, New York, NY 10014, 366-5438.

[1] Area code 917 serves cellular phones, pagers, and certain other services. The Bronx switches from 212 to 718 on July 1, 1992.

[2] *The New York Times* (April 16, 1991).

[3] Figures are based on rents and prices in all five New York City boroughs. Remember that rates in Manhattan tend to be higher. In addition, some New Jersey suburbs are more affordable than Manhattan.

[4] Arson is not included in these statistics.

[5] These organizations will sell directly to customers. They are not stores, so call first.

P H I L A D

Home of the Liberty Bell, Benjamin Franklin, cheesesteak, and the humble hoagie, Philadelphia is a city proud of its primacy: the first community theatre on the East Coast (Barnstormers), the oldest English-language theatre in continual use (Walnut Street Theater), the site of the world's first motion picture show, the home of one of the first colleges dedicated exclusively to the performing arts (Philadelphia College of Performing Arts). Founded more than three hundred years ago, old Philadelphia lives on in the cobblestone streets and colonial dwellings of Center City. Here, within a few blocks of each other stand Carpenters' Hall, where the First Continental Congress met; Independence Hall, where the Declaration of Independence was written; Christ Church, where Betsy Ross and George Washington worshipped. But despite this rich history, poor Philly suffers from an inferiority complex. With New York as a more glamorous sibling, oft- and unfairly-maligned Philadelphia makes up in brotherly love what it lacks in self love.

If in the twentieth century Philadelphia isn't as glamorous as it was in the seventeenth, it retains an East Coast intensity minus the sharp edges of a certain near neighbor. Not far from the lush countryside of Bucks County and Valley Forge, the city itself seems manageable, even comfortable. Here, artsy intellectualism is tempered by working-class ambience. (*Rocky* turns thirtysomething?) This birthplace of the American Constitution is a city of neighborhoods, many of which have strong ethnic and cultural identities. On an official level, the city's diversity is applauded and promoted; in reality,

FAST FACTS

1990 CENSUS
1,585,577 (−6.1%)

COUNTY
Philadelphia

TIME
Zone: Eastern
Telephone: 846-1212

AREA CODE
215

PHILADELPHIA CONVENTION AND VISITORS BUREAU
1525 John F. Kennedy Boulevard
Philadelphia, PA 19102
636-1666

VISITOR CENTER
3rd and Chestnut Streets
Philadelphia, PA 19106
597-8974 (voice and TDD)

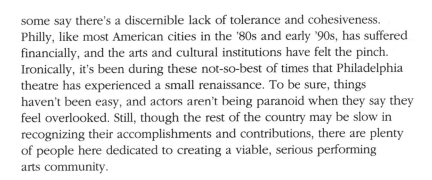

some say there's a discernible lack of tolerance and cohesiveness. Philly, like most American cities in the '80s and early '90s, has suffered financially, and the arts and cultural institutions have felt the pinch. Ironically, it's been during these not-so-best of times that Philadelphia theatre has experienced a small renaissance. To be sure, things haven't been easy, and actors aren't being paranoid when they say they feel overlooked. Still, though the rest of the country may be slow in recognizing their accomplishments and contributions, there are plenty of people here dedicated to creating a viable, serious performing arts community.

RECOMMENDED READING
Julie P. Curson, *A Guide's Guide to Philadelphia* (Philadelphia: Curson House, 1991).
John Edgar Wideman, *Philadelphia Fire* (New York: Henry Holt & Co., 1990).

MOVIES
Birdy (1985), *Clean and Sober* (1988), *Rocky* (1976), *Trading Places* (1983)

■■■■■CLIMATE

Situated a mere sixty miles from the Atlantic Ocean on the Delaware and Schuylkill Rivers, Philadelphia gets pretty wet, and rain can fall just about any time throughout the year. High temperatures combined with high humidity make for some uncomfortable summers, although the suburbs are slightly less sticky than the city. Snow, which can fall heavily in the northern suburbs, isn't too bad in the city and southern suburbs. Still, temperatures are generally moderate, and heat and cold waves don't usually last longer than a few days. Winter winds, however, can turn a cool day into a cold one. *For weather information call:* 936-1212.

NORMAL TEMPERATURES	Average Daily High	Average Daily Low
January	39°	24°
July	86°	67°

TEMPERATURE EXTREMES

Maximum Temp.	Annual No. of Days	Minimum Temp.	Annual No. of Days
90° and above	22	32° and below	97
32° and below	20	0° and below	1

NORMAL WEATHER CONDITIONS

Clear	Partly Cloudy	Cloudy
93	112	160

ANNUAL PRECIPITATION

ANNUAL PRECIPITATION	Days	Inches
All Precipitation	117	41
Snowfall	NA	21

TRANSPORTATION

Philadelphia is pretty easily negotiated by just about any means of transportation. Both Center City and the university area, west of the Schuylkill River, are quite doable on foot or by bike. Traffic isn't horrendous (except during rush hours) and pedestrian traffic rarely reaches mob proportions. Laid out in a grid pattern, streets running north-south are numbered, while many of the east-west streets are named for trees. Addresses on the east-west streets correspond to the nearest numbered streets (*i.e.*, 1105 Chestnut Street is between 11th and 12th Streets). On the numbered streets, addresses, appended N. and S., increase in either direction away from Market Street.

PUBLIC TRANSPORTATION
Southeastern Pennsylvania Transportation Authority (SEPTA). Philadelphia's public transportation authority coordinates several systems throughout the city and nearby suburbs. The system, the nation's fourth largest, has been in serious financial trouble in recent years. On April 16, 1991, *The New York Times* reported that significant cuts in service had already been made, and quoted the system's chief operations officer as saying "a total shutdown is a real possibility." In lieu of a shutdown, additional reductions in service seem likely. In the meantime, commuter lines continue carrying suburbanites in and out of Center City, which is compact enough that buses are reasonably fast and dependable, and timetables actually mean something. Buses are more popular than subways, which some people avoid, considering them unsafe, especially after dark.

The SEPTA fleet includes buses, streetcars, subways, and commuter rail (between city and suburbs). *For information call:* 580-7800; 580-7853 (TDD); 574-2780 (Paratransit service for people with disabilities).

Schedules are available at

- 15th and Market Street Information Center;
- Market Street E. Station, 10th and Market.

Exact change or a token is required. Transfers and suburban zones cost extra. Discount token packages and weekly and monthly passes are available at the 15th Street Ticket Sales Office, Market Street East, and Woolworth's at 1300 Chestnut Street. Children up to forty-two inches tall ride free; seniors and people with disabilities ride free during off-peak hours. (By the way, if you arrive in Philadelphia via Amtrak, use your ticket stub for a free subway ride into one of two Center City stations.)

The following is a list of terminals and additional transportation systems:

30th Street Station, 30th and Market Streets, Philadelphia, PA. Amtrak: 824-1600. SEPTA Commuter Rail: 574-7800.

Greyhound/New Jersey Transit, 10th and Filbert Streets, Philadelphia, PA. Greyhound: 931-4000. New Jersey Transit: 569-3752.

TAXIS

Taxis are metered and somewhat expensive. They're easiest to find at the train stations and in the busier areas of town and on main thoroughfares, like Market and Broad Streets, both of which slice through Center City.

DRIVING

Unlike those who live in surrounding suburbs, people who live and work in Philly itself can get around without a car. Most actors, however, need wheels (although some find they can manage without owning a car as long as they have occasional access to one). A Philadelphia actor is actually a Delaware Valley actor, and auditions, interviews, performances, and shoots can take place anywhere from Allentown, Pennsylvania to South Jersey, North Delaware, Baltimore, Washington, D.C., and New York. When going to Center City or the university area during the day, however, consider leaving the car at home; parking (most of it at short-term meters) is hard to find and, in several areas, forbidden during rush hours. Many of the narrow colonial streets are one-way and would be easier to negotiate if there weren't so many surprises, from small parks to large potholes.

▬▬▬▬HOUSING AND COSTS OF LIVING

Whether you want to live in Center City, in the surrounding neighborhoods, or in nearby suburbs, housing isn't too hard to come by. Prices aren't cheap, but they're certainly not the highest in the land, and finding a place to live isn't the gut-wrenching ordeal it is in many other cities. Housing hunters look at the listings in the Sunday *Inquirer* and in the *Welcomat,* a free weekly that comes out on Wednesdays and is delivered to residences and distributed in commercial building lobbies. Enlisting the help of the many no-fee real estate and management agencies is another option. Recommended areas are Queen Village, Mt. Airy, Fishtown, Graduate Hospital, West Philly, and Northeast Philly.

INTERAREA SHELTER INDEXES	Renters	Owners
Philadelphia	100	100

COSTS OF LIVING	
Total average annual expenditures	$29,564
Food at home	2,384
Telephone	499
Gas and motor oil	852
Public transportation	261
Personal care products and services	372

■■■■■■EMPLOYMENT

1989 Average Annual Pay
Philadelphia-Wilmington-Trenton: $25,069

1990 Average Unemployment Rates
Pennsylvania: 5.4%
Philadelphia metropolitan statistical area: 4.6%

1990 Average Weekly Unemployment Benefits
Pennsylvania: $188.40

■■■■■■CRIME

While some residents think there's a lot of crime in the city and others consider it quite safe, most people think of Philadelphia as pretty average. Of cities in this book for which statistics are available, Philadelphia has the lowest rate of aggravated assault (and the second-lowest city's rate is a full 35 percent higher), almost ties with New York for the lowest rate of reported rape, is at the low end of the burglary scale, and is somewhere in the middle when it comes to murder. But because the city feels relatively safe, there may be a tendency to let one's guard down. Paranoia is hardly called for, but in this city of a million and a half people, crime happens, making awareness an asset.

1990 CRIME RATES	Violent	Property
Total Crimes	21,387	94,277
Crimes per 100,000 People	1,349	5,948
Average 1 Crime per Every	74 people	17 people

■■■■■■MISCELLANEA

NEWSPAPERS
Philadelphia Inquirer (morning)
Philadelphia Daily News (evening)
Welcomat (weekly)

LIBRARY
Free Library of Philadelphia, 19th and Vine Streets, Philadelphia, PA 19103, 686-5322. More than a lending library, this is a historical institution.

POST OFFICE
Main Branch, 30th and Market Streets, Philadelphia, PA 19104, 895-8000.

THE BUSINESS

Being the perpetual bridesmaid to New York's bride affects culture and industry alike. This means performing artists are often overlooked by both producers and theatregoers, who'd rather head for Manhattan than see local talent, many of whom don't recommend moving to Philadelphia to be an actor. Instead, they say, come if an acting job brings you; while you're here, do some networking and see how you like it. Younger Equity actors, especially women, have a rough time getting work in Philly; some say the majority of Equity roles—female and male—are cast out of town. True or not, Equity actors should proceed with caution. And no matter what you do, if you've got credits from New York or another major center, be sure they're prominently displayed on your résumé.

Still, some optimism is warranted. Despite the New York fixation, there are enough people devoted to building and promoting a strong performing arts community that things might turn around within the next several years—but no promises. The Performing Arts League of

Philadelphia addresses the promotion and marketing of member organizations; there's talk of revitalizing the city's barely-alive film office; artistic directors and literary managers have been meeting regularly since early 1991 in order to create a supportive, increasingly visible theatre community. Philadelphia theatre's growing vibrancy hints that this could be just the place for the performer who, in the face of some resistance and a lot of frustration, is willing to take an active role in building something that might, or might not, turn out extremely well—and it's certainly not the first time that's happened in Philadelphia, now is it?.

RECOMMENDED READING

The Actor's Casting Guide (West Chester, Penn.: WildMann Productions, 1991). This is the first directory of casting resources in the Philadelphia-area market.

Hap Erstein, "Grass really is greener for theatre in Philly," *The Washington Times* (April 17, 1990).

▆▆▆▆ PROFESSIONAL ASSOCIATIONS

TALENT UNIONS

Actors' Equity Association (AEA), Liaison City.
   Members: 375
American Federation of Television and Radio Artists (AFTRA),
   230 S. Broad Street, 10th Floor, Philadelphia, PA 19102, 732-0507.
   Members: 1,677
Screen Actors Guild (SAG), same address as AFTRA, 545-3150.
   Members: 846
American Guild of Musical Artists (AGMA), Lafayette Building, 8th Floor,
   5th and Chestnut Streets, Philadelphia, PA 19106, 925-8400.

OTHER ASSOCIATIONS

Movement Theatre International, 3700 Chestnut Street, Philadelphia, PA 19104, 382-0600. MTI's purpose is to "promote the understanding of movement theatre and the development of the art form." A resource for mime, clown, circus, new vaudeville, and dance artists in Philly and around the world.

▆▆▆▆ LOOKING FOR WORK

Friends and colleagues are essential sources of information in the area. In addition, some theatres send casting notices to those actors who've worked or auditioned for them previously.

PUBLICATIONS

Stage: A Theatre Monthly, 9 E. Rose Valley Road, Wallingford, PA 19066,
565-2094. Published nine times a year (three double issues), *Stage*
runs audition notices (mostly non-Equity) and production listings, and
carries ads for classes, photographers, and so on. Distributed free of
charge to theatres and schools; a yearly subscription is very inexpensive.
Back Stage, 330 W. 42nd Street, New York, NY 10036, 212-947-0020.
The New York trade weekly is used by Philadelphians who commute
to New York for auditions, classes, and so forth. It is available by
subscription, at the Philadelphia Drama Bookshop, and at a number
of newsstands.

HOTLINES

Actors' Equity Association; AFTRA/SAG (see *Talent Unions,* p. 134)

BULLETIN BOARDS AND BINDERS

Philadelphia Drama Bookshop (see *Bookstores,* p. 141)

TALENT BOOKS AND TALENT BANKS

AFTRA/SAG. The *Philadelphia Talent Guide* is published every three
years.

TALENT SHOWCASES AND COMBINED AUDITIONS

League of Washington Theatres; National Dinner Theatre Association;
StrawHat Auditions. (For addresses, see Appendix B.)
Performing Arts League of Philadelphia, c/o The Wilma Theatre,
2030 Sansom Street, Philadelphia, PA 19103, 963-0249. This association
of professional companies and presenting organizations sponsors annual
auditions attended by member theatres. Auditions are announced
in *Stage.*

■■■■■■TALENT AGENTS AND CASTING DIRECTORS

There are only a few agents and casting directors in Philadelphia, and
actors who want to work in print, film, and broadcast (agents and CDs
are rarely involved in casting theatre) need to know them. Almost no one
signs exclusive contracts with agents; for many years, in fact, agents
played minimal roles in the casting process, as CDs called actors directly.
Recently, however, casting directors have started turning more frequently
to agents to provide talent, making it advantageous to list with an agent.
In addition, agents get some work the casting directors don't, and can
refer talent to agents in nearby areas like Baltimore, Delaware, and D.C.;
some may even submit actors for New York auditions.

At the time of this writing, the busiest casting companies are Walton-Wickline and Michael Lemon (the latter holds open hours every Monday except holidays from 1 to 5 p.m.). Reinhardt Agency and Greer Lange and Associates are two of the busier AFTRA/SAG franchised agencies. Agents and casting directors are considered relatively accessible; getting listed shouldn't be too difficult for actors with decent résumés and/or good training. Union and nonunion actors may pick up a list of casting directors and franchised agents at the AFTRA/SAG office, or refer to *The Actor's Casting Guide*. Send agents and casting directors P&Rs, and call to inquire about interviews or open hours.

▉▉▉▉▉ THEATRE

Philadelphia has an interesting theatre history. It was once an important stop on the Broadway try-out circuit, yet its activity ground to a near dead-halt during the 1970s. The early- to mid-'80s saw a resurgence of energy and interest, and by the end of the decade, Philly theatres were producing one world premiere after another; a few community theatres turned pro, new companies were popping up, and journalists began making comparisons to Chicago and talking about risky, cutting-edge theatre.

The theatre community extends both geographically (it includes suburbs and neighboring states) and categorically: professional, university, and community theatre peacefully coexist and sometimes intermingle. But here's the thing: Philadelphia's proximity to New York is both a blessing and a curse, for actors can commute easily enough, but so can producers and artistic directors, some of whom bypass local talent and head straight for the Apple. They do hold local auditions, but with varying results. Philly actors know very well which theatres snub them, and it makes them mad. The fact that it's become commonplace for actors living in New York to commute to Philadelphia for auditions doesn't help matters. Frustrated by an elitism that robs them of respect, not to mention jobs, Philadelphians with New York credits retain their New York addresses and answering services: that 212 area code and New York résumé give them added cachet. But despite the initial enchantment with a New York résumé, actors who stay around long enough eventually become local (and theoretically, less talented) actors.

But all is not bleakness; though the struggle for recognition is an arduous one, there is evidence of change. Several companies (among them Drama Guild, a leading local theatre) cast much of their '90-'91 seasons locally. In 1991, the Performing Arts League initiated an annual combined general audition. And in the last several years, many companies have been born or relocated here. What it comes down to is that there's a lot of union and nonunion professional theatre, from small, artist-initiated companies on up to commercial organizations. If there isn't as much as there is in other cities, well, there's also less competition. And Equity or not, actors almost always get paid. They may not get much, but they get something.

Philadelphia theatre is led by the Walnut Street Theatre, the Drama Guild, the Wilma Theatre, People's Light and Theatre Company, and the American Music Theatre Festival. Next are companies like Arden Theatre, Novel Stages, Cheltenham, and Bushfire Theatre; some are quite young, while others have been on the scene for many years. The third "tier" consists of lower budget, grass-roots organizations like Interact, Venture Theatre, Philadelphia Area Repertory Theatre, and Red Heel. There's also quite a bit of (primarily nonunion) dinner and mystery theatre in the city and surrounding suburbs.

Most theatres have general auditions once a year. Since auditions aren't always announced, actors should call individual theatres to find out when generals are held, and how to sign up. As for show-by-show auditions, simply call the theatre; you shouldn't have much of a problem getting a slot. And keep in mind that actors who love theatre here stay involved by wearing many hats, producing, directing, designing, and so on.

███████ FILM AND TELEVISION

The *Rocky* movies aren't the only features that have been shot in Philadelphia in the last couple of decades, though it sometimes seems that way. There's a statue of the pugilistic performer in the middle of the city, and it's been said that the success of that series generated increased interest in Philly as a location site. But though several successful films have been shot here in recent years, the fact is the city doesn't get terribly many theatrical and made-for-TV movies. Locals shake their heads and say there just isn't anything. Still, when films do come, a lot of people go to work as extras and in day-player and even contract roles. (The summer of 1991, for example, brought a low-budget feature for which all day-player roles were cast locally.) Principal casting is usually complete by the time projects arrive in Philly, but there is some good news: when a film's in town, as many as 50 percent of local SAG members go to work, and local actors work in films shot anywhere within the city's SAG jurisdiction, which includes all of Pennsylvania and Southern New Jersey.

No TV series are based here, and episodic television comes only rarely; unfortunately for locals, even the most well-known Philly-flavored show, "thirtysomething," was shot in L.A. The reality-based programs have stopped here for production, and the local PBS station and the network affiliates occasionally produce some dramatic shows.

CORPORATE AND COMMERCIALS

While Philadelphia's corporate production market is pretty strong, AFTRA's share of that market has room to grow. It's not a sickly share (a couple of major corporations produce a lot of industrials each year), rather one with a lot of potential. Between Delaware, Philadelphia, and the Philadelphia-Princeton corridor, a tremendous amount of production takes place; how many corporations become union signatories remains to be seen, although by mid-1991 there are indications that union production is picking up. In the meantime, nonunion production dominates. For work in corporate production, it's essential to be known to the busiest casting directors, although a number of production companies accept P&Rs and tapes directly from talent; check *The Actor's Casting Guide* for details.

The commercial market generates a lot of work for both union and nonunion actors. In this market, too, nonunion production may lead the way; after all, most national production, at least, is likely to originate in New York. And while some local clients prefer New York talent (it's not unheard of for an actor to go to New York for an audition, only to see the Philly-based producer riding the same train), casting in New York isn't always a sign of disrespect for Philadelphia actors. Sometimes it's simply a matter of diversity, for the local talent pool, while competent, isn't always deep enough. The higher-profile ad agencies and producers know they can cast most roles here, but for certain types and age categories, a trip to New York may be in order. Still, it works both ways: a lot of actors prefer to live in Philadelphia, but work in New York and Washington. After all, they can be at an audition in either city in a couple of hours. Back here in Philly, the typical commercial and corporate types—yuppie families, sales reps, executives—get the most work. The busiest age group is about thirty-five to fiftyish, and there's a real need for male execs in their forties. In voice-over, some ten-to-fifteen major players get most of the work, although there's some room for others who combine occasional v/o jobs with on-camera work.

CASTING DIVERSITY

In 1990, an actor who organized Philadelphia's first forum on multiculturalism in the theatre discovered that in the community there was little familiarity with—and much misunderstanding of—the concepts of nontraditional casting. Since that time, awareness and receptiveness have increased; in fact, nontraditional casting is rather in vogue right now, and if it doesn't always happen for the "right" reasons, well, at least it results in jobs for typically overlooked actors. Not all ethnically diverse hiring is the result of tokenism; Interact Theatre is known to cast multiracially, Bushfire Theatre and Freedom Theatre are well-established African American companies, and there's an annual Women's Theatre Festival.

In the corporate and commercial markets, men still dominate as spokespeople, but other opportunities for women have increased significantly. The demand for ethnic minority actors—particularly Hispanic, Asian, and black male—has also grown. The talent pool is small enough that casting such roles isn't always easy, and some ethnic minority actors have found quite a lot of opportunity. This doesn't mean, however, that there's a gold mine here for minority actors; remember, we're looking at an increase from almost nothing to, well, something.

ADDITIONAL OPPORTUNITIES

Bushfire Theatre, 224 South 52nd Street, Philadelphia, PA 19139, 747-9230. Throughout the theatre season, Bushfire's 52nd Street Writers Workshop has twice-weekly readings (call for schedules). Most are cast with actors who've appeared on the mainstage, but others actors may call or send a P&R.

Play Works, 623 South Street, Philadelphia, PA 19147, 592-8393. Dedicated to developing new works; projects include staged readings, productions, and community outreach. Auditions, held twice yearly, are announced in *Stage;* in addition, actors may submit a P&R.

Plays for Living, 311 S. Juniper, Room 802, Philadelphia, PA 19107. PFL "gives dramatic voice to compelling social problems by producing original . . . plays about critical . . . issues." Equity and nonunion performers may participate.

The Royal Pickwickians, 2008 Mt. Vernon Street, Philadelphia, PA 19130, 232-2690. Specializing in historical interpretation, the RPs provide actors as characters from history to school programs, museums, the Historical Society of Pennsylvania, and other audiences. They also produce murder mysteries and theme-based party and event entertainment. Non-Equity actors may submit P&Rs.

Singing City, 2031 Chestnut Street, Philadelphia, PA 19103, 561-3930. Since 1948, this volunteer choir "recognize(s) the influence music can have in improving the quality of life for individuals and for society." Some sight-reading is necessary; call for audition information.

Theatre Center Philadelphia, Playwrights Workshop, 622 South 4th Street, Philadelphia, PA, 336-3869. Actors interested in participating in

weekly readings may call the theatre, or attend readings (call for
schedule and information) and do some networking. Non-Equity only.

■■■■■TRAINING

Many theatre companies offer classes; students enrolled in Walnut Street
Theatre's program also serve as apprentices, taking small roles in the
company's productions. However, most professionals aren't satisfied with
the level of training available in town, and recommend commuting to
New York. Most area schools, they say, attract starry-eyed locals, not
professionals who need to stretch muscles or add skills. Still, there are
some recommended teachers and coaches, like those at the Wilma
Theatre. The Actor's Center, which teaches on-camera skills, is also well-
thought-of. As in any city, beware of the "so-you-want-to-be-a-model"
school of advertising.

CERTIFICATE/DEGREE PROGRAMS
Temple University, School of Communications and Theater, 13th and
    Norris Streets, Philadelphia, PA 19122-1801, 787-8748.
University of the Arts, Philadelphia College of Performing Arts, Theatre
    Department, 313 S. Broad Street, Philadelphia, PA 19102, 875-2232.
University of Pennsylvania, 34th and Walnut Streets, Philadelphia, PA
    19104, 898-5000.
Villanova University, Theatre Department, 108 Vasey Hall, Villanova, PA
    19085, 645-7545.

■■■■■AFFORDABLE ARTS

Philadelphia Drama Guild, Zellerbach Theatre of the Annenberg Center,
    3680 Walnut Street, Philadelphia, PA 19104, 563-7530. Half-price tickets
    are obtainable half an hour before curtain; you must show an Equity
    or eligibility card.
Venture Theatre, Stage III, Temple University Center City, 1619 Walnut
    Street, Philadelphia, PA 19103, 923-2766. Actors whose P&Rs are in
    Venture's files receive discounted preview admission. First-time
    attendance is free in exchange for a P&R, which then goes in the files.
Actor Nights. Several theatres have begun offering free-with-a-headshot
    or pay-what-you-can nights to area actors. Keep your ears open, or
    call theatres.
Half-Price Tickets. The Performing Arts League of Philadelphia operates
    three half-price ticket booths; locations were unavailable at the time
    of printing. For information call 963-0249.

RESOURCES

LIBRARIES

The Free Library houses an impressive theatre history archive. It doesn't, however, have the greatest collection of plays and theatre books (although there's a good selection of musical scores). Actors who have access to the University of Pennsylvania and Temple University libraries are in better luck.

BOOKSTORES

Philadelphia Drama Bookshop, 2209 Walnut Street, Philadelphia, PA 19103, 981-0777. Here's where you find scripts, directories, trade publications, and more. Owner Madeleine Kelly is dedicated to a strong performing arts community and is a wonderful resource; she really knows what's going on in Philadelphia's theatre scene.

Intermission, The Shop for the Performing Arts, 8405 Germantown Avenue, Chestnut Hill, PA 19118, 242-8515. Intermission carries scripts, directories, gifts, posters, and other items.

NETWORKING AND SOCIALIZING

Philadelphia is small enough that actors do most of their networking at auditions and play readings. Newcomers will need to jump in with both feet: try to get involved in readings, go to the Drama Bookshop, and talk to people at auditions. There are some popular bars and restaurants near theatres, including:

Moriarty's, 1116 Walnut Street, Philadelphia, PA 19107, 627-7676.
16th Street Bar and Grill, 264 S. 16th Street, Philadelphia, PA 19102, 735-3316.

SAN FRA

Is there anyone who doesn't like San Francisco? The land of cable cars, the Golden Gate, and the crookedest street in the world may not be everybody's favorite, but most people find something enchanting about the city by the bay. The morning fog, croons Tony Bennett, may chill the air, but who cares? When the fog lifts, the view of that bay, that sky, those hills across that bridge can brighten the saddest and soften the hardest of hearts. San Franciscans take quiet pride in their city (and whatever you do, *don't* call it Frisco); perhaps they're even a little snobbish about it. After all, they may reason, the city is as hip as New York (minus the craziness), as L.A. (without the sun-baked superficiality), and as Chicago (without the ultra-urban intensity). San Francisco's more than 700,000 residents represent, of course, the full range of social and political thought, but the city's powers-that-be come across as an arts-loving, somewhat patrician group that appreciates its theatre, but adores its symphony and ballet. If it sounds a little too bourgeois, remember this is also the place beatniks, hippies, and gays have comfortably called home; it's the city just over the bridge from Berkeley, the birthplace of student protest and the Free Speech Movement and the site of People's Park.

San Francisco's acting community, hardly confined to city limits, is spread throughout nine Bay Area

FAST FACTS

1990 CENSUS
723,959 (+6.6%)

COUNTIES
San Francisco
Alameda (Berkeley, Oakland)

TIME
Zone: Pacific
Telephone: 767-8900

AREA CODES
415 (San Francisco, San Mateo Counties)
510 (Alameda and Contra Costa Counties)
TELEPHONE NUMBERS IN THIS CHAPTER ARE
IN THE 415 AREA UNLESS OTHERWISE NOTED.

**SAN FRANCISCO CONVENTION AND
VISITORS BUREAU**
P.O. Box 6977
San Francisco, CA 94101
974-6900

VISITOR INFORMATION CENTER
Hallidie Plaza
900 Market Street
San Francisco, CA 94102
391-2000

counties. Some of "San Francisco's" major theatres (and many of its actors) are in Oakland and Berkeley; one of its LORT theatres is an hour south, in San Jose. But whatever the location, Bay Area actors take their art and work quite seriously. Perhaps only a handful of them make the leap to fame and fortune in Hollywood or the Apple, perhaps the work that's done here isn't as widely seen as it ought to be, but it's often good, interesting, actor- and/or playwright-oriented work.

RECOMMENDED READING
Herbert Gold, *Travels in San Francisco* (New York: Arcade Publishing, Inc., 1990). These essays are Gold's anecdotal strolls through "America's last great metropolitan village."
Dean Goodman, *San Francisco Stages: A Concise History, 1849-1986* (San Francisco: Micro Pro Litera Press, 1986). This is a great source for anyone seeking information on the San Francisco theatre scene.
John Miller, ed., *San Francisco Stories* (San Francisco: Chronicle Books, 1990).

MOVIES
Dim Sum (1985), *San Francisco* (1936), *The Times of Harvey Milk* (1985), *Vertigo* (1958)

■■■■■CLIMATE

While some people despair the absence of four distinct seasons, few could disagree that the Bay Area has one of the most liveable climates in the country. What the city lacks in freezing winters and sizzling summers it makes up for in its famous fog and cool bay breezes, and natives take not-so-secret pleasure at the sight of ill-prepared tourists shivering in their Bermuda shorts and goose pimples. Most of the surrounding cities and suburbs experience less of the fog, drizzle, and nighttime chill than San Francisco proper and on any given day can be a good ten degrees warmer. San Francisco summers are often pleasantly breezy; throughout the Bay Area, that season is generally warm and dry. Drought, in fact, has become a real problem, making at-home water conservation a way of life. *For weather information call:* 936-1212.

NORMAL TEMPERATURES	Average Daily High	Average Daily Low
January	57°	44°
September	73°	56°

TEMPERATURE EXTREMES		
Maximum Temp.	**Annual No. of Days**	
90° and above	2	
32° and below	—	

NORMAL WEATHER CONDITIONS

(Information not available.)

ANNUAL PRECIPITATION	Days	Inches
All Precipitation	67	21
Snowfall	NA	—

▬▬▬ TRANSPORTATION

With its famous hills and outlying residential districts, San Francisco may not be the most accessible or walkable place in the world, but getting around is rarely a hardship, and walking can be pleasant. Local public transportation is really pretty good; it's just a pity that San Francisco, built on hills and sand dunes, can't support a more extensive underground system. Most actors, with their less-than-routine schedules and a workplace that can encompass the entire Bay Area, have cars. San Francisco itself, however, is a great city in which to combine the use of public and private transportation.

PUBLIC TRANSPORTATION
Within the city, public transportation is made up of two independent but cooperative systems, MUNI and BART.

San Francisco Municipal Railway System (MUNI). The MUNI fleet includes buses, trolleys, streetcars (light rail), and cable cars. MUNI buses, streetcars, and trolleys go under- and mostly above-ground to cover the city extensively. MUNI's cable cars follow three routes in the city's northeastern corner, from Fisherman's Wharf to Market Street downtown.

For MUNI information call: 673-MUNI (6864); 923-6366 (TTY); 626-1033 (senior ID); 552-7908 (Paratransit door-to-door service for disabled). Free MUNI timetables are available where passes are sold, at MUNI Metro stations, and on MUNI vehicles. System maps are for sale at newsstands and at MUNI headquarters (brochures and schedules are also available), 949 Presidio, San Francisco, CA 94115, 923-6164.

MUNI requires exact fares; free transfers can be used twice within 1 1/2 hours. Regular cable-car fare is higher than that for other MUNI systems (and cable cars are a functioning part of the system, not just a tourist attraction). Discounts are offered for youth, seniors, and people with disabilities; children under age five ride free. Pass options include a monthly Fast Pass, and one- and three-day Passports, available at retail stores, the City Hall Information Booth, and MUNI headquarters.

Bay Area Rapid Transit (BART). BART is a rapid rail system that links San Francisco with Daly City to the south, and Contra Costa and Alameda Counties to the east. BART doesn't serve all of San Francisco; rather, it bisects the city at an angle, making stops along the way between Daly City and the Transbay Tunnel before branching out into the East Bay.

For BART information call: 788-BART (2278); 839-2220 (TTY); 464-7133 (information for disabled passengers).

BART fare tickets are purchased from in-station machines; fares vary according to distance travelled. There are discounts for children five to twelve, seniors, and people with disabilities; discount tickets must be bought at participating banks, stores, or at the Lake Merritt BART station. Children four and under ride free. Fast Passes, ticket books, and BART Plus passes are available for connecting with BART Express Buses and suburban bus systems. The MUNI Fast Pass is valid for rides within San Francisco. Purchase tickets in stations; be sure to save your ticket, as it operates the exit gate.

The following is a list of terminals and additional transportation systems:

Amtrak, Transbay Terminal, First and Mission Streets, San Francisco, CA, 982-8512. Train service actually begins and ends in Oakland, with shuttle bus service to San Francisco.

Caltrain Station, 4th and Townsend Streets, San Francisco, CA, 557-8661. Caltrain links San Francisco with San Jose, stopping in cities along the way.

Greyhound, Transbay Terminal, First and Mission Streets, San Francisco, CA, 558-6789.

TAXIS

Street hailing, while possible in the hotel/theatre/shopping district, isn't great throughout much of the city; your best bet is to order a cab by telephone. Taxis are metered and fairly expensive.

DRIVING

Driving can be quite a challenge in San Francisco's northeastern sector of one-way streets, cable cars, and hills. There's nothing quite like sitting on the upside of a San Francisco hill, waiting for a light to turn green, feet jammed on brake and clutch, hand gripping the stick. (Of course, you *could* drive an automatic.) On-street parking offers a challenge of a different sort, requiring less adrenalin and far more patience and cunning. In certain parts of town, finding a place to park can be next to impossible; always allow extra time for the hunt. (You could probably search any San Francisco car-owner's apartment and turn up a pile of parking tickets a-moldering in the back of a drawer.) Downtown, less-expensive parking lots and garages, as well as more available metered on-street parking, can be found south of Market Street, though parking there may mean walking extra blocks to your destination. But driving and parking downtown are exercises in frustration; better to take public transportation. When parking on hills, always use the emergency brake, and be sure to curb your wheels, turning them away from the curb when facing uphill, toward the curb when facing down; it's the law in San Francisco.

▄▄▄▄HOUSING AND COSTS OF LIVING

Lots of people have moved to the Bay Area in recent years, and housing costs have risen accordingly; the Bay Area, in fact, has become one of the country's most expensive places to live. Within San Francisco, housing has never been easy to find, and costs have risen steeply. One of the most effective ways to apartment-hunt is to walk or drive around the neighborhoods you like, keeping an eye out for "For Rent" signs. The Sunday *Chronicle* classifieds are a good source; you can also check bulletin boards at theatres. Some of the city's more affordable neighborhoods include the Sunset and Richmond districts (both largely residential, they're in the flatter western part of the city and tend to be grayer and foggier), Noe Valley, parts of the Haight, Portrero Hill, Bernal Heights, and parts of the Mission district.

More and more actors, especially those who want to own homes, live in Oakland and Berkeley, and several theatres and related organizations are located in those cities. Eastbay suburbs are also increasingly popular. The North Bay communities, across the Golden Gate Bridge from San

Francisco, are beautiful, but generally more expensive and a little isolated; the only way into the City is by vehicle over the Golden Gate bridge (or via a roundabout route through the East Bay), or by ferry.

INTERAREA SHELTER INDEXES	Renters	Owners
San Francisco	139	139
(Philadelphia)	(100)	(100)

COSTS OF LIVING	
Total average annual expenditures	$36,087
Food at home	2,617
Telephone	666
Gas and motor oil	957
Public transportation	591
Personal care products and services	386

■■■■■■ EMPLOYMENT

1989 Average Annual Pay
San Francisco-Oakland-San Jose: $27,568

1990 Average Unemployment Rates
California: 5.6%
San Francisco metropolitan statistical area: 3.3%

1990 Average Weekly Unemployment Benefits
California: $131.36

■■■■■■ CRIME

Depending, of course, on where she lives and works, a San Franciscan may feel pretty secure; after all, the city enjoys the lowest burglary rate of cities in this book, and rates of murder, rape, and aggravated assault are among the lowest. On the other hand, in 1990 San Francisco experienced the greatest increase over 1989 in motor vehicle theft of any city in this book for which statistics are available. Auto break-ins and vandalism appear to be on the increase as well, creeping into neighborhoods that historically have been among the most secure. Certain areas an actor might frequent during the day become iffy at night: though there are theatres and restaurants and even plenty of people South of Market and in the Mission, some caution is warranted.

1990 CRIME RATES	Violent	Property
Total Crimes	12,388	57,982
Crimes per 100,000 People	1,711	8,009
Average 1 Crime per Every	58 people	12 people

■■■■■ MISCELLANEA

NEWSPAPERS
San Francisco Chronicle (morning)
San Francisco Examiner (evening)
The San Francisco Bay Guardian (weekly)
S.F. Weekly

LIBRARIES
Main Library, Civic Center, Larkin and McAllister Streets, San Francisco,
   CA 94102, 557-4400, 557-4525 (Art and Music).
San Francisco Performing Arts Library and Museum (PALM), 399 Grove
   Street, San Francisco, CA 94102, 255-4800.

POST OFFICE
Main Branch, 1300 Evans Avenue, San Francisco, CA, 550-6500.

ADDITIONAL INFORMATION
Cityline, 512-5000. The *San Francisco Chronicle* maintains this free
   information line twenty-four hours a day. By pressing codes on a
   touch-tone phone, you can get information and updates on everything
   from the weather to news, sports, horoscopes, the stock market, your
   favorite soap opera, and so on.

THE BUSINESS

Because Bay Area actors are taken seriously in L.A., there has been a steady
southward exodus in recent years. The departure of San Francisco locals
should leave plenty of room for newcomers—but don't pack your bags
just yet. There's been an equal or greater influx of actors new to the Bay
Area, and while many consider the community supportive and the market
fairly open, increased competition has made breaking in more difficult.

   The theatre community here can get a little cliquish, although some
newcomers do just fine. It's not uncommon, however, for an actor to feel
stuck working at a certain level, unable to step up to the next rung of the

ladder. And in a community that takes particular pride in the integrity of its talent pool, actors with little training or experience may have it especially rough. There is, perhaps, less crossover between the legit and commercial markets than in many cities, as some actors in each category view the other category with some ambivalence. At the same time, crossover is possible for actors willing to get the necessary training and to actively pursue work in either market.

A few former San Francisco actors have done very well in Hollywood but, for the most part, film careers don't originate here. For one thing, L.A. is farther away than many non-Californians seem to realize. San Francisco talent is respected, yes, but that talent usually has to travel nearly four hundred miles south to be considered for principal film and television roles.

RECOMMENDED READING

Theatre Directory of the San Francisco Bay Area (San Francisco: Theatre Bay Area). The *Directory,* published biennially, contains listings and descriptions of member theatres, service organizations, agents and casting directors, training programs, and technical and photographic resources. It offers discounts for TBA members.

■■■■■■ PROFESSIONAL ASSOCIATIONS

TALENT UNIONS

Actors' Equity Association (AEA), 235 Pine Street, San Francisco, CA 94104, 391-3838.
Members: 784
American Federation of Television and Radio Artists (AFTRA), same address as Equity, 391-7510.
Members: 2,559
Screen Actors' Guild (SAG), same address/phone as Equity.
Members: 2036
American Guild of Musical Artists (AGMA), same address as Equity, 986-4060.

OTHER ASSOCIATIONS

Latin American Theatre Artists, 450 Geary Street, San Francisco, CA 94102, 771-0654. LATA's purpose is to promote the work and develop the craft of Latino theatre artists in the Bay Area. Activities include play readings, consultations, and referrals. Members receive a newsletter and priority casting in readings; their P&Rs are included in a casting file.
Theatre Bay Area, 657 Mission Street, Suite 402, San Francisco, CA 94105. 957-1557. TBA is "a resource and communications center for theatre artists, theatre companies and theatre lovers," with membership in the

many thousands. Services include group health insurance, a talent bank, library, annual combined auditions, job/audition information, discount tickets, and more. TBA publishes *Callboard* (see *Publications, below*), *Theatre Directory,* and *Sources of Publicity.*

■■■■■■LOOKING FOR WORK

PUBLICATIONS

Callboard. Published monthly by Theatre Bay Area, *Callboard* includes audition notices, articles, theatre listings, and advertisements for services and classes. It is available by subscription (included in TBA membership) or at bookstores and news kiosks at 1504 Haight Street and Castro near 18th Street.

San Francisco Chronicle. Though not a major source of performing arts information, column 470 in the classifieds has some audition notices.

HOTLINES

Actors' Equity Association; AFTRA/SAG (see *Talent Unions,* p. 149).

Theatre Bay Area Member Hotline (see *Other Associations,* p. 149). This line is for TBA members only.

Nancy Hayes Casting, 567-0108. Primarily lists calls for nonunion extra work.

BULLETIN BOARDS AND BINDERS

American Conservatory Theatre, 450 Geary Street, San Francisco, CA 94102. A.C.T.'s fourth floor bulletin board posts local and out-of-town audition notices; you don't have to be an A.C.T. student or company member to have a look.

TALENT BOOKS AND TALENT BANKS

Theatre Bay Area (for TBA members only).

Latin American Theatre Artists (for LATA members only).

TALENT SHOWCASES AND COMBINED AUDITIONS

AFTRA/SAG Equal Opportunity Showcase. Presented two to three times a year by the unions' EEO Committee, this showcase offers local members in good standing the opportunity to showcase themselves in nonstereotypical fashion to area producers, agents, and directors. Showcases are announced on the AFTRA/SAG hotline and in union newsletters.

Theatre Bay Area (see *Other Associations,* p. 149). Annual regional auditions are attended by numerous Bay Area theatres. Equity, eligible, and experienced nonunion actors may participate. Dates and sign-up information are announced in *Callboard.*

AGENTS AND CASTING DIRECTORS

In only ten years, San Francisco has gone from being a two-agency town to having somewhere in the neighborhood of twenty talent agents and casting companies. Finding out which agencies and casting companies are the best and the busiest isn't difficult; just ask around. In 1991, there were fifteen SAG-franchised agencies, thirteen of which were also franchised by AFTRA; half a dozen were franchised by Equity as well (though agents rarely handle theatre except for some of the touring shows that come to town). It's probably not hard to get an agent here, especially since signing an exclusive agreement isn't necessary. Finding an agent that really goes to bat for nonexclusive actors, however, is another matter, and a source of much dissatisfaction and complaint. Several years ago there was an agent-initiated trend toward exclusivity. More recently, flexibility has crept back into the system; however, quite a few actors are reconsidering the benefits of exclusive representation, the thinking being that agents are likely to work harder for signed talent. Of course, it's also possible that increased exclusivity will make getting an agent more difficult.

It's very necessary to have an agent (or agents) if you want to work in film and broadcast; most casting directors are too busy to call actors directly. Agented actors should send P&Rs (and follow-up material) to casting directors for their files. Unagented actors are certainly welcome to send them in; it may not do any good, but it can't hurt, and some actors recommend sending postcards or fliers and occasionally dropping by the office. Nancy Hayes Casting handles a lot of extra (as well as principal) casting; interested actors can register with her office between the hours of 11 a.m. and 4 p.m. weekdays. Bring a snapshot and a headshot.

THEATRE

During the '60s and '70s, San Francisco was known for nurturing theatre that was new and exciting. Here's where several of Sam Shepard's plays were developed; here's where the San Francisco Mime Troupe (with roots in the '50s) was born; here's where the American Conservatory Theatre settled down for good. As the years went by, the theatre community expanded, its members grew a little older, and the bad-for-the-arts '80s came along. Though no fewer than four of the city's major Off-Broadway-type theatres closed their doors in the last decade, most have survived. If, in their maturity, their offerings are slightly less brash or "cutting-edge" than they once were, each theatre retains a distinct identity. In the meantime, new companies have been born to carry on with the riskier business; the early '90s, in fact, indicate a reemergence of the different and the daring. (In fact, San Francisco is unusual in that some members of the theatre community complain that local critics are biased in favor of the experimental and avant garde, and go out of their way to pan more traditional presentations!) Finding space, however, grows increasingly difficult, even though in the '80s several more affordable spaces became available as a result of the revitalization of parts of the once-blighted area known as South of Market.

Whatever the social and economic climate, it seems, the acting community continues its love affair with the stage, and a lot of theatre happens in the Bay Area. The premiere LORT theatre, A.C.T., has been joined in stature by the Berkeley Repertory Theatre. Then there are the California Shakespeare Festival, the San Francisco Shakespeare Festival, and San Jose Repertory Company. It was never easy to get work at A.C.T., which tends to cast out of town (and to bring in young actors from the theatre's training program). Unfortunately, the same can now be said of most of the LORT companies, many of which do some casting out of town and hold local per-show auditions on invitation-only bases.

At the next level of the hierarchy are Bay Area Theatre Contract companies, led by the Magic Theatre and the Eureka Theatre. The BAT contract is also used by companies like the San Jose Stage Company and the Marin Shakespeare Festival. Numerous other companies—some old, some new, some Equity, some not—round out the scene, representing a wide range of styles and sensibilities.

Monologues are a favored method of auditioning here. Most auditions are by appointment, although in 1991 some companies started holding open calls. Either way, if you don't get a slot, go the day of the audition and ask to be put on a waiting list. Noneligible actors can go to Equity calls and ask to be seen if there's time.

The Bay Area can be a good place to build up credits and play good roles. This doesn't mean, however, that it's easy to break in, especially at the higher levels, and it's probably not the easiest place to get an Equity card. In the early '80s, when the number of Equity theatres could be counted on a woodcarver's hand, local actors, tired of working for no pay, formed the Bay Area Theatre Workers Association. BATWA has all but faded into the sunset, but it served an important purpose, for eventually San Francisco was made an Equity office city, and most of the established theatres were brought into the union. A Bay Area Theatre (BAT) Contract was created, as was the Bay Area Project Policy, an agreement somewhat akin to New York's Showcase code. BAPP primarily is used on a per-show basis and doesn't always require that salaries be paid, making it possible for Equity actors to work with small, seat-of-the-pants companies. With LORT, BAT, and Guest Artist contracts, along with BAPP and LOAs, then, most theatres that endure for any length of time have some relationship with Equity. Non-Equity actors can and do work (and get paid) at these theatres without necessarily getting their cards. For completely nonunion productions, a contract created by BATWA is available though rarely used.

The touring musicals that come into presenting houses do some local casting, though not enough to keep musical theatre actors very busy. There are locally-produced musicals, but the major theatres don't do them. The zany *Beach Blanket Babylon,* which after nearly two decades is a San Francisco institution, has kept some musical theatre actors very steadily employed. There are several cabaret stages, although the health of that market seems to fluctuate every few years, and the area has a solid history of supporting stand-up comedy and improv.

▌▌▌▌FILM AND TELEVISION

Despite its attractiveness as a location spot, the Bay Area doesn't get loads of film and TV production. The San Francisco Film and Video Commission has made efforts to attract producers, however, and there are those who say production is on an upswing. San Francisco is popular for its unique look, while the surrounding areas can stand in for any number of locales.

Still, local actors can't count on television and theatrical film to keep them busy. KQED, the local PBS station, occasionally produces dramatic programming, and the area gets an occasional pilot and several features each year (including hometown girl Danielle Steel's novels-into-TV-movies, when they happen). When production comes, most of the casting is done in L.A., leaving extra and day-player roles to be filled locally. In general, it's only in films that shoot entirely in the Bay Area that locals play featured roles. There are some bright spots, though, including the fact that San Francisco is often a stop when there are national searches for soaps and films. There's very little TV work, although in 1991, the pilot "Bay City Stories" cast all but five roles here. "Midnight Caller," in residence for several years, did a great deal of local casting.

As in most theatre-oriented cities, strong stage actors get many of the film and television auditions; some people say the same handful of actors auditions over and over, while everyone else has a hard time getting seen for the screen. Agents do get the L.A. breakdowns and make submissions, and tapes occasionally get sent. But L.A. is nearly four hundred miles away, and it's extremely rare that a screen career is launched from the Bay Area.

▌▌▌▌CORPORATE AND COMMERCIALS

With several major corporations headquartered in the Bay Area, the commercial and corporate markets are quite strong. Recession notwithstanding (certainly Silicon Valley has seen better days), corporate production has remained many Bay Area actors' bread and butter. Actual production may be down slightly at the time of this writing, and the nonunion market has increased. But while some 85 percent of union industrials are produced under AFTRA contracts, SAG industrials earnings were up slightly in 1990. (AFTRA earnings data were unavailable.) For union work, it's best to have an agent (or agents), since some corporations go right to the agencies, bypassing casting directors. There are several companies, however, that accept P&Rs directly from actors, so the unagented aren't completely out of luck; in fact, industrials may be the only film/broadcast market in which it's possible to get cast without having an agent.

The local and regional commercial markets are quite strong. At least 90 percent of union spots are under SAG contracts, and for 1990, the Bay Area had the fifth-highest SAG commercial earnings of cities in this book. Some growth is indicated in the national market; the area is favored as a commercial test market, and popular for automobile advertising, half-hour-long "infomercials," and production for Asian/Pacific-Rim markets. Extreme character types may not find a great deal of work, although some have managed to carve out niches for themselves. Comedy and improv have always been popular in San Francisco, and local ad agencies do a fair amount of casting from comedy troupes and stand-up clubs.

CASTING DIVERSITY

The Bay Area, with its history of social activism and progressive politics and its increasingly diverse population, has been in the forefront of the nontraditional casting movement. A 1987 regional symposium increased local awareness, and while there's progress yet to be made, the situation is better here than in many places. Companies like the San Francisco Mime Troupe (a grandparent of sociopolitical/street/multicultural theatre), TheatreWorks, Thick Description, and New Traditions are committed practitioners of casting diversity. Other theatres practice nontraditional casting with varying degrees of success.

Actors with disabilities have appeared on one or two of the major stages. Some theatres have good records of casting ethnic minority actors, although there have been complaints that those actors are rarely cast in anything but very small or ethnically-specific roles. There has been increasing interest in the work of Asian American playwrights due, probably, to the area's increasing Asian population. San Francisco has long had a large Chinese population; the more recent influx of Southeast Asians has brought the Asian population to 29 percent of the 1990 total.

The area supports a number of constituent-specific theatres including the Lorraine Hansberry Theatre, A Travelling Jewish Theatre, Asian American Theatre, Teatro de la Esperanza, and Turtle Bay Ensemble, a still-young

American Indian company. Theatre Rhinoceros presents work on gay and lesbian themes, and throughout the years there have been several women's companies as well as companies of disabled actors and dancers.

Some local agents and casting directors believe they have quite a bit of freedom here to submit the best actor of any kind for a given role. The best film/broadcast market for ethnically diverse casting is corporate, which tends to reflect the work force for which it's produced. Still, although progress has been seen in that market as well as in commercials, there isn't as much diverse casting as one might expect to find in the Bay Area. The voice-over market hasn't really opened up to women, but many area corporations have made conscious efforts to utilize women as on-camera narrators, and Asian and black actors appear to be working more frequently in commercials and industrials.

ADDITIONAL OPPORTUNITIES

Kaiser Permanente Educational Theatre Program, P.O. Box 12916, Oakland, CA 94604, 510-596-1000. This hospital produces health education programs; non-Equity actors work full-time throughout the school year. Auditions are announced in *Callboard;* you can also send a P&R.

New Traditions Theatre Company, 1610 Martin Luther King Jr. Way, Berkeley, CA 94707. Actors interested in participating in monthly play readings can send P&Rs to this company dedicated to developing multicultural theatre.

Performing Arts Workshop, Fort Mason Center, Landmark Building C, Room 265, San Francisco, CA 94123-1382, 673-2634. This is a nonprofit organization with several performing arts programs, including Artists in Schools and Theater for Elders. Salaried nonunion jobs are announced in *Callboard, Dance Bay Area,* and the *Bay Guardian,* or send a P&R and cover letter.

Pier 39, P.O. Box 193730, San Francisco, CA 94119-3730, 981-8030. The annual Street Performers Festival (June) presents mimes, jugglers, and comedians. The December Croon-Alike Contest searches for someone who can sing like Bing. Proceeds from both events benefit local organizations.

Playwrights' Center of San Francisco, 3225 Laguna Street, No. 3, San Francisco, CA 94123, 763-2727. "Dedicated to the creation, development and production of new stage works," the Center sponsors readings and an annual play contest, "DramaRama." Auditions are held twice each year. The group meets every Friday night at Fort Mason (Blue Bear, Building D, 2nd Floor); interested actors may attend; bring a P&R.

The Playwrights' Foundation, P.O. Box 460357, San Francisco, CA 94146-0357, 777-2996. Auditions for this annual summer festival of new play readings and/or productions are announced in *Callboard* and on the Equity hotline.

San Francisco Bay Revels, 2531 9th Street, Berkeley, CA 94710, 510-841-6628. Equity and non-Equity actors can appear as mummers in the annual Christmas Revels. Auditions are announced in *Callboard,* or send your P&R and ask to be put on the audition mailing list.

School Tours. A number of theatres, including Berkeley Rep, Berkeley Shakespeare, and San Jose Rep, have companies that tour schools.

Student Film. Write to San Francisco State University Department of Cinema, Attn: *Actors Book,* 1600 Holloway Avenue, San Francisco, CA 94132, 338-2466. Send a P&R for inclusion in the *Actors Book,* which is kept on file to be used by student filmmakers.

■■■■■■TRAINING

It should come as no surprise that there's training aplenty in the Bay Area, including college and university programs, theatre institutes, private schools, and individual teachers. Training is available in a variety of acting techniques, in acting for the camera, in movement, voice, speech, and audition skills, and there are some very highly-regarded teachers. A.C.T.'s programs (the Young Conservatory, the Academy, and the Summer Training Congress) attract students from all over the country. The Jean Shelton Actors Lab has been training actors for over twenty years. Each of these schools has a distinctive flavor, and there are people who have strong opinions—some favorable, some not—about either or both. Theatres like the Eureka, the Asian American, and Marin Theatre Company offer classes; many more private schools and instructors are listed in *Callboard*.

CERTIFICATE/DEGREE PROGRAMS

American Conservatory Theatre, 450 Geary Street, San Francisco, CA 94102,749-2350.

City College of San Francisco, Drama Department, 50 Phelan Avenue, San Francisco, CA 94112, 239-3132.

San Francisco State University, Department of Theatre Arts, 1600 Holloway Avenue, San Francisco, CA 94132, 338-1341.

University of California, Berkeley, Dramatic Art/Dance Department, 101 Dwinelle Annex, Berkeley, CA 94720, 510-642-1677.

■■■■■■AFFORDABLE ARTS

San Francisco Ticket Box Office Service (STUBS), 433-STBS. Half-price day-of-performance tickets are sold at the following locations:

- Union Square, Stockton Street across from Maiden Lane;
- Embarcadero One, street level, near Battery and Sacramento Streets.

Theatre Bay Area. Participating theatres, listed in *Callboard,* offer discounted tickets; customers must show a TBA membership card.

San Francisco Shakespeare Festival, Golden Gate Park, Liberty Tree Meadow. Free shows run every Saturday and Sunday at 1:30 during late summer. Bring a picnic and something to sit on; arrive about an hour ahead of time.

Equity Hotline (see *Talent Unions,* p. 149). The hotline sometimes announces free or discounted tickets for Equity members.

Ushering. Here's another free-viewing option; call theatres directly for information.

■■■■■■■ RESOURCES

LIBRARIES

Performing Arts Library and Museum (see *Libraries,* p. 148). PALM's archival collection includes "both national and international holdings, but focuses principally on . . . the San Francisco Bay Area."

Theatre Bay Area (see *Other Associations,* p. 149) has a library of theatre-related material and some scripts, available to members.

BOOKSTORES

Drama Books, 134 9th Street, San Francisco, CA 94103, 255-0604.

Limelight Film and Theatre Books, 1803 Market Street, San Francisco, CA 94103, 864-2265.

A Show Business, 1975 Diamond Boulevard, Concord, CA 94520, 510-671-3390.

Cody's, 2454 Telegraph Avenue, Berkeley, CA 94704, 510-845-7852. Though not specifically a theatre bookstore, Cody's has a respectable selection of scripts.

■■■■■■■ NETWORKING AND SOCIALIZING

Newcomers would be wise to join Theatre Bay Area (see *Professional Associations,* p. 149) or at least subscribe to *Callboard.* Participating in TBA's twice-yearly general auditions is a good way to get seen by area theatres. Bay Area actors like to study, and classes provide a way to meet people in the community. Doing volunteer work at a theatre is another networking option; just don't expect it to lead right to the stage.

S E A T

If you're old enough, you may remember the TV series "Here Come the Brides," whose theme song sang the praises of a place with "the bluest sky you ever seen . . . and . . . hills the greenest green."[1] That show was set during a time when men were lumberjacks, women mail-order brides, and Seattle barely a city. Nowadays, women looking for husbands go to Alaska, but less than a hundred years since Seattle became a gateway to the North and Far East, the city is a boom town again, drawing more newcomers (or so it seems) every year. Anyone who's been a Seattleite for at least five years claims the right to gripe about the phenomenon; some reserve their harshest epithets for people who, weary of overcrowded, polluted Southern California, migrate northward to overcrowd and pollute Seattle. Of course, not all the newcomers come from California; they also come from the north, the east, and farther east: Cambodia, Thailand, Viet Nam.

Civilians aren't the only ones flocking to Seattle: plenty of actors, betting that this will be the next Chicago (theatre-wise, that is), have made the move as well. But Seattle, stuck up in a corner of the country, has neither the population not the resources to make a Chicago-sized splash. Make no mistake: as a theatre town, Seattle is a player, but while it's probably safe to say that Seattle theatre has already come into its own, outsiders may continue to think of the region as up-and-coming—and Seattle actors, smiling all the way to rehearsal, will think that's just fine.

FAST FACTS

1990 CENSUS
516,259 (+4.5%)

COUNTY
King

TIME
Zone: Pacific
Telephone: 555-TIME (8463)

AREA CODE
206

INFORMATION OFFICE
Vance Hotel
666 Stewart Street
Seattle, WA 98102
461-5840

INFORMATION
SEA-TAC International Airport
Seattle, WA
Lower Concourse (Across from baggage carousels 1 and 9)
433-4679
433-5218

SEATTLE-KING COUNTY CONVENTION AND VISITORS BUREAU
520 Pike Street, Suite 1300
Seattle, WA 98101
461-5800

Of course, they come for more than just theatre. They come for the comparatively sane lifestyle and reasonable costs of living (which have been affected adversely, though not yet drastically, by the increasing population); they come for the greenery, the mountains, the water, even the coffee, all of which are inspiringly abundant. In his book *Hunting Mr. Heartbreak,* Jonathan Raban says he found "an extraordinarily soft and pliant city. People who come to Seattle could somehow recast it in the image of home, arranging the city around themselves like so many pillows on a bed."[2] But if Seattle sounds like an American Shangri-La, a few words of warning: the secret's been out for quite a while. Prices, freeway traffic, and tensions have increased along with the population. And as a theatre town, well, it's like other theatre towns: right for some, not-so-right for others.

RECOMMENDED READING
Jon Bowermaster, "Seattle—Too Much of a Good Thing?," *New York Times Magazine,* (January 6, 1991).

Theresa Morrow, *Seattle Survival Guide* (Seattle: Sasquatch Books, 1990). Here is an impressive, astonishingly comprehensive guide to everything about living in Seattle.

MOVIES
The Fabulous Baker Boys (1989), *It Happened at the World's Fair* (1963), *Say Anything* (1989)

■■■■■ POPULATION

The 1990 census may not reflect a dramatically increasing population, but ask some Seattle-ites, and you'll get a St. Helens-like response. After all, the population has been increasing steadily for several decades now.

■■■■■ CLIMATE

Seattle is as famous for rain as it is for the Space Needle and Mount Rainier. The funny thing, though, is that the city actually gets little more rain annually than many other cities. There's a lot of drizzle, however, so what local precipitation lacks in quantity, it makes up in constancy. People who thrive on sunshine, who find gray skies oppressive, may not do well here. On the other hand, all that moisture makes for lush springtimes, whose explosive colors and fragrances thrive even under overcast, threatening skies. With a rainy season that can last a good eight to ten months a year, the surrounding mountains are often shrouded in mist. On clear days, when the sky is a brilliant, clear blue, locals say "the mountain's out," meaning they can see nearby Mount Rainier. Despite all the dampness, Seattle enjoys relatively moderate temperatures, and few extremes. Almost every winter, however, sees one big, brutal snowstorm for which everyone is less than prepared; caught unawares, the city comes to a screeching (albeit snow-muffled) halt. *For weather information call:* 728-RAIN (7246).

NORMAL TEMPERATURES	Average Daily High	Average Daily Low
January	45°	36°
July	75°	56°

TEMPERATURE EXTREMES

Maximum Temp.	Annual No. of Days	Minimum Temp.	Annual No. of Days
90° and above	2	32° and below	18
32° and below	2	0° and below	—

NORMAL WEATHER CONDITIONS

Clear	Partly Cloudy	Cloudy
71	93	201

ANNUAL PRECIPITATION	Days	Inches
All Precipitation	151	36
Snowfall	NA	8

■ TRANSPORTATION

Like Rome, Seattle was built on seven hills. Bordered by Puget Sound to the west and Lake Washington to the east, the city lies on several juts of land that fit together like puzzle pieces amid a jumble of lakes, bays, rivers, islands, and peninsulas. Despite all the topography, navigating the city isn't particularly difficult. People get in and out of the various neighborhoods by bus and car, and most of the more commercial areas, once you're there, are quite doable by foot: the downtown area, for example, is completely walkable. (Don't cross against the light, however—you could get ticketed.) Most avenues run north-south, most streets, east-west. Beyond the downtown area, streets have directional prefixes and suffixes; the system, however, isn't entirely consistent, so until you really know your way around, check maps and pay close attention to those prefixes and suffixes.

PUBLIC TRANSPORTATION

Metro Transit. It's funny: though the American Public Transit Association has voted Metro the top transit system in the nation, a lot of Seattle residents stick to their cars. Still, most agree that the system isn't at all bad and will get you almost anywhere—it just might take a while. All bus routes lead to downtown, which serves as the system hub; the newish Metro Tunnel, which gets buses underground and off downtown streets, eases some congestion and speeds things up a little. Much of the fleet, by the way, is made up of nonpolluting electric buses. In total, it includes buses, monorail, and waterfront streetcar. *For information call:* 553-3000; 684-1739 (TDD); 624-PASS (Pass sales); 553-3060 (disabled/senior reduced fare permit).

Schedules and passes are available at
- Westlake Tunnel Mezzanine, underground at 4th and Pine;
- Exchange Building, 821 2nd Avenue at Marion.

Passes are also sold at Seafirst Bank cash machines; schedules are available on buses and at libraries, shopping centers, 7-Eleven Stores, and Bartell Drugs.

Fares are based on a two-zone, peak/off-peak system. Zone 1 trips are those within city limits, Zone 2 go beyond, and peak fares are slightly higher than off-peak. Exact fare is necessary, and dollar bills are accepted. When heading toward downtown, pay as you board; when riding away from downtown, pay as you exit. Transfers are free and can be used several times within a designated period of time. There are discounts for students, seniors, and the disabled, and children under five ride free. Numerous pass options, including weekend and holiday fares, are available. Best of all is the downtown Ride Free Area, where rides are gratis between 4:00 a.m. and 9:00 p.m. every day (this does not apply to the Waterfront Streetcar or the Monorail).

The following is a list of terminals and additional transportation systems:
Amtrak, King Street Station, King Street and 3rd Avenue S., Seattle, WA, 464-1930.
Greyhound, 8th Avenue and Stewart Street, Seattle, WA, 624-3456.

TAXIS

Taxis are hardly a way of life for most Seattleites. Street hailing rarely bears fruit; better to call for a cab or try in front of one of the big hotels. Taxis are metered.

DRIVING

Living within city limits it's possible, if not always convenient, to make do on Metro buses. Most actors, however, find they need cars for coming home from the theatre late at night, and for getting to and from production houses and theatres in Tacoma and even Spokane. Still, with local traffic increasing and parking often hard to find, your best bet may be to have a car but use buses as often as possible. Driving downtown, where parking is nearly impossible, is usually a mistake; the commercial parts of Queen Anne (especially around Seattle Center), Capitol Hill, and the University District are also parking trouble spots. Some merchants participate in the Easy Street Token program in which customers spending a minimum of $20 receive a token that can be traded for discount parking or free metro rides.

A number of actors consider themselves part of what is laughingly called the "I-5 Repertory"—those who work in cities along Interstate 5: Seattle, Portland, Ashland, San Francisco (requiring a slight detour), all the way down, in some cases, to L.A. and San Diego. Of course, you can do that by train; the Seattle-Portland run takes only about four hours.

◼◼◼◼ HOUSING AND COSTS OF LIVING

The population growth of recent years, not surprisingly, has had an adverse affect on the very thing that attracts so many people to Seattle: readily-available, decent, affordable housing. The situation hasn't reached crisis level, but things aren't what they used to be, when the mere mention of the size and cost of a Seattleite's home could send a New Yorker into a frenzy. Some of the lovelier and more conveniently-located neighborhoods like Queen Anne, once quite reasonable, are now out of reach for many people. The market appears to be stabilizing, however, and it's possible, if one is persistent, to find housing in areas like Beacon Hill, youthful Capitol Hill, and family-oriented West Seattle. The competition for moderately-priced houses and apartments means hunters should check the Sunday *Times* when it comes out on Saturday.

INTERAREA SHELTER INDEXES	Renters	Owners
Seattle	86	93
(Philadelphia)	(100)	(100)

COSTS OF LIVING

Total average annual expenditures	$30,915
Food at home	2,644
Telephone	607
Gas and motor oil	986
Public transportation	453
Personal care products and services	354

███████ EMPLOYMENT

1989 Average Annual Pay
Seattle-Tacoma: $23,608

1990 Average Unemployment Rates
Washington: 4.9%
Seattle metropolitan statistical area: 3.5%

1990 Average Weekly Unemployment Benefits
Washington: $169.12

███████ CRIME

Seattle may not be quite as laid-back as some people think. Increased crime rates are to be expected with an increased population. Unfortunately, that population now reportedly includes Los Angeles gang members. In 1990, among cities included in this book for which statistics are available, Seattle had the second lowest murder rate; the numbers of burglaries and rapes, however, were at the high end of the scale. And despite a low incidence of aggravated assault, there have been gay-bashing incidents, primarily in the Capitol Hill area. Drug trafficking has also increased.

Seattleites probably worry less about crime and personal safety than do the inhabitants of, say, New York or Los Angeles, although the chances of being the victim of some kind of crime (violent or property) are actually greater here. Perhaps the relative lack of worry stems from the fact that crime here seems less random, more localized. Perhaps there's a certain comfort that comes with seeing police patrolling on mountain bikes. Keep in mind that popular areas like Pioneer Square and Pike Place Market—in fact, most of downtown Seattle—which bustle with activity during the day and evening, get real spooky late at night.

1990 CRIME RATES	Violent	Property
Total Crimes	7,780	57,542
Crimes per 100,000 People	1,507	11,146
Average 1 Crime per Every	66 people	9 people

■■■■■■■ MISCELLANEA

NEWSPAPERS

Seattle Post-Intelligencer (morning)
The Seattle Times (evening)
Seattle Weekly
News/Herald (weekly)

LIBRARY

Seattle Public Library, Main Branch, 1000 4th Avenue, Seattle, WA 98104,
    386-4683.

POST OFFICE

Main Branch, 301 Union at 3rd Street, Seattle, WA, 442-6340.

THE BUSINESS

People are always looking for the next best thing, right? When the word got out that Seattle was a great place to live, many actors, sick of or uninterested in living the tough life in New York or the weird life in L.A., took their pictures and résumés and headed northwest. Two things happened: Seattle gained national recognition as a theatre town, and Seattle grew overcrowded with actors. Today, despite an acting community filled with transplants, some say there's always room for more, especially in the still-growing, ever-changing fringe theatre scene. Others, eager to be in on the *next* big thing, think the torch has already been passed to Portland, which today hints at being where Seattle was several years ago.

There's no doubt that the Northwest is currently hot: witness the "Twin Peaks" and "Northern Exposure" (set in Alaska, but filmed near Seattle) trend of the early '90s, the popularity of Northwest writers and artists, even all those winding-mountain-road car commercials. Seattle, with friendlier-to-the-dollar British Columbia practically in its backyard, may never be a production hot spot, but it enjoys a certain small popularity. Most important, however, look to the area's theatre scene. Seattle-Tacoma has about a dozen Equity theatres, and some major Broadway shows have been developed here. In less than half a dozen years, the fringe scene has flourished, with small, mostly non-Equity companies multiplying by about a thousand percent—no kidding. But while theatrical activity has increased, so has the competition, and there are those who wish Seattle had a big door they could close to keep newcomers out. The theatre actors who stay busiest are those who work the entire Northwest, or even the entire coast, and Seattle can be a place to make the connections that lead to theatres in Alaska, Oregon, and California.

RECOMMENDED READING

Misha Berson, "A Tale of Two Cities," *The Seattle Times/Seattle Post-Intelligencer* (May 26, 1991).

Wayne Johnson, "Talent, energy and new ideas star in Seattle's many fringe theatres," *The Seattle Times/Seattle Post-Intelligencer* (June 10, 1990).

Ellen Taft, ed., *The Actor's Handbook* (Seattle: Capitol Hill Press, Inc., 1991). Written by a team of local actors, the *Handbook* is an invaluable resource for performers in Seattle and Portland; updated supplements are published periodically. Exclusively available in Seattle at The Play's the Thing (see *Resources,* p. 173); also at Powell's in Portland, in New York and L.A., and by mail from Capitol Hill Press, P.O. Box 12222, Seattle, WA 98102-0222.

■■■■■ PROFESSIONAL ASSOCIATIONS

TALENT UNIONS

Actors' Equity Association (AEA), Liaison City.
Members: 407

American Federation of Television and Radio Artists (AFTRA), 601 Valley Street, No. 200, Seattle, WA 98109, 282-2506.
Members: 979

Screen Actors' Guild (SAG). Caretaker city; see AFTRA office.
Members: N/A

American Guild of Musical Artists (AGMA), 5051 148th Avenue N.E., J-21, Bellevue, WA 98007, 282-0804, 881-7235.

OTHER ASSOCIATIONS

The Goliath Project, P.O. Box 31612, Seattle, WA 98103, 547-6331. This membership organization, dedicated to furthering better understanding of Middle Eastern arts and issues, produces a play a year. Those interested in acting and/or joining can call or send a P&R.

League of Fringe Theatres (LOFT), 1710 37th Avenue, Seattle, WA 98122, 328-4321. This nonprofit membership corporation is "dedicated to

bringing the experience of fringe theatre to a wider public." Its
activities include the Annual Seattle Fringe Theatre Festival. Individual
members receive discount admission at member theatres, audition
priority at LOFT generals, a newsletter, and discounts on workshops.

Seattle's Loosely Affiliated Physical Performers (SLAPP), 5628 20th Avenue
N.E., Seattle, WA 98105, 525-8367. SLAPP is a networking organization
for physical theatre performers, offering resources and support via
monthly meetings/master classes, a newsletter, and more. Members
also have access to a mailing list and bulk mailing permit.

The Actor's Handbook lists additional associations.

■■■■■ LOOKING FOR WORK

PUBLICATIONS

There is no local trade paper. The following newspapers are worth
checking, although none are complete sources of audition information.

Seattle Post-Intelligencer. See the Friday "Auditions" column.

Seattle Weekly. See the "Callboard" column.

Seattle Times. See the Thursday classifieds.

HOTLINES

Equity (see *Talent Unions,* p. 165).

League of Fringe Theatres (LOFT), 637-7373 (see *Other Associations,*
p. 165).

BULLETIN BOARDS AND BINDERS

The Play's the Thing (see *Resources,* p. 173); *AFTRA* (see *Talent Unions,*
p. 165). Bulletin boards at both places have announcements and a few
audition notices.

TALENT BOOKS AND TALENT BANKS

Contact Seattle, c/o LOFT, 1710 37th Avenue, Seattle, WA 98122,
323-4321. Jonathan Harris maintains a picture and résumé file that is
made available to theatres and producing organizations. Send a P&R
with a letter designating what category you should be in. Harris
founded both LOFT and Contact Seattle, which may be merged into
one organization.

TALENT SHOWCASES AND COMBINED AUDITIONS

Northwest Drama Conference. (For address, see Appendix B.)

Regional Equity Actors (REACT). REACT sponsors local auditions for
regional theatres across the country; participating actors pay a low fee
to cover the cost of bringing casting/artistic directors to Seattle.

League of Fringe Theatres (LOFT). Twice-yearly general auditions for LOFT theatres are announced on the LOFT hotline.

TALENT AGENTS AND CASTING DIRECTORS

There was a time, they say, when a decent-or-better theatre actor could get signed with an agent without too much trouble. Times have changed, competition has grown fierce, and it's no longer quite so easy. Actors sign exclusively with agents, and since each agent handles all areas (except theatre), one is all that's needed.

Some agencies are known for having carved out a particular niche or having a certain work style. To learn who's who, ask other actors; ask casting directors who they work with. If you can't get signed with one of the two or three top agencies, try the others. Be sure, however, to get the word of mouth on any nonfranchised agent you're considering signing with. If you have no luck at all, despair not: there are actors here who manage to work in film and broadcast *sans* agents. It's probably more difficult, but unagented actors can market themselves directly to casting directors. Unless they're just too busy, many casting directors (and again, there are a top two or three) will call unagented actors directly. Casting directors, like agents, rarely work in theatre, although theatres may contact them when they have difficulty casting a role.

THEATRE

Presenting houses aside, Seattle's theatre hierarchy is topped by LORT theatres Seattle Repertory Theatre (a Tony Award winner that has premiered some Broadway-bound plays), Intiman Theatre, Fifth Avenue Musical Theatre, and A Contemporary Theatre (ACT). Next come SPT and LOA companies like Tacoma Actor's Guild, the Empty Space, Bellevue Repertory Theatre, Seattle Shakespeare Festival, Seattle Group Theatre, The Bathhouse Theatre, Center Stage, and New City Theatre. Some of these formerly small, struggling companies are now bigger, better-established, struggling companies.

While many of the major theatres develop and produce new plays, dependence on grant and subscriber dollars makes risk-taking a little, well, risky. Of course, that's not unique to Seattle. What is unique is the absolute explosion of what is known as fringe theatre, which consists of dozens of small companies, most of which are non-Equity, although a few use Guest Artist contracts or LOAs. The development of the fringe theatre scene has resulted in increased opportunities for non-Equity actors, and it's probably easier (though not necessarily easy) to break into non-Equity than into Equity theatres. However, while Equity actors have been unable to appear in most fringe productions, in December 1991, national Equity Council approved on a year-long trial basis an umbrella plan that brings a number of nonunion theatres under the auspices of a single producer of record for the purpose of hiring Equity actors.There's no official definition of fringe theatre, but if you strike out the Equity Contract theatres, community theatres, and the non-Equity commercial houses, what you're left with is mostly fringe. Fringe theatre isn't necessarily experimental or political, though some of it is. While the movement keeps growing and there's a feeling that anything can happen, finding appropriate, affordable space gets increasingly difficult. Auditions for fringe theatres may be announced on the LOFT hotline, in the newspapers, and by word of mouth.

In the early '90s, Seattle's Equity membership increased by about one third in less than two years. So many actors have come here that, despite a supportive, friendly atmosphere, it can be hard to break in. The major theatres hire locally, but do more out-of-town casting than local actors would like. It's rough on newcomers, and even on many who are no longer so new. (Although if you come from the Twin Cities, you might feel right at home. There's been enough of a migration that some Seattleites complain you have to be from Minneapolis to get cast here!) Not long ago, an Equity actor new to Seattle could call Equity houses and arrange to do a couple of monologues. That's less common these days, making it important to attend the theatres' annual general auditions. (Noneligible performers are seen as time permits.) Try to time your arrival in Seattle so that you don't miss the generals at those companies that interest you the most; for information, contact the theatres or check *The Actor's Handbook,* which includes an audition schedule. (And prepare some monologues, which are a favored method of auditioning here.)

REACT (stands for Regional Equity Actors) Auditions offer eligible performers a wonderful opportunity to audition for regional theatres around the country. Artistic directors come in for a couple days of auditions; participating actors pay a small fee to cover travel expenses. REACT and Equity theatre general auditions are announced on the Equity hotline (sometimes inaccurately called the REACT hotline).

Musical theatre actors have more opportunity in nonunion and community theatre. There aren't a lot of Equity musicals around, although the numbers have increased, and the imports sometimes hire a few local actors; cabaret, open to everyone, is also popular.

Seattle audiences are fairly sophisticated. This is a city of literate folk, people who, it's said, would rather read a book than watch TV. People who go kayaking and mountain climbing one weekend might well go to see a play the next.

FILM AND TELEVISION

Washington is a reasonably popular location state and, for several years now, local actors have been able to count on a nice little handful of films coming in to shoot. Principals, of course, are cast before production arrives, but locals work as day players and (usually nonunion) extras, and there's almost always an actor or two who ends up with, if not a really meaty part, a good two or three weeks' work. Every so often, film features shooting in Vancouver, B.C. and Portland (an increasingly popular production site) do some casting in Seattle. In addition, local agents subscribe to the breakdowns from L.A. and make submissions accordingly, though only rarely does anything come of it.

The early '90s are a time of flux and transition for Washington's film and video markets. While state and local politics and budgetary crises have some people worried, others think the state will emerge stronger than before. The successes of two notable television series gives some people reason for hope. "Twin Peaks" certainly gave the region a boost. True, only the pilot was shot locally (the diner, the lodge, and the waterfall are less than an hour from Seattle), but when the show headed to L.A., several local actors went along to be series regulars. "Northern Exposure" came next and settled in for a while. Set in Alaska but headquartered in Bellevue (just across Lake Washington from Seattle) and on location in nearby Roslyn, WA, the show has utilized quite a few local actors as day players and guest stars; one local is a series regular. Seattle also has its own local comedy show. An ensemble effort, "Almost Live" (patterned after guess which national Saturday night show), hires additional actors as needed.

Seattle gets a few national searches for soap operas each year, as well as its share of reality-based programming shoots. But actors here don't count on television; rather, it's wonderful when it comes along and even better if it stays put for a while. Whether the current interest in this particular corner of the nation is infatuation or true love remains to be seen.

CORPORATE AND COMMERCIALS

Seattle's reasonable healthy corporate and commercial markets are pretty evenly split between union (primarily AFTRA) and nonunion production. (The region's largest employer, the Boeing Company, in fact, produces quite a lot of both union and nonunion training and industrial films and videos.) Throughout fluctuations in the corporate and commercial markets, a fair-to-middling number of Seattle actors have been able to support themselves working in front of the camera. Actors would do well to bring a P&R to each audition, making sure that commercial credits are listed on the résumé (it's wise, then, to have a separate theatre-legit film résumé).

The increasing use of comic and dramatic scripts has opened the corporate market to a wider range of "types" in recent years. Still, most work remains the province of the typical corporate spokesperson. While some producers hire independent CDs, others go right to agents. Agented or not, however, actors can contact some corporations and production companies directly. *The Actor's Handbook* lists those that accept P&Rs and tapes.

Although local and regional production keep the commercial market strong, a decent number of nationals shoot here, too; some people believe that the migration from southern California has helped strengthen the market, as industry people set down roots in and around Seattle. But location is the biggest draw for national spots, and when they come, they're often cast here. The popular commercial look has been described as "whitebread" and outdoorsy. Actors who can portray the Northwest "yuppie"—healthy and wholesome, dressed by Eddie Bauer, munching granola bars behind the wheel of a Saab—have the best shot. And with all those automobile ads, those who look like they belong in commercialdom's typical "car family" can do very nicely. The radio market has been strong for many years and will apparently stay that way. Here, as in so many places, about a half-dozen people (including a few women) do extremely well in voice-over.

■■■■■■CASTING DIVERSITY

Perhaps it's because Seattle has only a 25 percent ethnic minority population, but when it comes to having a real understanding of nontraditional casting issues, the city is a step or two behind several of the other cities included in this book. In the commercial and corporate markets, men may work twice as often as women except, perhaps, when it comes to doing voice-overs and spokespeople; surprisingly, in those still-male-dominated markets, women are making visible progress. Ethnic minority actors may fare pretty well in corporate production; in film and broadcast in general, black women probably do better than black men. But only a small percentage of local breakdowns actually specify ethnic minority actors, and those agents and casting directors that attempt more diverse casting are often told no.

"Northern Exposure" has meant some work for American Indian actors, many of whom live in Canada. The city's largest ethnic minority population is Asians and Pacific Islanders, including a lot of relatively recent immigrants from Southeast Asia. The Asian acting pool may be small, but it does exist.

Some fringe theatre companies are devoted to multiculturalism, as is the well-established Equity company, Seattle Group Theatre. There are just a few constituent-specific theatre companies in town, like the Northwest Asian American Theatre and The Alice B. Theatre; there are also two or three Christian ensembles, like Taproot Theatre Company.

Seattle's more established theatres, while supportive of the ethnic performing arts communities, tend to remain rather segregated. They do produce the occasional "black play," and cast black (mostly male, and often from out of town) actors in rather traditional roles. Most opportunities, however, are in fringe, and perhaps community, theatre. In the more established companies and the commercial theatres, opportunities come primarily with the every-so-often specifically-integrated or ethnic minority scripts.

Seattle does have a smaller minority acting pool than many cities, and a few ethnic minority actors do work steadily. But many leave Seattle because there just isn't enough work for them here. There is reason for some optimism, however: the city is an artistically fertile one, and many members of the acting community believe that, despite the problems, this is a place that will continue to grow and change. In Seattle, they believe, just about anything can happen.

ADDITIONAL OPPORTUNITIES

The Actor's Handbook is an excellent resource for further opportunities, including youth- and community-oriented teaching programs that employ professional performers.

Book It, c/o Pasqualini-Smith Studio, 919 E. Pike Street, Seattle, WA 98122, 632-7683. Book It is dedicated to "bringing fiction alive onstage [by performing] each story in its entirety, preserving all of the author's words." Send a P&R or call for further information.

Jackstraw Productions, 4261 Roosevelt Way N.W., Seattle, WA 98105-6999, 634-0919. This relatively new producer of radio drama accepts résumés and voice tapes from narrators and those with the ability to do different voices.

New City Theatre, 1634 11th Avenue, Seattle, WA 98122, 323-6801. This popular fringe theatre produces a Playwrights' Festival each fall and a Directors' Festival every spring. General auditions—one for each festival—are held twice a year. A lot goes on at New City, one of the oldest and most visible fringe theatres.

Northwest Playwrights Guild, P.O. Box 95259, Seattle, WA 98145,
    365-6026. The Guild's Playwrights-in-Progress project uses actor
    volunteers for staged readings. NWPG's other readings series and
    festivals are produced in conjunction with theatre companies in both
    Seattle and Portland. Anyone can join NWPG; actors interested in
    participating in readings can send a P&R.
Plays That Work, 1107 E. Republican, Seattle, WA 98102, 325-6801.
    Equity and non-Equity actors interested in participating in these
    plays dealing with social issues may send P&Rs; Program Director
    Carla Granat casts completely nontraditionally and frequently casts
    older actors.
Readings. Several theatres, including ACT and Seattle Rep, workshop
    new plays as part of the development process; let them know you're
    interested when you attend general auditions.

TRAINING

While there's no dearth of schools and teachers, some people say there's
a dearth of training, especially for experienced actors who want to do
some polishing or work out between jobs. Several casting directors teach
on-camera skills. By using the *Handbook* and networking with other
actors, it should be possible to find some quality acting and related-skills
classes. Since this is a theatre-oriented town, however, it's probably wise
to come with solid training already under one's belt.

CERTIFICATE/DEGREE PROGRAMS

Cornish College of the Arts, Theatre Department, 710 E. Roy Street, Seattle,
    WA 98102, 323-1400 Ext. 320.
University of Washington, School of Drama, DX-20, Seattle, WA 98195,
    543-5140.

AFFORDABLE ARTS

Ticket/Ticket, 324-2744. Half-price day-of-performance tickets are sold
    at two locations:
    • Broadway Market, 401 Broadway East
    • Pike Place Market Information Booth, 1st and Pike
Professional Discounts. A good number of Seattle theatres sell half-price
    or discount day-of-performance tickets to members of the performing
    community. *The Actor's Handbook* has a list, or call theatres directly.
Ushering. This is another option; again, call the theatres.

■ RESOURCES

LIBRARIES

Seattle Public Library, Main Branch, 1000 4th Avenue, Seattle, WA,
386-4683. The main branch of the public library has a pretty good
selection of plays, and often holds copies of currently auditioning
plays on reserve.

University of Washington Drama Library, Hutchinson Hall, Seattle, WA
98105, 543-5148.

BOOKSTORES

Cinema Books, 4753 Roosevelt Way N.E., Seattle, WA 98105, 547-7667.

The Elliott Bay Book Company, 101 So. Main Street, Seattle, WA 98104,
624-6000.

The Play's the Thing, Drama Bookstore, 514 E. Pike, Seattle, WA 98122,
322-PLAY. In Robin Kilrain's inviting place, actors can find plays and
theatre-related books, peruse New York, L.A., and San Francisco trade
publications in the upstairs lounge, and check the bulletin board for
auditions and announcements. A recessed area in the center of the
floor serves as a stage for informal play readings.

Tower Books, 20 Mercer Street, Seattle, WA 98109, 283-6333.

■ NETWORKING AND SOCIALIZING

Several fringe theatres are in the Capitol Hill area (Seattle's answer to
Greenwich Village), and the restaurants on and around Broadway are
filled with youthful, creative types, both seated at tables and serving food
and drink. Performers also stop in at:

The Play's the Thing (see *Resources,* above). Patrons sip coffee and read
the national trade papers in the upstairs lounge. The downstairs area is
available for informal readings.

---

[1]   *Seattle,* by Jack Keller, Hugo Montenegro, and Ernie Sheldon.
[2]   Jonathan Raban, *Hunting Mister Heartbreak: A Discovery of America* (New York:
      Edward Burlingame, HarperCollins, 1991).

W A S H I N G

There's an undercurrent of excitement in the District of Columbia—
something in the air. No matter how one feels about politics and
government, clearly there's a whole lot of movin' and shakin' goin' on.
From the imposing neoclassical architecture of the Supreme Court, the
Capitol, and the White House, to the quiet eloquence of the Vietnam
Veterans Memorial; from limo-ed diplomats to passels of press passes
swinging on chains 'round neck after neck;
from international powerbrokers to
international tourists lining up each day to
look at the Bill of Rights, Washington is
unique. Locals call it a one-company town;
some call it a troubled, decaying city "which
is sort of deteriorating in front of our eyes . . .
a very sad city."[1]

It is without question an international city,
and a transient one at that: many are called,
but just as many are called away, politics,
media, and foreign relations being what they
are. Covering an area of sixty-nine square
miles, the District is a fairly manageable
place, with a good mix of urban bustle and
neighborhood ambience. And while the
neighborhoods are many, the distinctions and
dividing lines aren't always terribly obvious.
Oh, you know when you're on Capitol Hill,
of course, and downtown is full of museums
and monuments and important-looking
buildings. But many of Washington's
primarily residential neighborhoods meld
easily from one to the other, and within each,
most shops and restaurants are clustered
along several streets and blocks.

You don't have to live in the District
to be a Washingtonian; many people do, of
course, but those who live nearby are

FAST FACTS

1990 CENSUS
606,900 (-4.9%)

COUNTY
District of Columbia

TIME
Zone: Eastern
Telephone: 844-2525

AREA CODES
202 (D.C.)
301 (Maryland)
703 (Virginia)
ALL PHONE NUMBERS IN THIS
CHAPTER USE THE 202 AREA CODE,
UNLESS OTHERWISE NOTED.

**VISITOR INFORMATION
CENTER**
1455 Pennsylvania Ave., NW
Washington, D.C.
789-7038

**WASHINGTON CONVENTION
AND VISITORS ASSOCIATION**
1212 New York Avenue, NW,
6th Floor
Washington, D.C. 20005
789-7000

174

Washingtonians, too. The fact is, all District suburbs are in neighboring states, and countless "native" Washingtonians have always worked in D.C. while living in the suburbs and cities of Maryland and northern Virginia, just a short Metro ride away.

The actor's Washington, too, stretches well beyond the District. There are plenty of theatres in D.C., and a handful in those nearby cities and suburbs. Even then, for many actors, the playing field stretches to Baltimore and sometimes even Philadelphia and beyond; commercial and corporate actors travel between Washington and Baltimore as a matter of course. But wherever "Washington" actors hang their hats, theirs is a community both stimulating and livable.

RECOMMENDED READING

Robert L. Price, ed., *The Washington Post Guide to Washington,* 2d ed.
    (Washington, D.C.: The Washington Post Co., 1989).
What's Past Is Prologue. This booklet, a work-in-progress of the Theatre
    Legacy Project, takes a look at the history of Washington theatre. It is
    available from the Helen Hayes Awards.

MOVIES

All the President's Men (1976), *Mr. Smith Goes to Washington* (1939),
No Way Out (1989)

██████ POPULATION

While the 1990 census still shows a largely African American population in Washington, it also shows an 11 percent loss of that group, and a smaller decrease in the white population, since 1980. Other population groups, including American Indians and Asians or Pacific Islanders show significant increases, although the numbers are still relatively small.

██████ CLIMATE

Neither quite a northern nor a southern city, Washington enjoys a fairly moderate climate. Winters, while cold, are less than brutal, and generally last only a few months. There's snowfall, but temperatures rarely drop below the high 20s. Spring, with cherry blossoms bursting pink throughout the city, is lovely, as is fall, although strong winds can turn a warm day suddenly chilly. Summer can endure well into September, and while temperatures rarely soar above the mid 80s to low 90s, the humidity can be absolutely stifling, and thunderstorms are not infrequent. *For weather information call:* 936-1212.

NORMAL TEMPERATURES	Average Daily High	Average Daily Low[2]
January	43°	27°
July	88°	70°

TEMPERATURE EXTREMES

Maximum Temp.	Annual No. of Days	Minimum Temp.	Annual No. of Days
90° and above	37	32° and below	70
32° and below	10	0° and below	—

NORMAL WEATHER CONDITIONS

Clear	Partly Cloudy	Cloudy
98	105	162

ANNUAL PRECIPITATION	Days	Inches
All Precipitation	112	39
Snowfall	NA	17

▄▄▄▄▄▄TRANSPORTATION

Washington is a walkable city if you've got stamina and comfortable shoes. Within the District, a car is not strictly necessary and, since parking is never easy, is often best left at home. Metrobus and Metrorail (subway) cover extensive ground within the city and surrounding suburbs.

A planned city, D.C. is divided into quadrants, with the Capitol providing the directional dividing line: the two 1st Streets border the eastern and western edges of the Capitol grounds, with the numbers increasing as you move outward in both directions. The two A Streets begin above and below East Capitol Street, which runs from the center of the eastern side of the Capitol building; the alphabet then unfolds in either direction as you go north and south. Although most of the city lies within the NW quadrant, it's imperative that you know the directional suffix of any street address. That part of the system is easy to learn; what makes it confusing are those avenues, named for states, that cut diagonally—and ubiquitously—through the city. Until you really know your way around, pay attention: you may think you're heading due east, for example, only to discover you've diverted onto a diagonally-running avenue.

PUBLIC TRANSPORTATION

Washington Metropolitan Area Transit Authority (WMATA). The Washington Metro is a fairly extensive system connecting points both within the District and between the District and surrounding suburbs; it's possible, in fact, to pass through Maryland, the District, and Virginia during a single ride. The Metrorail (subway) system is easy to use, clean, and reliable. A brochure entitled *All About the Metro System* is an invaluable aid, providing a map, station operating hours, a complete fare schedule, and a chart showing the stops nearest numerous points of interest. The WMATA fleet includes buses and subways. *For information call:* 637-7000; 638-3780 (TDD); 962-1825 (On-Call services for the handicapped); 962-1245 (reduced-fare I.D. for disabled).

Maps and schedules are available at subway entrance kiosks and by mail. Write for the brochure *All About the Metro System:* Metro Marketing Department, 600 5th Street, NW, Washington, D.C. 20001, 962-1234.

Subway entrance is via Farecards, which are purchased from machines (have coins and crisp bills ready) at every Metrorail station. Cards can be purchased for a single trip or for several; turnstiles code the card at the station of entry and deduct the appropriate fare upon exiting. Fares vary according to destination and peak/non-peak hours, and a chart showing the value of every trip is posted clearly at all stations. Buses require change or tokens, and transfers are free; you can also transfer from Metrorail to Metrobus; be sure to get transfers from machines located just beyond entrance turnstiles. Seniors, students, and people with disabilities ride at a discount, and many bus and/or subway pass options are available.

The following is a list of terminals and additional transportation systems:
Amtrak, Union Station, Massachusetts Avenue and North Capitol Street, NE, Washington, D.C., 484-7540.
Maryland Rural Commuter System (MARC), Union Station, 800-325-RAIL (7245). MARC provides service to Baltimore and Baltimore/Washington International Airport.
Greyhound, 1st and L Streets, NE, Washington, D.C., 565-2662.

TAXIS

With some 9,000 taxis registered in D.C., street hailing is a way of life. Of course, as in any other taxi town, trying to grab a cab during rush hours and rainstorms can be maddening. Fares within the District are based on a zone system, with a surcharge for each additional passenger and for trips during evening rush hour (4:00 to 6:30 p.m.). Suburban rides are metered. With many District newcomers driving cabs, it's wise to know exactly where you're going before getting in.

DRIVING

With so many people heading downtown to work in the federal government each weekday, traffic is rather difficult. It's a good idea to leave the car at home when venturing into the city; public transit makes things easier, and bike riders do well here, too. Parking, rarely a problem in the suburbs, is always a problem here, where space is hard to come by and meter people are vigilant. Since acting jobs can take place well outside the District, most actors find it necessary to have a car. Those who live in the city or close to a suburban Metrorail line may not always use their cars, but theatres and production houses can be located anywhere in the area, and Washington actors also work in Baltimore, thirty-three miles away. Actors Center members (see *Other Associations,* p. 182) sometimes use their hotline to arrange rideshares for out of town auditions.

■■■■■■■HOUSING AND COSTS OF LIVING

"Washington," says writer Joel Garreau, "has been transformed . . . into fourteen emerging cities."[3] This means that many Washingtonians don't actually live here. Instead, they live in cities like Rockville, Maryland and Tyson's Corner, Virginia, and suburbs like Bethesda and Chevy Chase, Maryland. With so much to choose from, housing isn't that hard to find, and while D.C. itself has plenty of fans, many people prefer the nearby communities, where they can more easily balance home and family life with work. That the Metro spiderlegs out to a number of those communities widens the choice. Since most area actors consider the entire D.C./Baltimore region their market, another option is to live in the Corridor, the area between the two cities. Other areas recommended for decent, affordable housing are Takoma Park (considered an "artistic" community), Alexandria, and Arlington. In the city, Dupont Circle is a pleasant, busy neighborhood with lots of restaurants and art galleries; Woodley Park, just slightly farther north, has similar appeal and is more affordable. The northeast quadrant is seeing a lot of renovation; the area near Catholic University is especially recommended. *City Paper,* a free weekly published on Thursdays, is recommended for housing classifieds. Bulletin boards throughout the capital, like that at the Chesapeake Bagel Shop on Connecticut Avenue in Dupont Circle, also provide housing information.

INTERAREA SHELTER INDEXES	Renters	Owners
Washington, D.C.	107	114
Baltimore	89	98
(Philadelphia)	(100)	(100)

COSTS OF LIVING	
Total average annual expenditures	$37,254
Food at home	2,317
Telephone	666
Gas and motor oil	949
Public transportation	542
Personal care products and services	455

■■■■■EMPLOYMENT

1989 Annual Average Pay
Washington, D.C.: $28,103

1990 Average Unemployment Rates
Washington, D.C.: 6.6%
D.C.-Maryland-Virginia: 3.4%

1990 Average Weekly Unemployment Benefits
Washington, D.C.: $212.32
Maryland: $170.00

■■■■■CRIME

Our nation's capital has a rather bad rep for crime—from political corruption to a violently angry underclass—doesn't it? Not only does D.C. have the highest murder rate in the nation, its rate is 75 percent higher than that of Dallas, which has the second highest rate among cities in this book. Among cities in this book for which statistics are available, aggravated assault is in the middle of the scale, burglary in the high-middle, and reported rape at the low end. In fact, D.C. has the unique distinction of being the only city in which the numbers are higher for murder than for rape; still, in 1990, the incidence of rape increased by an alarming 63 percent over 1989! Like every city, Washington has its special problems, including high-crime neighborhoods. Interestingly, a number of years ago, four theatres made their homes along an unsavory stretch of 14th Street from P to T Streets. Their presence hasn't exactly transformed the neighborhood, but it has

brought about some improvement; restaurants and artists' spaces have
been added and as time goes on, more and more theatregoers venture
into what has come to be known as the 14th Street Theatre District.

1990 CRIME RATES	Violent	Property
Total Crimes	14,919	50,720
Crimes per 100,000 People	2,458	8,357
Average 1 Crime per Every	41 people	12 people

MISCELLANEA

NEWSPAPERS
The Washington Post (morning)
City Paper (weekly)

LIBRARIES
Library of Congress, 10 1st Street, SE, Washington, D.C. 20540, 707-5458.
   Containing more than 84 million items in 470 languages, the library is
   open to anyone over high school age. For reference and research only,
   it's not a lending library. (For more information, see *Resources,* p. 189.)
Public Library Main Branch, Martin Luther King Memorial Library,
   1901 G Street, NW, Washington, D.C. 20001, 727-1221.

POST OFFICE
Main Branch, 900 Brentwood Road, NE, Washington, D.C., 682-9595.

MUSEUMS
Folger Shakespeare Library, 201 E. Capitol Street, SE, Washington, D.C.
   20003-1094, 544-4600. In addition to the collection (see *Resources,*
   p. 189), there is a Shakespearean Theatre modeled after an
   Elizabethan theatre. The small museum has changing exhibitions of
   Renaissance and Shakespearean manuscripts, with a first folio almost
   always on display.
Ford's Theatre, 511 10th Street, NW, Washington, D.C. 20004, 426-6924.
   It contains Lincoln memorabilia and is a functioning theatre.

THE BUSINESS

There's something satisfying about being an actor in Washington, D.C.
True, actors have their share of frustrations and disappointments. The rest

of the country doesn't seem to consider D.C. a major theatre center on the level of, say, Chicago or even Minneapolis or Seattle. This isn't a place, like Florida, North Carolina, or Vancouver, B.C., that filmmakers flock to when they want to avoid shooting in New York or Los Angeles. And it's not as though everything is easy here: like their counterparts everywhere, some D.C. actors struggle financially, balancing acting income—when it comes—with survival jobs. And yet, the region has a lot to offer.

For starters, many actors enjoy being part of a relatively small, supportive community. Of course, this is a conservative city, primarily middle class, and the attendant social atmosphere has an affect on the kind of theatre that gets made. There may be a lot of serious, devoted theatre folk, but the region isn't brimming with risk-taking, boundary-pushing companies, though there are a few. Naturally, not everyone who wants to is able to break into the theatre scene here, but those that do find they can do some good, honest work.

People don't grow rich and famous here, and this certainly isn't the place to get "discovered" or to do lots of theatrical film and television. (Washington does get some production; in fact, in 1990 earnings, Washington, D.C. was the fastest growing SAG branch in the country.) But no small number of actors manage to earn at least a healthy portion of their living doing commercials and industrials. The D.C.-Baltimore area places surprisingly high in SAG earnings for these markets.

Of course, things don't work out well for everybody, but when all's said and done, many people find Washington is a place where they can do stage work they can be proud of, make (at least part of) a reasonably decent living in front of the camera, and live a relatively sane existence.

RECOMMENDED READING

The Actor's Casting Guide (West Chester, PA: WildMann Productions, 1991). This guide to Philadelphia and the Delaware Valley is included here because of that region's proximity to Washington.

Robert Martin, "Capital Gains: Stages Offering Classics and Contemporaries Dominate the D.C. Scene," *Back Stage* (January 19, 1990).

■■■■■ PROFESSIONAL ASSOCIATIONS

TALENT UNIONS

Actors' Equity Association (AEA), Liaison City.
    Members: 251 (D.C.), 221 (Baltimore)
American Federation of Television and Radio Artists (AFTRA), The Highland House, 5480 Wisconsin Avenue, No. 201, Chevy Chase, MD 20815, 301-657-2560.
    Members: 2,634

Screen Actors Guild (SAG), same address/phone as AFTRA.
  Members: 1,162
American Guild of Musical Artists (AGMA), 918 16th Street, NW,
  Washington, D.C. 20006, 466-3030.

OTHER ASSOCIATIONS

Actors' Center, P.O. Box 50180, Washington, D.C. 20091, 638-3777. This
  service organization provides members with an audition hotline and
  produces a newsletter, annual audition, and annual talent showcase.
  Attending their workshops, held every Saturday morning, is a good
  way to meet people and network. Highly recommended, especially for
  newcomers to the business or the area.
African Continuum Theatre Coalition, P.O. Box 90075, Washington, D.C.
  20090, 832-6249. This is an organization whose purpose it is to
  give visibility, strength, and nurturance to Washington's black theatre
  community. Members include theatre artists and professionals of
  all kinds.

■■■■■LOOKING FOR WORK

PUBLICATIONS

City Paper. This free weekly (Thursdays) has a few audition notices;
  most are for community theatre and workshops.
The Washington Post. Theatre audition notices run in the Friday edition's
  "Weekend" section, and sometimes in the Sunday paper.

HOTLINES

Equity; AFTRA/SAG (see *Talent Unions,* p. 181).
Actors' Center (see *Other Associations,* above). This hotline is for
  members only.

BULLETIN BOARDS AND BINDERS

Backstage Books, 2101 P Street, NW, Washington, D.C. 20037, 775-1488.
  On one wall of the shop are the weekly *Washington Post* audition
  notices; on another are notices for student films, showcase
  auditions, and more. Another wall displays business cards advertising
  services (such as photography, massage, and instruction) of interest
  to store patrons.

TALENT BOOKS AND TALENT BANKS

The Actors' Center (see *Other Associations,* above) keeps a P&R file of
  all its members.
The AFTRA/SAG Talent Directory is updated every two years.

League of Washington Theatres, 410 8th Street, NW, Suite 600,
   Washington, D.C. 20004, 638-4270. The League maintains an extensive
   talent file; all area actors can send in a P&R for inclusion.
Producers' Audition Hotline, P.O. Box 742, Olney, MD 20830, 301-924-5700,
   800-950-2834 (outside the Washington area). Voice talent can pay to
   have their demos included in this talent bank utilized by producers,
   casting directors, and others throughout the Mid-Atlantic region.
   Interested voice-over talent may call the office at numbers listed above.

TALENT SHOWCASES AND COMBINED AUDITIONS

East Central Theatre Conference; National Dinner Theatre Association;
   Southeastern Theatre Conference. (For addresses, see Appendix B.)
Actors' Center (see *Other Associations,* p. 182). AC members may
   participate in the February auditions and the December Scene
   Showcase. Slots for the auditions are filled by lottery; inclusion in the
   Showcase is by audition.
AFTRA/SAG (see *Talent Unions,* p. 181). 1991 was the year of the first
   annual AFTRA/SAG talent showcase. Inclusion is by audition;
   participants present scenes, monologues, or songs to producers,
   casting directors, and other professionals.
League of Washington Theatres (see *Talent Banks,* above). The League's
   annual auditions are a week-long summer event, open to all actors
   who can supply enough P&Rs for distribution to attending producers,
   artistic directors, and casting personnel. Reported to be effective, the
   auditions are announced in the *Washington Post* and on the Actor's
   Center Hotline (or write to the League).

■■■■■■TALENT AGENTS AND CASTING DIRECTORS

For practical purposes, there's little distinction between casting directors
and talent agents here, and the terms "casting company" and "casting
agency" are used interchangeably to describe the half-dozen or so
companies in the Washington-Baltimore area. (There are numerous
additional companies that work primarily with models.) As of this writing,
only Characters Agency is franchised by AFTRA and SAG for all areas,
and so functions solely as a talent agency. The two busiest companies,
Central Casting and Taylor Royall, are franchised (and so act as agents)
for all areas except theatrical film, for which they work as casting
directors. Some casting agencies also serve as paymasters. It's no surprise
that, with so many heads wearing so many hats, there are glitches in
the system, and change may be in the offing. In the meantime, it's
important that both union and nonunion actors familiarize themselves
with union regulations, including actors' rights and responsibilities.

Agencies/casting companies rarely get involved in theatre, working primarily in the film and broadcast markets.

It's probably not too difficult to get accepted by at least a couple of the casting companies, especially for union members with strong résumés. Casting agencies are always looking for new faces, since clients often shy away from using actors they consider overexposed. But having P&Rs on file is no guarantee of being sent out, so it's necessary to do follow up, keeping oneself and one's work visible. Nobody signs exclusive contracts with the agencies, and many actors are registered with several; others are quite satisfied to work with a single agency. Newcomers can get a list of agencies from the Actors' Center or AFTRA/SAG, then call each company to find out the preferred contact procedure. Central Casting holds open hours every Thursday from 10 a.m. to noon (call to confirm the schedule). The agents there have a reputation for "brutal honesty," and if they don't like what they see, they'll say so. Many actors register at both Central's D.C. and Baltimore offices. Taylor Royall, which handles the entire region from their sole office in Baltimore, requires P&R submissions by mail; since they respond by mail, be sure to include your mailing address. By the way, with just a single photo repro house (in Rockville, Maryland) specializing in actors' headshots, many actors send their photos to New York for quantity reproduction.

■■■■■THEATRE

Washington may never be viewed as a major theatre center, but actors who live and work here know that the area holds its own. It's the home of some pretty famous theatres, like the Kennedy Center, Ford's Theatre, the National Theatre, and The Shakespeare Theatre. The National and Ford's are presenting houses, while the Kennedy does some presenting and some producing. Regional companies Arena Stage and The Shakespeare Theatre tend to cast some principal roles in New York (and to some degree, the Shakespeare relies on star power), but both theatres also have longtime resident companies. In addition, the Shakespeare uses students and apprentices from its training programs in small roles and as understudies. The Arena casts nonmember locals as walk-ons and understudies, and this system can be a source of frustration for experienced actors who find it hard to break through the glass ceiling that keeps them from playing leads, although recently there have been small signs of improvement. Growing awareness of nontraditional casting issues, in fact, may be partly responsible for increased local casting.

Washington has a strong small-theatre movement that was energized some ten to fifteen years ago when a handful of companies, like the Source, GALA Hispanic, the Studio, the Roundhouse, and Woolly

Mammoth, appeared on the scene. The League of Washington Theatres has been instrumental in creating a cooperative community of both large and small theatres. A new theatre or two springs up every year now, and each year seems to see another company converting to an Equity SPT Contract. Some locals say non-Equity actors have an advantage here (they can work at both the nonunion and the SPT theatres), although the local Equity liaison committee works hard to encourage nonunion theatres to use Equity actors under Guest Artist Contracts and Letters of Agreement. Equity or not, most theatres pay something, though very few companies employ actors on a full-time, salaried basis. Musical theatre is done primarily at dinner theatres; there are several in the area. Actor-produced showcases have become popular in recent years, and community theatre is quite strong.

Despite the vitality and relative success of many small theatres, it's not a great town for new plays, nor is there as much avant-garde or political theatre as one might expect. Audiences are conservative, and finances being what they are, producing new and/or controversial works can be risky; Peter Sellars' tenure at the Kennedy Center, for example, apparently was just too much for Washington. But there are exceptions: the Source Theatre annually produces a festival of new plays, and theatres like Woolly Mammoth and Scena have audiences devoted to their unusual, riskier works. In addition, two relatively new companies, Potomac Theatre Project and Theatre of the First Amendment have had quite a bit of success producing plays addressing social and political themes.

The actor new to the area should take advantage of as many local talent showcases and general auditions as possible, make use of the hotlines, and pound the pavement. That means sending P&Rs to theatres (get a list from the Equity liaison committee) and following up by calling to ask for meetings or auditions, or offering to do a couple of monologues. Many theatres are pretty open to newcomers, though some show a recent trend away from open calls, except when there's difficulty casting roles from among actors whose work they know. Theatre staff members do, however, attend the League and Actor's Center auditions. It may not be as easy as it once was to break into theatre here, but many actors who get known stay busy. Moving to a higher rung, however, can be difficult, and eventually the town grows too small for some actors, who succumb to the "regional theatre blues." But despite the difficulties, many actors laud Washington theatre and consider this a great place to get started.

◼◼◼ FILM AND TELEVISION

There just isn't a great deal of theatrical film and television here, although the local film bureaus work hard to attract production, and there's even talk of building a soundstage in the District. Though the film and television markets haven't been great for local actors, the region, which includes Maryland and extends south to Richmond, Virginia, does get some production. Each year sees perhaps a half-dozen films and even a TV pilot or two. In recent years, several episodes of "America's Most Wanted" have kept locals working, some PBS programming has been shot here, and a few local cable stations have been doing some mostly small-scale, nonunion dramatic programming.

Producers coming in on location may hire local casting agencies to handle everything from contract players to extras; others do their own principal casting and hire a local company to provide extras only. Some directors, unfortunately, won't even consider casting anything more than extras and bit players locally. Recently, Virginia, a right-to-work state, has been getting quite a bit more film work than D.C. or Maryland. For that reason, some D.C.-Baltimore actors are registered with agencies in Richmond, although Richmond-based productions often hire a D.C. company to handle, if not principal, at least extra casting.

CORPORATE AND COMMERCIALS

Washington-Baltimore actors do very nicely in the corporate and commercial markets; in 1990 the area had the fourth-highest SAG commercials and industrials earnings in the nation. Guess who one of the biggest producers of industrials is: the U.S. government. From the military to the IRS, the EPA, and the rest of the federal alphabet soup, many departments and agencies hire local talent for industrials and training films. Several even have their own production departments, as do numerous corporations and private agencies headquartered in the area. Actors who are the right type—conservative, clean-cut chairmen of the board—can do well as narrators and spokesmen. Yes, they are men most of the time. (And those who have experience working with an ear prompter are at an advantage.) There's also a decent market for yuppie and middle-class mom and dad types, and some need for the blue-collar look; there's far less work for athletic, ditsy, thug-like, and other offbeat characters. Many producers of industrials are SAG signatories; the nonunion market, while probably not gigantic, has shown some growth. AFTRA/SAG can provide a list of area signatories and of "frequent-use" signatories; some production houses keep in-house casting files, and can be contacted directly.

The bulk of the industrial work is located in and around D.C. Far more commercial production happens in Baltimore, however, although some commercials are produced in the District. Fortunately for D.C. actors, the two cities make up one big, happy market. The unions' local hire designation encompasses fifty-mile radii from both Baltimore's Inner

Harbor and the Washington Monument, and actors regularly commute between the two cities. (For many, this requires being registered with agencies in both areas.) A lot of political advertising is produced here, but that's a tough market to crack. Those character types who don't do well in corporate do a little better in the commercial market, where things may be starting to loosen up. In the busy print market, "upscale casual" is the most popular look, and there's quite a bit of work for older models.

■■■■■■CASTING DIVERSITY

Multicultural representation on the stage has increased significantly since 1987, when the League of Washington Theatres sponsored a symposium on nontraditional casting. Now more ethnic minority actors than ever attend League auditions, and in 1991, the League made a concerted effort to reach out to actors with disabilities. Ethnic minorities are filling administrative and artistic positions at theatres, production of plays by minority writers has increased, and the Arena Theatre has created a program to develop ethnic minority designers and technicians. In 1991, for the first time, the *Washington Post* sent a reviewer to cover a Spanish-language production at GALA Hispanic Theatre. The region has also seen a bit of cross-gender casting, and many theatres are good about casting against type. At this point, in fact, you'd have to look hard to find a Washington theatre that is *not* practicing nontraditional casting to some degree.

The Shakespeare Theatre, which has consistently utilized color-blind and color-inspired casting, has a liaison program with Howard University and the University of South Carolina; students spend a year studying at the theatre and fill small roles in company productions. There is an ongoing effort to establish an Asian theatre company; in its early stages as of this writing, the group is presenting readings and offering classes. But all is not rosy. The District has taken a leadership role in casting diversity, but some people wonder if it will last. At the time of this writing, there is no consistently-producing black theatre with a permanent space in this largely black-populated city. The African Continuum Theatre Coalition (ACT Co., winner of a *Washington Post* Award for Distinguished Community Service) is making efforts to better organize black theatre, and the city's Commission on the Arts and Humanities has developed an initiative to help strengthen black theatre.

Though non-Hispanic white men continue to work more than anyone else in the corporate and commercial markets, there have been increased opportunities recently for women and ethnic minorities. African American actors are working more frequently, and there's been an enormous demand of late for Asian and Hispanic (including bilingual) actors. In fact, the Hispanic and Asian talent pools are small, and actors who are the right types (see *Corporate and Commercials,* p. 186) might do well here.

████ ADDITIONAL OPPORTUNITIES

Discovery Theatre, Susan Swarthout, Arts and Industries Building, 900 Jefferson Drive, SW, Room 1401, Smithsonian Institution, Washington, D.C. 20560, 357-1500. This organization presents performing arts programs to school groups. Dancers, puppeteers, theatre artists, musicians, and storytellers may submit materials; a video is helpful, or invite Ms. Swarthout to a performance. October through June residency, although some actors are jobbed-in. Non-Equity only.

The Royal Pickwickians, 2008 Mt. Vernon Street, Philadelphia, PA 19130, 215-232-2690. This group also casts in D.C.; see the Philadelphia chapter for details.

Washington Revels, Mary Swope, Producer, Box 39077, Washington, D.C. 20016, 364-8744. Auditions for non-Equity actors for the Christmas mummers play are held in September. The casting notice can be found in the *Washington Post,* or call for information.

Washington Theatre Festival, Source Theatre, 1835 14th Street, NW, Washington, D.C. 20009, 462-1073. The Source produces an annual summer festival of new plays presented in a variety of locations. Auditions are in June.

████ TRAINING

In addition to private teachers and coaches, actors will find interesting options for study offered by several theatres and organizations. AFTRA/SAG holds very low-cost workshops each month; Actors' Center members may participate in that organization's free Saturday morning workshops. The Studio Theatre Acting Conservatory is another popular option; classes range from basic acting, voice, and movement to classics, styles, directing, auditioning, Young Peoples Workshops, and more. There are three well-reputed programs at The Shakespeare Theatre: an intensive thirteen-week long minority workshop for college interns, a five-week summer intensive, and the twelve-week Saturday Program; this last is most appropriate for working professionals.

CERTIFICATE/DEGREE PROGRAMS

American University, Department of Performing Arts, 4400 Massachusetts Avenue, NW, Washington, D.C. 20016-8053, 885-3420.

Catholic University of America, Department of Drama, Washington, D.C. 20064, 635-5351.

Howard University, Department of Theatre Arts, 6th and Fairmont Streets.,
   NW, Washington, D.C. 20059, 806-7050.
University of Maryland/Baltimore County, Theatre Department, 5401
   Wilkens Avenue, Baltimore, MD 21228-5398, 301-455-2949.

■■■■■AFFORDABLE ARTS

Ticketplace, F Street Plaza between 12th and 13th Streets, NW,
   Washington, D.C., 842-5387 (TIC-KETS). Half-price day-of-performance
   theatre, music, and dance tickets are available through this project of
   the Cultural Alliance of Greater Washington.
National Theatre, 1321 Pennsylvania Avenue, NW, Washington, D.C.
   20004, 628-6161. This Shubert Theatre offers half-price tickets to
   qualifying seniors, disabled, students, and military personnel.
Actor's Center. Comps and low-cost tickets are often announced on the
   hotline, as are discounts on photography, classes, and other services.
Comps. The smaller theatres are good about reciprocal comping; if you're
   a member of, or are known to have worked at, one theatre, you
   shouldn't have a problem getting into others on slow nights.
Shakespeare Free-for-All. Shakespeare Theatre's free summer
   performances are presented in the Carter Barron Amphitheatre in
   Rock Creek Park. Watch for announcements in *The Washington Post*
   and elsewhere.

■■■■■RESOURCES

LIBRARIES
Library of Congress
   • Motion Picture, Broadcasting and Recorded Sound Division
   • Performing Arts Reading Room
   1st Street between E. Capitol Street, SE, and Independence
   Avenue, SE, Washington, D.C., 707-5000, 887-5677 for recorded
   schedule of weekly screenings.
Performing Arts Library, Terrace Level, John F. Kennedy Center for the
   Performing Arts, Virginia and New Hampshire Avenues, NW. This is
   part of the Library of Congress; the 4,000-volume reference collection
   includes microform, listening, and viewing equipment.
Folger Shakespeare Library, 201 E. Capitol Street, SE, Washington, D.C.,
   544-4600. You must apply for a reader's card (only available
   to postgraduate students and credentialed theatre professionals) to
   gain access to this private collection of Shakespeare and
   Renaissance materials.

BOOKSTORES

Backstage Books, 2101 P Street, NW, Washington, D.C. 20037, 775-1488.
The only performing arts bookstore in the area, Backstage carries a full
line of scripts, books, tapes, vocal selections, and periodicals, as well
as costumes, theatrical makeup, and gifts. It also posts casting notices
and other announcements.

▋▋▋▋NETWORKING AND SOCIALIZING

Newcomers would do well to get themselves to the Actor's Center and to
Backstage Bookstore, both of which serve as resource and information
centers for the acting community. Involvement in Actor's Center programs
is one way to meet people. This is a good city in which to get involved
in play readings; submit P&Rs to theatres, and attend auditions announced
on hotlines or in newspapers. The following restaurants are popular
with actors:

Dante's, 1522 14th Street, NW, Washington, D.C. 20036, 667-7260.
Herb's, 1615 Rhode Island Avenue, NW, Washington, D.C. 20036,
333-HERB.
Trio Restaurant, 1537 17th Street, NW, Washington, D.C. 20036, 232-6305.

---

[1] Art Buchwald in an interview with Mark Seal, *American Way* (April 1, 1991).
[2] Low temperatures shown here are among the highest in the area; suburban
temperatures can vary as much as ten to fifteen degrees.
[3] Joel Garreau, "The Suburbs: The Emerging Cities," in *The Washington Post Guide
to Washington,* 2d ed., ed. Robert L. Price (Washington, D.C.: The Washington
Post Co., 1989).

The *Sourcebook* is intended for both experienced and inexperienced actors. It assumes you understand the basics of an actor's career, i.e., what constitutes a good picture or résumé, the difference between talent agents and casting directors, what it means for an agency to be franchised by talent unions, and your rights and responsibilities as a union member. However, if you need more information of that kind, I encourage you to get it; your use of this book will only be enhanced. The books listed here, in addition to several mentioned throughout the text, are good sources.

Beecham, Jahnna, Zoaunne Le Roy, and Adale O'Brien. *See the U.S.A. with Your Résumé: A Survival Guide to Regional Theatre.* New York: Samuel French, Inc., 1985. Provided here are lists of essential goods and services in seventy-one LORT cities. Though by now some information is probably out of date, the book includes useful tips on negotiating contracts, setting up temporary living quarters, income-tax record keeping, and good capsule descriptions of listed cities.

Boyer, Richard, and David Savageau. *Places Rated Almanac: Your Guide to Finding the Best Places to Live in America.* Rev. ed. New York: Prentice-Hall Travel, 1992.

Charles, Jill. *Directory of Theatre Training Programs II.* 2d ed. Dorset, Vt.: Theatre Directories, 1989.

———. Regional Theatre Directory, 1990-91. Dorset, Vt.: Theatre Directories, 1991.

———. *Summer Theatre Directory, 1990-91: A National Guide to Summer Employment for Professionals and Students.* Dorset, Vt.: Theatre Directories, 1991.

Eaker, Sherry, comp. and ed. *The Back Stage Handbook for Performing Artists.* 2d ed., rev. and enl. New York: Back Stage Books, 1991.

Hammond, David, ed. *Opportunities for Actor Training and Apprenticeships with the League of Resident Theatres.* New York: LORT Training Project Task Force.

U.S.A. Reports. Long Island City, N.Y.: Television Index, Inc. This publication, updated semiannually, lists franchised agents and/or personal managers in Ariz., Calif., Colo., Conn., D.C./Md., Fla., Ga., Hawaii, Ill., Kans., La., Mass., Mich., Minn., Mo., Nev., N.J., N.Mex., N.Y., Ohio, Oreg., Pa., Tenn., Tex., Utah, Va., Wash., Wis.

The combined auditions listed here are some of those that are held in or near cities covered in this book; this is not a complete list of auditions held in the United States. Please bear in mind that unless an audition is specifically geared toward Equity hiring, Equity theatres in attendance may be hiring only non-Equity apprentices or Equity Membership Candidates.

Illinois Professional Auditions, Illinois Theatre Association, Theatre Building, 1225 W. Belmont Avenue, Chicago, IL 60657, 312-929-7288. Held annually in the spring in Chicago for "students in or completing university degree programs, new-to-Chicago, nonunion actors, and community theatre actors."

Indiana Theatre Association, Butler University Theatre, 4600 Sunset Avenue, Indianapolis, IN 46208, 317-283-9666. Held annually in February, usually in Indianapolis. Equity and experienced student and non-Equity actors may attend.

Michigan Theatre Association, P.O. Box 726, Marshall, MI 49068, 616-781-7859. Held annually in February, usually in Lansing. Primarily for students and community theatre actors; some Equity theatre apprenticeships.

Mid-America Theatre Conference, The University of Kansas, 356 Murphy Hall, Lawrence, KS 66045-2175, 913-864-3511. Held annually in March in different cities in a nine-state region including Minneapolis and Illinois. Does some Equity hiring, although it's mostly non-Equity.

National Dinner Theatre Association (the same contact as Michigan Theatre Association, above). Held annually in March in different locations, generally east of the Rockies and central U.S. Hires Equity and non-Equity professionals, though mostly non-Equity.

New England Theatre Conference, NETC Central, 50 Exchange Street, Waltham, MA 02154, 617-893-3120. Held annually in March in the Boston area. Mostly non-Equity, mostly summer stock, though attended by some year-round theatres.

The Northwest Drama Conference, Inc., University of Alaska at Anchorage, Department of Theatre and Dance, 3211 Providence Drive, Anchorage, AL 99508. Held annually in February in different northwest locations. Non-Equity, primarily for students.

Southeastern Theatre Conference, 506 Stirling Street, University of North Carolina at Greensboro, Greensboro, NC 27412, 919-272-3645. Held annually in March in different cities in a ten-state region, and in Atlanta in September. Experienced Equity and non-Equity, though Equity theatres may hire apprentices only.

Southwest Theatre Association, Don Williams, Lubbock Christian University, 5601 19th Street, Lubbock, TX 79407. Held annually in late February in Lubbock, Texas. Equity and non-Equity.

StrawHat Auditions, P.O. Box 1226, Port Chester, NY 10573-8226. Held annually in late March in Manhattan. Non-Equity summer stock; primarily attended by eastern and midwestern theatres.

Summer Theatre Support Group (to contact, see Straw Hat Auditions, above). This is still in the formative stages at the time of this writing, planning spring and fall Equity auditions. Profits above expenses will be donated to charitable organizations. Watch trade papers for further information.

Wisconsin Statewide Theatre Auditions, Department of Continuing Education in the Arts, 726 Lowell Hall, 610 Langdon Street, Madison, WI 53703, 608-263-7787. Held annually in February in Madison. Auditions are for acting jobs as well as for transfers from high school and community colleges to four-year college/university acting programs. Some Equity theatres attend.

SOURCES OF INFORMATION

Average Annual Pay: "Average Annual Pay Levels in Metropolitan Areas, 1989," U.S. Department of Labor, Bureau of Labor Statistics.

Climate: "Local Climatological Data: Annual Summary," National Oceanic and Atmospheric Administration, U.S. Department of Commerce.

Costs of Living: "Consumer Expenditure Survey," U.S. Department of Labor, Bureau of Labor Statistics (1988-89).

Crime Statistics: "Uniform Crime Report 1990 Preliminary Annual Release," U.S. Department of Justice, Federal Bureau of Investigation.

Interarea Shelter Indexes: Brent R. Moulton, "Interarea Indexes of the Cost of Shelter Using Hedonic Quality Adjustment Techniques," unpublished working paper, U.S. Bureau of Labor Statistics (1991).

Population: U.S. Department of Commerce, Bureau of the Census, 1990 Census.

Unemployment Rates and Benefits: Unpublished reports, U.S. Department of Labor, Bureau of Labor Statistics.

As an actor and singer, Andrea Wolper has worked in both New York and California. Her fiction and nonfiction writing has appeared in *New York Woman, The Sun, Back Stage, The Paper Bag,* and other publications, and several of her pieces were included in *The Back Stage Handbook for Performing Artists, Revised and Enlarged Edition.*